Escape Finance

Escape Finance

How to prepare for economic collapse or geopolitical chaos

Elias van

Mindful Pages

Published in 2025

ISBN: 9789371343183 (PB)
ISBN: 9789371344111 (eBook)

Published by

Mindful Pages
Imprint of Alpha Editions LLC
312 W. 2nd St #1834
Casper, WY 82601, USA

This book was developed using advanced writing tools to support the drafting and ideation process. All content has been thoughtfully curated, refined, and reviewed to ensure quality and relevance.

Content

Introduction
The Mirage of Stability

For much of the modern era, the idea of financial security has been almost inseparable from the notion of wealth accumulation. Be it property deeds, pension statements, savings accounts, or share portfolios, such symbols have long stood as emblems of safety—woven tightly into the cultural narrative of success and respectability. From a young age, we're taught to link money with comfort, liberty, even a certain kind of moral worth. Those who navigate the financial labyrinth are celebrated as prudent, while those who stumble are often dismissed as careless. But what if the game itself is rigged—not to safeguard, but to siphon?

This book begins with a quiet but radical suggestion: that the security we've been conditioned to seek in financial systems is, for the most part, a mirage. Not because money is powerless—it plainly isn't—but because the structures through which it flows are more fragile, more politicised, and more philosophically hollow than we generally care to acknowledge. The architecture of contemporary finance, from fiat currency to national pensions, rests on intricate scaffolding made of engineered belief. It has the aura of permanence, but lacks the substance. It feels intimately tied to our individual lives, but in truth, it's profoundly impersonal.

We find ourselves living in a moment of overwhelming complexity. Global supply chains stretch thin across continents, interlaced and precarious. Digital economies now depend less on tangible goods and more on strings of code and the ever-fluctuating tides of sentiment. Behind every trade deal or stimulus package lurks a geopolitical subtext, simmering just beneath the surface. And the average person—diligent, savvy, even cautious—is deeply entangled in financial systems designed not for their benefit, but to serve distant and opaque interests. Troublingly, these systems aren't breaking down. They are, in many ways, operating exactly as they were meant to.

This is not, let it be said from the outset, a manifesto for burying bullion in your backyard or hoarding dried lentils in your larder. *Escape Finance* is not a book for alarmists or survivalists. It is, rather, a call to reclaim agency—to wrest back a sense of control in a world where the odds increasingly seem stacked against the individual. It is a reckoning with the idea that what once passed for prosperity has in many cases become a subtle form of servitude. And it is an argument that genuine resilience—resilience that endures—cannot be built on trending investment tips or confident market predictions, but on clarity of mind, agility of thought, and a deliberate stepping back from the most precarious edges of the system.

At its core, modern finance depends on belief. Fiat currencies, those slender lifelines of national economies, hold value not by virtue of any intrinsic worth, but because we collectively agree to pretend they do. We trust that governments will remain solvent, that laws will remain steady, that tomorrow will look enough like today to be predictable. So long as this trust holds, the machinery hums. But once it wavers—just a little—the unraveling can be swift and dramatic. Argentina. Zimbabwe. Lebanon. Cyprus. Russia. These are not sepia-toned anecdotes from some forgotten past. They are urgent reminders of how quickly capital can vanish, how easily civil liberties can be clipped, and how consistently governments will prioritise the survival of their institutions over the dignity of their citizens.

Escape Finance begins with a stark, liberating truth: your financial wellbeing is not secured by doubling down on the prevailing system. It is secured by learning to detect its weaknesses before they surface. By questioning the stories we are told. By cultivating a mindset that favours flexibility over conformity. This isn't about rebellion for its own sake—it's about the art of financial disengagement. Not retreating from society, but refusing to anchor your future to its most volatile structures.

What you'll encounter in this book isn't just economic strategy; it's a broader worldview. The notion of escape finance is not confined to spreadsheets or balance sheets. It stretches into the realm of psychology, philosophy, and personal design. It challenges us to reconsider what we mean by "wealth" or "freedom." It suggests that value lies not in what can be amassed, but in what can be mobilised. Not in static ownership, but in dynamic access—especially when the winds shift. It moves the focus away from passive returns and towards sovereign capability, from the false security of diversification to the more demanding but rewarding terrain of autonomy.

Expect to have your assumptions questioned. Diversification across similar risk environments is no shield—it merely spreads your exposure. Inflation, public debt, currency devaluation, rising authoritarianism—these aren't black swan events. They're part of the operating manual. And government safety nets? Pensions, welfare, deposit protections—they're mathematical fictions, increasingly stretched by demographic trends and economic drift. Worse still, they lull the public into a kind of fatalistic optimism, an emotional paralysis that delays real preparation.

Still, this book is not a screed of despair. It is a framework. A reorientation. What follows is a pragmatic, unvarnished blueprint—from diagnosing institutional decay to designing exit strategies grounded in principle and pragmatism. You will learn how to read the tea leaves of geopolitics not as background noise, but as actionable insight. You will explore uncorrelated assets that do not bend to central bank policy or election cycles. You will be invited to think not like an investor, but like a sovereign—someone who doesn't wait for the storm to pass, but builds a craft strong enough to sail through it.

Picture this book as your departure gate—not to some utopian elsewhere, but to a deeper awareness. It is not about fleeing civilisation; it's about seeing clearly where your dependencies lie. Once you grasp the scale of your entwinement with systems beyond your control, the only sensible question becomes not *if* you should begin your disentanglement, but *how soon.*

The person this book is written for is neither cynic nor coward. They are a strategist—perhaps one who has grown quietly suspicious of the smiles on financial billboards. They notice the tightening loop of digital oversight, fiscal pressure, and policy overreach. And rather than await the inevitable, they act. Not with noise, not with fury, but with foresight and calm resolve.

There are no illusions here. You will not be promised secrets to beat the market or schemes to shortcut your way to wealth. What you will find is more enduring: the intellectual tools and psychological shifts required to build structural independence in a time of cascading fragility. You will learn to spot the cracks before they become chasms. And, more importantly, you'll be equipped to construct a life whose bedrock lies not in promises made on paper, but in the tangible resilience of skills, relationships, and discernment.

In the end, this is a book about freedom. Not the glossy kind hawked in advertisements, but the authentic, hard-earned sort. The kind that comes from the quiet confidence of knowing you could walk away if you had to—not because you wish to, but because you're prepared. That is the essence of escape finance: not abandoning the world, but refusing to be shackled by it.

Welcome to *Escape Finance.* You are not here by coincidence. You are here because, at some level, you've started to question the official script. You've begun to suspect that the thing we call "stability" is often a costume. And you are ready—finally—to stop playing along.

Chapter 1
The Currency of Illusion

If money embodies power, then modern finance is best understood as large-scale illusion management. Few human inventions have exercised such sweeping authority over perception, policy, and personal behaviour—yet paradoxically, few remain so shrouded in misunderstanding. Ask around and you'll find most people can sketch a rough idea of what a currency is. Fewer still can explain where that currency derives its value. And rarer than both is the individual who can tell you what might cause that value to collapse, quietly and catastrophically.

This chapter opens, unflinchingly, with a confrontation: that what we so often accept as economic "truth" is less grounded in fact than in collective fabrication. Our financial lives are not secured by vaults of gold, acres of land, or repositories of hard assets—but by belief. Not conviction rooted in principle, mind you, but belief manufactured through repetition. We believe in value. We believe in growth. We believe money behaves as we've been told it should. But these beliefs are built more on narrative than evidence, more on policy than on permanence. And those shaping them—the institutions we're conditioned to trust—are seldom working in the service of the individual.

Consider the world's dominant currencies—the dollar, the euro, the pound, the yuan. Each is fiat by construction. No gold standard. No tangible backing. Their worth arises not from intrinsic value, but from confidence—faith, really—in the stability of the issuing state. This trust, while essential, is neither rational nor robust. It is engineered. It is brittle. And it is constantly nudged along by those who benefit from its persistence. The word *fiat* itself comes from Latin: *let it be done.* We conjure our money into existence through decree, not substance.

This simple, unsettling truth opens the door to a cascade of implications—many of which mainstream finance would rather keep sealed. For once money floats untethered from physical reality, it becomes a tool not of commerce but of control. It can be created out of nothing, taxed at will, quietly drained of value, or eroded through inflation—a silent confiscation masquerading as economic necessity. And make no mistake: inflation is not some unintended side effect. It is central to the operation.

Inflation is often discussed as if it were akin to rain or humidity—something that just *happens*. "Prices are going up," people say, shrugging. "Everything's getting more expensive." But inflation is not weather. It is policy. A mechanism designed, at least in theory, to discourage hoarding, stimulate spending, and grease the wheels of economic motion. But in reality? It functions as a creeping form of expropriation—quietly draining the purchasing power of those least equipped to hedge against it. The saver, the pensioner, the wage-earner—all find their efforts worth less with each passing year. The treadmill of labour and life spins faster, but the ground beneath remains unstable.

Running parallel to this is the defining engine of our economic era: debt. Debt is no longer a feature of the system—it *is* the system. Growth is no longer a product solely of innovation or productivity, but of expanding credit. Governments borrow to sustain spending. Corporations borrow to finance expansion. Individuals borrow simply to stay afloat, as wages stagnate and living costs climb. The entire edifice leans ever more heavily on leverage. And when interest rates rise—as, inevitably, they must—the facade of affordability collapses. Defaults rise, liquidity dries up, and what looked like prosperity is revealed for what it was: a delicate pyramid built on deferred reckoning.

Debt is not merely a domestic issue, either. It is geopolitical. Nations borrow in currencies they do not print. They become beholden to transnational lenders, subjected to terms crafted in distant boardrooms. When geopolitics flare—when sanctions hit, when currencies are devalued, when capital flows reverse—ordinary citizens are caught in the crossfire. Overnight, savings vanish, access to funds disappears, and the illusion of control is exposed as nothing more than consent withdrawn. All under the noble guise of "stability" and "macroeconomic management."

And yet, perhaps the most beguiling fiction of all is the story we tell ourselves about risk: the myth of diversification. For decades, the gospel of prudent investing has been clear—spread your bets. Don't put all your eggs in one basket. A portfolio should be diversified: equities, bonds, commodities, geographies. Sensible, isn't it? Sensible, that is, until one begins to notice that most of these baskets are woven from the same brittle fibres. When nearly every asset class is propped up by fiat currency, reliant on central bank liquidity, and vulnerable to global debt contagion, diversification becomes, at best, cosmetic. At worst, it ensures one suffers in more places at once.

In periods of calm, diversification feels clever. In moments of crisis, it can feel like exposure multiplied. True resilience demands a deeper reckoning. It asks awkward questions. Who controls the asset? On what assumptions is its value predicated? And what happens if those assumptions are weaponised, disrupted, or discredited? Risk mitigation that fails to account for structural fragility is not strategy—it's self-deception.

All of this—our submission to inflation, our complicity in debt, our overconfidence in diversification—is made possible by a force that is both intimate and invisible: the psychology of money. Money is not merely a unit of exchange. It is a vessel of emotion. It carries our fears, our aspirations, our self-worth. We chase it not just to survive, but to feel secure, admired, whole. And that emotional entanglement leaves us dangerously exposed.

We tell ourselves reassuring tales: the markets always rebound. Property values always rise. Pensions will be there when we retire. Even as evidence to the contrary accumulates, we resist change—because the alternative is too disruptive to contemplate. And this isn't just a problem for the uninitiated. Highly educated, professionally successful individuals fall into the same trap. They believe they are diversified, liquid, well-insulated. Until they are not. Until the ATM stops working. Until the capital controls tighten. Until the "safe" assets turn out to be unobtainable at the moment they are most needed.

This chapter peels back those illusions—not to induce panic, but to foster clarity. It will probe the architecture of economic fragility, not as anomaly but as intention. It will challenge the orthodoxy of diversification, not out of contrarian impulse, but because prudence demands more than surface-level analysis. And it will explore the inner terrain of money—how our deeply human instincts around status, security, and identity warp our responses to risk.

The aim here is not to abandon the world of finance, but to break free from its most pernicious deceptions. To push beyond comforting slogans and enter a mode of sober, forensic inquiry. To begin crafting a vision of wealth that accounts not merely for return on investment, but for sovereignty of access. Not just for accumulation, but for endurance.

At its core, *The Currency of Illusion* is about vision. About seeing money not as a fixed resource, but as a tool—dynamic, fragile, manipulable. Once you understand this, the old rules begin to look suspect. You stop assuming that the same institutions that extract your labour and wealth will suddenly protect you when the storm hits. And you start building—not out of fear, but out of awareness. You begin constructing a financial life capable of withstanding what others still pretend is unthinkable.

The collapse of belief always precedes the collapse of structure. Better, then, to dismantle the illusion voluntarily—while time, and options, remain. Only then can you begin to build something with staying power. Not because it grows unchecked, but because it survives wisely.

Fiat and Faith

In the architecture of modern civilisation, there is no instrument more quietly powerful, more universally accepted, or more profoundly misunderstood than fiat currency. It passes through our lives invisibly—earned, spent, hoarded, and traded—yet few pause to consider the foundation upon which its value rests. It is not gold. It is not labour. It is not even productivity. The value of fiat currency is trust, and that trust is not incidental. It is manufactured. It is cultivated. It is, in many cases, deliberately manipulated. And increasingly, it is misplaced.

Fiat currency—derived from the Latin *fiat*, meaning *let it be done*—is money by decree. It has value because a government declares it so, and because the public, in turn, agrees to believe it. That belief underpins everything from household budgets to sovereign debt markets. But the magnitude of this consensus illusion is rarely appreciated. Trust in fiat is not a side effect of a stable system—it is the core technology. The paper note, the digital bank balance, the central bank policy—they are all expressions of collective faith in institutions, continuity, and control.

This is not a flaw of fiat; it is its defining feature. But it is also its vulnerability. Because once currency is severed from any intrinsic anchor—be it precious metal, basket of commodities, or labour equivalence—it becomes susceptible to abuse, distortion, and catastrophic collapse, all without violating a single technical rule of the system. The mechanism functions. The belief fails.

To understand this fragility, it helps to examine the post-Bretton Woods era. When the United States formally decoupled the dollar from gold in 1971, it marked the end of hard money and the beginning of a fully trust-based monetary order. What followed was a rapid expansion of global fiat systems, all predicated on the perceived strength of their issuing governments and central banks. But unlike gold-backed systems, which enforced a degree of fiscal discipline, fiat systems granted policymakers near-total freedom to inflate, debase, and reconfigure currency to suit political agendas.

Inflation, often described euphemistically as "price stability targeting," became the accepted lubricant of economic growth. But inflation is, in essence, the sanctioned dilution of value. A £100 note in 1990 and a £100 note in 2025 are not equivalent—though they bear the same numbers, their purchasing power, and thus their real-world impact, are starkly different. And when this dilution becomes chronic—as it has in countless historical cases—it begins to erode not just wealth, but the foundational trust that gives currency its legitimacy.

Consider Zimbabwe in the late 2000s, where hyperinflation reached 89.7 sextillion percent. The currency became so worthless that citizens used trillion-dollar notes as novelty items or wallpaper. Or Venezuela, where the bolívar collapsed under the weight of political dysfunction and monetary abuse, triggering food shortages and mass migration. These are not merely distant catastrophes. They are instructive examples of what happens when trust evaporates. And though such extremes may seem unlikely in the developed world, the underlying conditions—rising debt, declining productivity, unchecked monetary expansion—are alarmingly familiar.

Yet trust in fiat does not rest solely on economic fundamentals. It is propped up by narrative. Central banks are no longer just stewards of monetary stability—they are psychological managers. Their language is studied obsessively by investors. A single phrase from a Federal Reserve chair can shift trillions in capital flows. This is not accidental. Modern monetary policy is part finance, part theatre. Forward guidance, quantitative easing, emergency backstops—these are not just tools for managing liquidity; they are instruments of narrative control.

And this control is fragile. In 2020, at the onset of the COVID-19 pandemic, the U.S. Federal Reserve injected over $3 trillion into the financial system in a matter of months. Other central banks followed suit. The justification was crisis mitigation. The effect was asset inflation—equity markets soared even as real economies contracted. This decoupling revealed an uncomfortable truth: that markets are now sustained less by productive output than by the anticipation of continued monetary intervention. That is not confidence in value. That is dependence on stimulus.

This dependence extends to political domains as well. Fiat currencies have become tools of geopolitical strategy. The weaponisation of the dollar through sanctions, for instance, has profound implications for global trust in fiat. Nations like Russia and China have begun diversifying away from dollar reserves, not simply for economic reasons, but to reduce exposure to Western political influence. The more a currency is used to enforce geopolitical will, the more it invites alternatives—and the more it exposes the soft underbelly of fiat: its reliance on cooperative belief.

Even domestically, this trust is showing signs of strain. Consider the erosion of confidence in pension systems, the rising scepticism towards central banks' independence, and the growing popularity of decentralised assets like Bitcoin. These are not just fringe sentiments. They are indicators of a broader awareness that the traditional architecture of value is no longer assumed to be neutral, permanent, or even reliable. The rise of digital currencies, in particular, challenges fiat's monopoly by offering competing frameworks for trust—trust in code, trust in cryptography, trust in decentralised consensus.

But let us be clear: fiat is not about to vanish. It remains the dominant system, backed by legal tender laws, tax obligations, and military might. What is changing, however, is the nature of belief. The public no longer views fiat as sacred. It is beginning to see it as strategic—something to be used when convenient, hedged when necessary, and exited when possible.

This shift in mindset has profound implications. Because once people stop believing that their currency is a stable store of value, they begin to behave differently. They save less in cash. They invest in assets with perceived real-world utility—land, commodities, skills. They seek exposure to alternative stores of value. And eventually, they begin to build systems parallel to the mainstream: peer-to-peer exchanges, barter economies, private currencies. History is replete with such examples. Parallel economies have emerged in wartime, under hyperinflation, during political upheaval—and always as a rational response to the collapse of trust in fiat.

The behavioural psychology of money adds another dimension to this unraveling. Our attachment to currency is not purely rational—it is emotional, cultural, and deeply embedded in our sense of control. Studies in behavioural economics show that people treat losses in monetary terms more seriously than equivalent gains—a phenomenon known as loss aversion. This makes fiat devaluation particularly insidious: it reduces wealth in ways that people often do not fully perceive until it is too late. A 2% annual inflation rate may seem negligible, but over twenty years, it halves your purchasing power. Yet few respond to this as they would to an outright theft.

Why? Because the decline is slow, sanctioned, and abstract. Fiat, unlike gold or real estate, does not rust or crumble. It remains numerically whole. The illusion of value persists long after the reality has shifted. This psychological latency is one reason why fiat systems endure longer than their fundamentals would suggest. The pain is delayed, dispersed, and disguised.

In light of this, the question is not whether fiat will continue to function—it will, in some form, for the foreseeable future. The question is whether it will continue to be trusted, and by whom. As centralised control increases—through digital currencies issued by states, tighter capital controls, and programmable monetary instruments—the very mechanisms that sustain fiat may become the reasons individuals begin to reject it. A programmable currency can enforce spending restrictions, expiry dates, even political penalties. Such features may be sold as efficiency or security. But they come at the cost of sovereignty.

And here lies the core dilemma: fiat currencies offer convenience, scalability, and legal interoperability—but at the expense of autonomy, transparency, and long-term stability. Trust in fiat is therefore not just economic—it is ethical. It is a question of whether individuals are willing to place their futures in the hands of opaque, politicised institutions whose incentives do not align with their own.

Fiat and Faith is a study in that tension. It is an invitation to see beyond the numbers on a bank screen or the promise of central bank stability. It is a call to interrogate the stories we have been told about what money is, and who benefits from our belief in it. Because when trust is no longer implicit, it must be earned. And when it cannot be earned, it must be reimagined.

Understanding this dynamic is the first step towards financial sovereignty. Not by abandoning fiat outright, but by refusing to be enslaved by its illusions. By building systems, portfolios, and mindsets that function independently of institutional trust. By recognising that faith, when misplaced, becomes risk—and when redirected, becomes power.

The Hidden Mechanics of Economic Fragility

Economic collapse is not the failure of a system. It is often the realisation that the system has been functioning exactly as designed. What appears, in the aftermath, as a series of shocks—spiking inflation, collapsing currencies, sovereign defaults, and geopolitical turmoil—is rarely unpredictable. On closer examination, these events follow patterns. They are embedded not at the periphery of the financial order, but at its core. The mechanics of fragility are not outliers. They are features.

This chapter begins with a premise many economists quietly acknowledge but seldom discuss in public discourse: *modern economies are built for momentum, not balance.* Growth is essential. Stagnation is feared. Retraction is unthinkable. And to keep the machine moving, central banks, governments, and global institutions lean heavily on tools that inevitably generate instability over time—namely inflation, debt, and geopolitical leverage. These are not emergency measures. They are structural dependencies. Understanding them is not just an intellectual exercise—it is a prerequisite for survival.

Take inflation. Most are taught to view it as a manageable side effect of prosperity—a natural outcome of increased demand in a growing economy. But inflation, particularly in fiat-based systems, is policy-driven, not accidental. Central banks aim for a "targeted" inflation rate (typically 2%) under the belief that moderate price growth encourages spending and investment. Yet this framing conceals its corrosive impact. Over time, even modest inflation quietly erodes purchasing power, diminishes savings, and penalises financial caution. A person saving diligently at a 1% interest rate in an economy with 3% inflation is not preserving wealth—they are bleeding it.

And inflation rarely remains moderate. Once it gains momentum, it becomes difficult to rein in without inducing recession. The 1970s stagflation crisis in the United States is illustrative: inflation rates soared into double digits, eroding wages and asset values alike. Paul Volcker's Federal Reserve had to raise interest rates to nearly 20% to restore stability, plunging the economy into painful contraction. The lesson was clear but largely ignored in subsequent decades: inflation may be engineered, but it is not easily controlled.

In recent years, the post-pandemic policy response has reignited these dynamics. Trillions of dollars, euros, pounds, and yen were injected into global economies in response to COVID-19 disruptions. This unprecedented monetary expansion, paired with disrupted supply chains and rising commodity costs, triggered a resurgence in inflation unseen in over four decades. The initial narrative—that inflation was "transitory"—collapsed under the weight of reality. What emerged instead was a broader realisation that central banks had become trapped: raise rates too slowly, and inflation persists; raise them too fast, and credit markets seize. In either case, fragility is exposed.

Which leads directly to the second mechanic: debt. If inflation is the erosion of value, debt is the amplification of fragility. Modern economies are not merely debt-based—they are debt-dependent. Government deficits fund everything from healthcare to defence. Corporate leverage finances growth and share buybacks. Household borrowing props up consumer demand. This web of obligations is so vast, so structurally embedded, that it is no longer an aberration—it is the model.

The numbers are staggering. As of 2024, global debt exceeds $300 trillion, over three times global GDP. This figure is not just unsustainable; it is unrecoverable. There is no plausible path to repayment under current economic structures. Instead, debt is rolled over, refinanced, and increasingly monetised by central banks—a process that further inflates currency supply and feeds the inflationary cycle. What results is a self-reinforcing loop: more debt requires more currency creation, which triggers more inflation, which demands higher rates, which increases the cost of servicing existing debt. Eventually, the system consumes itself.

This cycle is not hypothetical. It has real-world consequences. Countries like Japan now spend over 40% of government revenue on interest payments. The United States has crossed the threshold where annual interest payments exceed military spending. And emerging markets, many of which borrow in foreign currencies, find themselves perpetually vulnerable to capital flight, currency devaluation, and IMF conditionality. The architecture of debt ensures that fragility is both domestic and global.

But perhaps the most overlooked mechanism of instability is geopolitical tension—not as an external risk, but as a built-in pressure valve of the global economic order. Since the end of World War II, global finance has been deeply entangled with geopolitics. The Bretton Woods system, the petrodollar arrangement, the rise of multilateral development banks—all reflect the strategic use of monetary policy as a lever of international influence.

Today, that entanglement is intensifying. Sanctions are used not just to punish aggressors but to reshape global financial flows. Trade agreements are structured to favour strategic alliances over free-market logic. Technological decoupling between China and the West is redefining global capital allocation. Even semiconductors—once a niche concern—have become economic weapons, targeted through export bans and national subsidies.

Consider the U.S. decision to freeze Russia's foreign reserves following the invasion of Ukraine. It marked a tectonic shift: for the first time, a G20 nation saw its sovereign assets effectively confiscated by a rival bloc. The signal was unmistakable. Global reserves are no longer politically neutral. This has pushed many nations to reconsider their holdings in U.S. dollars, accelerating the move toward currency diversification, bilateral trade agreements, and even digital alternatives like central bank digital currencies (CBDCs). But these "solutions" introduce new forms of fragility: surveillance risk, programmability, centralisation of control.

Geopolitical fragility is not limited to state actors. It filters down to corporations, supply chains, and individuals. A factory closure in Taiwan can stall global electronics production. A policy shift in Washington can bankrupt companies half a world away. A cyberattack on a banking network can paralyse commerce in minutes. The supposed resilience of globalised markets has been revealed as brittle, conditional, and heavily contingent on political goodwill that is increasingly in short supply.

What emerges from this landscape is a clear conclusion: *the global economic system is not designed to withstand sustained disruption.* It is designed to defer, disguise, and distribute fragility. Policy makers are incentivised to delay hard choices, voters are conditioned to expect intervention, and markets are built to price risk only after it becomes unmanageable. Stability is simulated, not structural. And the longer it is simulated, the more catastrophic the eventual reset becomes.

This is not a call for alarmism. It is an argument for understanding. For those who believe that diversified portfolios, regulated banking systems, or policy safeguards offer protection, this chapter is a challenge. Inflation is not contained. Debt is not accidental. Geopolitical tensions are not background noise. *They are core functions of the machine.*

To navigate this reality requires a shift in thinking. Stop assuming that crises are interruptions. Begin to see them as recalibrations. Build models of wealth and life that are not premised on uninterrupted growth, but on adaptive capacity. Think beyond the balance sheet. Consider geography, liquidity, access, control. Recognise that fragility is not something to be feared if it is seen early—but it is lethal when denied until impact.

Ultimately, economic fragility is a test of vision. Not of whether you can predict the exact moment of collapse, but whether you can read the mechanics before they stall. The objective is not perfection. It is preparedness. And that begins by accepting a hard truth: the machine is not broken. It was never built to be safe. It was built to run—until it doesn't.

The Myth of Diversification

There is perhaps no idea more universally accepted—and less rigorously interrogated—in personal finance than diversification. Its appeal is intuitive, its logic seemingly unassailable: *don't put all your eggs in one basket.* This aphorism has been repeated so frequently, across so many contexts, that its underlying assumptions are rarely questioned. But beneath its veneer of prudence lies a critical flaw: *diversification across systems that are structurally compromised is not protection—it is distributed exposure.*

Modern portfolio theory (MPT), formalised by Harry Markowitz in the 1950s, remains the backbone of financial advice across the globe. It offers a model in which risk can be reduced—not eliminated—by allocating assets across different classes, sectors, and geographies. By spreading investments, MPT suggests, one can offset the volatility of some positions with the stability of others. The idea is elegant. In theory, it holds. But in practice—especially in an age of globalised interdependence, correlated crises, and institutional fragility—it no longer functions as promised.

The problem begins with the assumptions baked into traditional diversification strategies. MPT presumes that asset classes behave independently, or at least with low correlation. That is no longer the world we inhabit. When central banks around the globe coordinate interest rate policies, when equity markets from Tokyo to Toronto react in tandem to signals from the Federal Reserve, and when monetary debasement is a shared policy rather than a national aberration, the lines between diversification and duplication blur. A global portfolio of stocks, bonds, and real estate may *appear* diverse on paper, yet functionally behave as a single trade—particularly during periods of stress.

The 2008 financial crisis exposed this dynamic with clarity. Portfolios diversified across U.S. equities, European bonds, mortgage-backed securities, and even emerging markets all sank together. Correlations, which had appeared low in times of growth, converged toward one during the downturn. The illusion of independence evaporated. Diversification had not hedged against systemic collapse—it had embedded investors deeper within it.

This is not merely an historical anomaly. It is a structural feature of the modern financial machine. Globalisation has created unprecedented levels of financial connectivity. Supply chains are multinational. Currency markets are interlocked. Debt is held across borders. As a result, when one major economy falters, the shock reverberates through every node of the system. A sovereign debt scare in Italy sends tremors through German banks. A tech correction in California deflates pension funds in Seoul. Diversification, once a strategy to mitigate risk, becomes a conduit for contagion.

Moreover, the instruments of diversification themselves are not neutral. Exchange-traded funds (ETFs), index funds, and algorithmically rebalanced portfolios—all sold as solutions to volatility—are often built upon the same infrastructure: centralised exchanges, fiat-denominated assets, and custodial institutions. When those structures are challenged—by liquidity crises, cyber attacks, regulatory overreach, or capital controls—the entire framework buckles. Investors who believed they were hedged suddenly find that access, not allocation, is their most pressing problem.

It is also worth noting the psychological aspect of diversification. It offers not just theoretical protection, but emotional reassurance.

The act of spreading investments feels like responsible behaviour. It aligns with a societal preference for moderation, and it appeals to a managerial class that prizes risk-adjusted metrics over existential resilience. But this emotional comfort can be deceptive. It creates a sense of preparedness that discourages deeper scrutiny. In effect, diversification becomes a substitute for understanding—a way to *appear* sophisticated without confronting the full spectrum of risk embedded in the system.

This becomes particularly dangerous when diversification is used to justify exposure to fundamentally unstable environments. Consider the portfolio that includes Chinese equities for growth, European bonds for stability, and U.S. real estate for income. On the surface, it looks well balanced. But such a strategy may involve capital tied up in autocratic jurisdictions, exposure to negative-yield debt, and reliance on asset classes propped up by speculative leverage. If the legal system of one country seizes assets, if another enters a debt spiral, or if housing markets implode under tightening liquidity, the illusion of safety is quickly shattered. The portfolio was diversified—but only in geography, not in system logic.

This distinction is critical: *diversification across systems with similar failure modes is not true diversification.* When fiat currencies are under simultaneous stress, when real estate is inflated globally by cheap credit, and when equities are all priced off the same discounted cash flow models sensitive to interest rates, the risk is not isolated. It is replicated. The collapse, when it comes, is not partial—it is holistic.

True risk management requires a redefinition of diversification. It must move beyond asset classes and into *systems thinking*. Ask not only *what* you own, but *where it lives*, *how it functions*, and *what assumptions it relies upon*. Is your wealth accessible during a capital freeze? Is it denominated in currencies exposed to political risk? Does it rely on digital platforms that can be shut down, or intermediaries that may be insolvent when needed most?

The answers to these questions are uncomfortable precisely because they disrupt conventional wisdom. They challenge the financial orthodoxy taught in business schools, promoted by fund managers, and reinforced by decades of bull market behaviour. But they are essential if one is to build wealth that is not only profitable but *resilient.*

This is not a rejection of diversification as a concept. It is a demand that it be reimagined for the world as it is—not as it was. In a system where institutional risk is pervasive, geographic boundaries offer little insulation, and liquidity can disappear in hours, diversification must include:

Asset sovereignty—the ability to *own* and *control* your capital without dependency on fragile intermediaries.

System agnosticism—holding value across frameworks not governed by a single monetary or regulatory authority.

Access redundancy—ensuring that you can reach your wealth under multiple conditions: online and offline, digitally and physically, domestically and internationally.

Behavioural antifragility—building mental models that prepare you to act decisively under stress, not freeze in the hope that "markets will rebound."

One might hold precious metals stored in-country, decentralised digital assets protected by cold wallets, land or productive assets in stable regions, and tradeable skills that retain value across environments. This is not diversification in the conventional sense. It is a form of *parallel robustness*, designed not to maximise theoretical returns, but to preserve real-world agency when systems falter.

Ultimately, the myth of diversification is not that it doesn't work—it's that it works until it matters most. And in those moments, what you need is not statistical correlation, but structural independence. Not risk parity, but *sovereign optionality*. The goal is not to be right in ten scenarios. It is to survive in the one that actually unfolds.

In the pages ahead, we will go deeper into these alternatives—not as speculative hedges, but as strategic imperatives. Because in a collapsing paradigm, the conventional map of safety becomes not just outdated—but dangerous. And those who continue to rely on diversification as doctrine, without interrogating its underlying assumptions, may find that they were never hedged at all—only scattered across a system that cannot save them.

Money as a Psychological Construct

Few forces shape human behaviour as profoundly, and as invisibly, as money. Yet despite its centrality to modern life, money is rarely examined for what it truly is: not a fixed economic object, but a fluid psychological construct. It governs choices, relationships, ambitions, and even our sense of self. But its power does not derive from gold reserves, production metrics, or digital ledgers. *It stems from belief.* Belief in its stability, in its function, and—perhaps most dangerously—in the stories we tell ourselves about what it means.

This chapter argues that until we dismantle these internalised narratives, we remain financially vulnerable—regardless of income, education, or asset size. Because financial fragility is not merely structural. It is also cognitive. *How we think about money determines how we behave in times of uncertainty.* And those behaviours, more than any market force, are what often separate those who preserve sovereignty from those who forfeit it.

To grasp the psychology of money, we must first understand that money itself is an abstraction. It has no intrinsic value. A £20 note is not inherently more useful than a scrap of printed paper. A digital bank balance is merely an expression of encoded trust, regulated by invisible systems. And yet, our emotional responses to these symbols are intense, often irrational, and deeply ingrained. Why?

From an early age, we are conditioned to equate money with success, competence, safety, and even self-worth. It is presented as a scorecard in the game of life—accumulate enough, and you are deemed responsible; fail to do so, and you are labelled careless or incapable. These associations are reinforced culturally, institutionally, and emotionally. They create a potent psychological framework where money becomes not just a means of exchange, but a proxy for identity and control.

This is not a neutral framework. It introduces several well-documented behavioural distortions—cognitive biases that operate quietly but decisively in our financial lives.

Loss aversion is one of the most pervasive. First identified by psychologists Daniel Kahneman and Amos Tversky, it refers to the fact that we experience the pain of losing money more acutely than the pleasure of gaining it. In practical terms, this bias leads people to cling to failing investments, avoid calculated risks, or delay exits from collapsing systems—simply because the emotional cost of acknowledging a loss outweighs the rational benefits of taking action.

Closely related is the *endowment effect*, wherein we overvalue what we already own, regardless of its actual utility or market worth. This is why people remain emotionally attached to property in politically unstable regions, or why they hesitate to shift out of fiat currencies even when they intellectually recognise the risk of devaluation. The familiarity of ownership creates psychological inertia.

Perhaps most insidious is the *normalcy bias*—the tendency to assume that future conditions will resemble the past, even in the face of mounting evidence to the contrary. This bias creates paralysis in the face of systemic change. Individuals with otherwise sharp judgment may dismiss warning signs—capital controls, inflation spikes, political polarisation—because they conflict with deeply held assumptions about economic continuity. The belief that "it won't happen here" is not a logical assessment. It is a psychological defence mechanism.

All of these traps are intensified by the media and financial industries, which have a vested interest in maintaining certain narratives. Stability sells. Volatility frightens. And so the system reinforces the illusion that responsible citizens need only stay the course: keep your pension in national funds, your savings in regulated banks, your trust in central banks. When cracks appear, they are explained away as temporary. Structural decline is framed as cyclical adjustment. To question the narrative is to risk being labelled paranoid, pessimistic, or unpatriotic.

Yet the historical record contradicts these assurances. No fiat currency has lasted indefinitely. No empire has avoided economic strain. No centralised financial system has proven immune to corruption, decay, or external shock. The fragility is not hypothetical. It is observable. The only variable is how individuals interpret—and act upon—that fragility.

This is where psychological clarity becomes strategic advantage. To operate intelligently within a collapsing or compromised system, one must separate *money as tool* from *money as emotion*. This means recognising when fear is driving inaction. It means acknowledging sunk-cost bias when it clouds exit decisions. And it means dismantling the belief that safety is defined by conformity.

For example, many middle-class professionals in Western nations continue to view home ownership as the ultimate marker of financial maturity. This belief persists despite evidence that housing markets in urban centres are increasingly driven by speculative bubbles, political risk, and unsustainable debt. The emotional script—*owning a home means stability*—remains stronger than the structural data. This creates vulnerability, especially when mobility, liquidity, and optionality may be far more valuable than a fixed physical asset.

Similarly, the idea that a steady income and a retirement plan equate to security is a psychological holdover from a different era—one in which states were solvent, demographics were favourable, and economic growth was relatively predictable. To remain psychologically attached to that model today, without questioning its assumptions, is to confuse nostalgia with prudence.

Yet none of this is meant to suggest that detachment from money is the goal. On the contrary: *a rational, strategic relationship with money is essential.* But that relationship must be continuously updated, questioned, and adapted to current realities. It must be resilient not only in terms of asset class, but in terms of cognitive flexibility.

The 2022 bank runs in Lebanon, the capital controls in Argentina, the freezing of Russian foreign reserves, the digital surveillance policies tied to Chinese digital yuan—all illustrate the speed and scope with which financial landscapes can shift. Those who responded effectively were not always the wealthiest or best educated. They were the ones who had mentally decoupled from outdated models. They had already moved psychologically from dependence to autonomy.

In this context, financial preparedness begins not with spreadsheets, but with introspection. Ask yourself: *What do I believe about money that might no longer be true? What assumptions have I inherited without scrutiny? What risks do I downplay because they are emotionally uncomfortable?* These are not rhetorical questions. They are diagnostic tools.

Ultimately, the psychology of money is not about managing feelings—it is about recognising how unexamined feelings manage us. When systems fail, the gap between knowledge and action is psychological. Those who act early are not necessarily braver. They are less encumbered by internal narratives that confuse familiarity with safety, or consensus with truth.

To build a sovereign financial life requires both structural strategy and psychological rigour. It demands the humility to question deeply held beliefs, the courage to exit when others remain, and the clarity to define safety in terms that reflect actual control—not institutional reassurance.

Money is not merely something we use. It is something we *believe in.* And those beliefs, if left unexamined, become the very chains that keep us exposed to the collapse we think we're avoiding. The mind, then, is the first line of defence. And the most strategic financial pivot is not always in markets—but in mindset.

Chapter 2
Systemic Vulnerability and the Illusion of Control

When most people picture collapse, they see something loud and cinematic: empty shelves in supermarkets, locked bank doors, crowds on the streets, governments scrambling to contain the fallout. But in reality, collapse—when it truly begins—rarely plays to that script. It arrives more subtly, often disguised as continuity. Promises hold, until they don't. Institutions appear composed, even as the scaffolding beneath begins to strain. What makes systemic breakdown so perilous is not simply the weakness in the infrastructure, but the widespread assumption that someone, somewhere, is managing the risk.

That assumption, that quiet confidence—it is the illusion. And it doesn't persist because it's anchored in verifiable truth. It survives because of belief. A belief gently propped up by legislation, slogans, and the soft-spoken reassurances of politicians and financial leaders. The notion that modern economies are too regulated to fail, that your pension is inviolable, that deposit insurance will always hold, that central banks are infallible backstops—these are not laws of physics. They are stories. Stories told often enough to feel like reality.

Chapter Two opens with a challenge to this very architecture of belief. Because to prepare honestly for instability, one must first understand its architecture—not as anomaly or administrative error, but as a baked-in feature of systems that were never truly designed to shield the individual. Most state financial guarantees—whether in the form of social security, deposit insurance, health entitlements, or unemployment assistance—depend on three underlying assumptions: perpetual economic growth, demographic alignment, and stable governance. Remove just one, and the structure begins to lurch.

expansion over long-term resilience. This is not an accident. It is the product of deeply embedded incentives that favour growth at all costs, even when that growth comes at the expense of systemic stability.

At the heart of this design is the financial cycle itself. Most people are familiar with the concept of a business cycle—periods of boom and bust—but far fewer grasp the mechanics behind credit cycles, which are longer, more volatile, and vastly more dangerous. Credit expansions fuel asset bubbles, inflate consumption, and support political promises. But they also create cumulative fragility. As debt levels rise, economies become increasingly sensitive to interest rates, liquidity conditions, and investor sentiment. A small policy error, a geopolitical misstep, or a shift in narrative can unwind trillions in paper wealth almost overnight.

The 2008 global financial crisis is often explained through the lens of subprime mortgages and Wall Street greed. But the deeper story is structural: a system addicted to leverage, enabled by financial innovation (credit default swaps, synthetic CDOs), and legitimised by regulatory institutions that had no incentive to interrupt the party. When the music stopped, governments and central banks intervened—not to reform the system, but to restore it. The result was not resilience. It was a reset, with even greater fragility embedded in the next cycle.

Post-2008, central banks entered a new phase of interventionism. Interest rates were slashed to zero or below, quantitative easing became permanent, and financial markets came to rely not on earnings or productivity, but on central bank liquidity. This is the era of *monetary moral hazard*—where risk-taking is rewarded because failure is socially underwritten. The problem, of course, is that moral hazard compounds. When market actors believe that bailouts are inevitable, they double down on fragility. The system becomes not just leveraged, but conditioned for failure.

Yet the most misunderstood dimension of systemic fragility is not financial—it is psychological. The illusion of control is a deeply embedded cognitive bias. As long as the system functions in day-to-day life—cash machines dispense money, markets open at 9:30, salaries arrive on schedule—people assume the structure is fundamentally sound. This belief is reinforced by institutions whose credibility rests on projecting competence: central banks, finance ministries, major media outlets. When risks are raised, they are often dismissed as alarmist. Even when the data is public—rising sovereign debt, widening wealth inequality, deteriorating trust in institutions—most people default to inertia. They assume that if collapse were imminent, "someone" would be doing something. That belief is not just naïve. It is systemically useful.

This isn't merely an issue of individual psychology. It is baked into institutional design. Political cycles are short-term—typically four to six years—while the costs of financial fragility accumulate over decades. There is little incentive for policymakers to implement painful reforms that deliver no immediate political benefit. Fiscal prudence, regulatory restraint, and monetary tightening are all career liabilities in boom periods. This is how fragility becomes institutionalised: when those charged with governance are incentivised to preserve appearances rather than confront risk.

Consider the global sovereign debt situation. As of this writing, total government debt exceeds $100 trillion, with debt-to-GDP ratios at historic highs in many developed nations. Servicing this debt is feasible only under ultra-low interest rates—conditions that cannot be sustained indefinitely without distorting capital allocation, penalising savers, and fuelling inflation. Yet raising rates risks triggering debt crises, market crashes, and fiscal insolvency. This is a *trap*, not a cycle. And it's one that is reproduced across jurisdictions.

Emerging markets face a parallel dynamic. They are often dollar-indebted, export-reliant, and institutionally weak. When the global credit tide recedes, these nations face currency collapses, capital flight, and IMF-imposed austerity. Again, this is not misfortune. It is structural dependency. The global financial system operates as a hierarchy, with developed nations exporting risk and developing nations absorbing it.

Technology has further amplified fragility by accelerating the speed of contagion. Financial transactions occur at near-light speed. Capital flight, flash crashes, algorithmic trading errors—these can unravel months of economic planning in minutes. The system is not only complex; it is brittle at scale. A bank run no longer requires queues outside branches; it takes a trending hashtag. And while digital innovation brings efficiency, it also concentrates power—placing outsized influence in the hands of a few platforms, exchanges, and data monopolies whose internal mechanics remain opaque to regulators and users alike.

This raises a deeper philosophical question: why does a civilisation with such immense technological prowess remain so financially fragile? The answer lies in the disconnect between complexity and comprehension. The more advanced a system becomes, the harder it is for any single actor—or even institution—to fully grasp its vulnerabilities. Complexity creates opacity, and opacity creates dependency. People stop asking *how* the system works, and focus instead on *how to extract from it* while it lasts.

In this environment, collapse is not just probable—it is cyclical. And most people are blindsided because they are trained to interpret each crisis as an isolated failure, not a structural pattern. The dot-com bust, the global financial crisis, the Eurozone sovereign debt crisis, the pandemic-induced shutdowns—these are treated as separate events, each with its own causes and solutions. But step back, and a pattern emerges: risk builds in silence, is rationalised during expansion, and is met with panic when the cycle turns.

The real danger is not the crisis itself. It is the interval of complacency that precedes it. That is when leverage builds, oversight relaxes, and warnings go unheard. Those who wait for clarity often find themselves too late. By the time fragility becomes visible, options have narrowed. Capital controls are imposed. Markets shut. Banks freeze withdrawals. Laws are rewritten. The public narrative shifts—from "there's nothing to worry about" to "nobody could have seen this coming"—despite the fact that many did.

This chapter is not an indictment of capitalism, central banking, or technological innovation. It is an indictment of systemic denial. Of the comforting idea that someone, somewhere, is managing the risks with foresight and competence. The truth is more sobering: *the system is fragile because it is incentivised to be.* Until that changes, collapse is not a matter of if, but when.

To see clearly in this environment is not an act of cynicism. It is a form of preparation. If the system is structured to break periodically, then one must build personal and financial strategies that assume failure as a feature—not a glitch. This begins not with fear, but with understanding. Because once you accept that the architecture is fragile by design, you stop waiting for the crisis. You start positioning for it.

That is what this chapter will explore. Not just the mechanics of fragility, but the psychology that obscures it. Not just the patterns of collapse, but the incentives that reproduce them. And most critically, how to think, act, and prepare in a world where the next crisis is already embedded in the current design.

The Safety Net Illusion

There is a quiet doctrine embedded in the financial lives of most citizens: *the belief that the state will step in if things go wrong.* This belief is not the result of direct evidence. It is cultivated—by political narratives, policy rhetoric, and institutional design. Deposit insurance, public pensions, unemployment benefits, bailouts—these are marketed as guarantees, structured as entitlements, and internalised as assurances. They form what is commonly referred to as the financial "safety net." Yet, as history repeatedly demonstrates, *the reliability of these safety nets disintegrates precisely when they are needed most.*

The psychological comfort derived from state-backed guarantees is immense. It allows individuals to take economic risks, delay financial planning, and mentally outsource the consequences of systemic shocks. But this comfort rests on a fundamental misunderstanding: that governments and their financial institutions possess unlimited capacity to absorb economic stress. In reality, they do not. They operate within constraints—fiscal, monetary, demographic, and political. And when these constraints tighten, the promise of protection often gives way to triage, austerity, or outright default.

To understand the illusion, we must examine the underlying design of these guarantees, and how they behave under pressure. Consider deposit insurance. In most developed countries, bank deposits are insured up to a certain limit—£85,000 in the UK, €100,000 in the EU, and $250,000 in the US. This scheme is intended to prevent bank runs and reassure depositors. But the mechanism is neither infinite nor automatic. Insurance funds are typically underwritten by a pool of bank contributions, not by state treasuries. In a small, localised failure, these funds may suffice. In a cascading crisis, they do not. The state must then choose whether to monetise the shortfall—by issuing debt or printing money—or allow losses to cascade. The outcome depends not on law, but on political and economic conditions at the time.

Cyprus in 2013 offers a sharp example. When two of its largest banks faced insolvency, the government implemented a controversial "bail-in" of uninsured depositors. Accounts exceeding the €100,000 limit were frozen, and in many cases, partially confiscated to recapitalise the banks. For many, this was the first realisation that *insured* does not mean *safe*, and that legal guarantees can be suspended or reinterpreted under the logic of emergency.

Pensions, another pillar of the safety net, are equally vulnerable—though less visibly so. Public pension systems are generally structured as pay-as-you-go (PAYG) schemes: current workers fund the benefits of current retirees. This design assumes demographic and economic stability—steady birth rates, full employment, and a broad tax base. But this assumption no longer holds in much of the developed world. Ageing populations, low fertility rates, and rising life expectancy have inverted the dependency ratio. In countries like Japan, Italy, and Germany, there are now fewer than two workers supporting each retiree. Even the United States, with a comparatively younger demographic profile, faces long-term insolvency in its Social Security and Medicare programmes.

What governments do under such pressure is rarely to default outright. Instead, they recalibrate promises: increase retirement ages, reduce cost-of-living adjustments, raise payroll taxes, or change eligibility criteria. These are forms of *stealth default*—legal, incremental, and politically palatable. Yet for the individual who has structured their retirement around the original terms, the effect is the same: the safety net shrinks just as reliance on it becomes acute.

Unemployment benefits, housing subsidies, food assistance—similar dynamics apply. These are discretionary expenditures that depend on fiscal space and political will. In times of mass unemployment or economic contraction, they are either expanded—at great cost—or reduced to preserve fiscal solvency. The 2008–2010 austerity measures across southern Europe, driven by the Eurozone debt crisis, saw deep cuts to social services, healthcare, and public-sector wages in countries like Greece and Spain. The promises of social protection collapsed under the weight of creditor demands and sovereign bond market dynamics.

The illusion persists because these systems function in ordinary times. Deposits are reimbursed. Pensions are paid. Healthcare is delivered. But this consistency is deceptive. It conceals the *conditional nature* of the guarantees. They are contingent on fiscal health, monetary credibility, and institutional trust—all of which deteriorate in crisis.

And herein lies the psychological trap. People mistake consistency for resilience. They believe that because something has *always worked*, it will *continue to work*—even as underlying fundamentals decay. This is a classic cognitive bias: extrapolating from the past while ignoring structural deterioration. It explains why so few reposition before the net frays—why retirees are left exposed, savers lose access to funds, and citizens are blindsided by benefit cuts.

This illusion is reinforced by political rhetoric. Leaders, especially during campaigns, speak of safety nets as if they were immutable rights. Pensions are "guaranteed." Deposits are "safe." No one says, "Your benefits will be recalibrated in line with debt service obligations." But this is often what happens. And the disconnect between promise and delivery—when it finally appears—feels like betrayal, not correction.

There is also an ethical complexity to consider. Safety nets were not designed to create dependency. They were intended to manage tail risks—illness, job loss, old age—not to serve as lifelong income strategies. But over time, especially in high-income economies, they have become substitutes for personal financial resilience. This is not entirely the fault of the individual. Wages have stagnated. Housing has financialised. Education and healthcare have inflated faster than general CPI. In such a landscape, leaning on state guarantees becomes not a choice, but a survival strategy.

Yet the danger of this dependency is precisely what this chapter aims to illuminate. If the structure you rely on is brittle, then the sense of control it provides is a mirage. The safety net, rather than insulating you from risk, *increases your exposure*—by lulling you into deferring preparation.

This does not mean one should reject all state systems. It means recognising their limits and planning *around* them. Consider insured deposits as *convenient*, not *guaranteed*. View public pensions as *supplementary*, not *sufficient*. Treat unemployment support as *a bridge*, not *a destination*. And above all, ensure that your financial life does not rest on the sustained solvency of institutions whose incentives, constraints, and political mandates you neither control nor influence.

The deeper insight here is that financial sovereignty requires not just assets, but *clarity*. Clarity about what is promised. Clarity about what can be delivered. And clarity about what is at stake when belief in the system outruns its capacity to provide.

This chapter will explore these themes in greater detail—examining the historical failure points of safety nets, the mechanisms by which guarantees are rescinded, and the psychological defences that keep people from seeing the erosion until it's too late. Because ultimately, the most dangerous feature of a safety net is not that it can break. It's that it can give you the false impression you don't need to build your own.

Geopolitical Fault Lines

Global finance does not operate in a vacuum. It is shaped—and frequently destabilised—by the friction between nation-states. While monetary policy, debt issuance, and investment flows may appear technical or apolitical at first glance, they are, in reality, tightly entangled with power, territory, and ideology. To ignore geopolitics in the analysis of financial stability is to misread the very terrain on which modern economies are built. In fact, it is often at the **intersections of diplomacy, conflict, and strategic competition** that the most profound economic collapses originate—not as direct acts of war, but as unintended consequences of geopolitical strain.

The notion of a geopolitical "fault line" is not metaphorical. These are actual stress zones—geographic, economic, and ideological—where global interests collide, and from which systemic risk can propagate. Today's fault lines are neither obscure nor speculative. They are recognisable and active: the Taiwan Strait, the South China Sea, the Russian-Ukrainian frontier, the Persian Gulf, the Korean Peninsula, the Sahel, and the Arctic shipping routes. These regions are more than potential military flashpoints; they are deeply embedded in global economic infrastructure—energy, semiconductors, rare earths, shipping lanes, currency zones, and cyber networks.

What makes these zones so economically consequential is that modern markets are both highly integrated and politically exposed. A single act of provocation in one of these regions can derail entire sectors. In 2022, when Russia invaded Ukraine, the immediate fallout was not only human and territorial—it was monetary. Sanctions, swift removals from the global payment system, central bank asset freezes, and ruptured energy contracts reshaped the financial strategies of nations overnight. For Russia, it meant decoupling from the Western financial grid and accelerating internal rouble-based trade and external yuan-denominated settlements. For Europe, it precipitated a scramble for alternative gas supplies, fiscal bailouts of households and utilities, and a reconsideration of monetary policy amidst energy-driven inflation. The lesson was sobering: *currency systems are not neutral—they are weapons, and they can be turned off.*

Sanctions represent a particularly potent form of financial warfare. Designed to punish, isolate, or coerce, they increasingly act as both a deterrent and a provocation. The freezing of Iranian central bank assets, Venezuela's exclusion from SWIFT, the blocking of Russian sovereign reserves—all illustrate the extent to which financial tools are now deployed to achieve political ends. But this use of finance as a diplomatic weapon is not costless. It encourages targeted states to build *parallel financial systems*—trading in local currencies, creating alternative messaging networks like Russia's SPFS or China's CIPS, accumulating gold reserves, or experimenting with blockchain-based cross-border settlement systems.

From a systemic standpoint, this bifurcation creates a dual risk. First, it erodes trust in the existing dollar-based order, accelerating de-dollarisation not as a fringe movement, but as a strategic imperative for politically exposed economies. Second, it introduces friction into global trade, investment, and capital flows. If dollar access becomes conditional on political alignment, states will hedge against that dependency by building fragmented systems. This reduces efficiency, but more critically, it *reduces the elasticity of the global financial system*—its ability to absorb shocks by reallocating capital swiftly across borders. Financial protectionism, like trade protectionism, raises the risk of misallocated capital and slows down crisis recovery.

Taiwan represents another high-risk node—not because of its size, but because of its centrality to global supply chains. The Taiwan Semiconductor Manufacturing Company (TSMC) produces over 90% of the world's most advanced semiconductors. These chips are not just components—they are infrastructure, embedded in everything from smartphones to weapons systems. A blockade, sabotage, or forced reunification effort by China would not only be a geopolitical shock; it would induce a global economic seizure. Central banks could not print their way out of a semiconductor shortage. It is not an abstract risk. The scenario is repeatedly gamed by defence analysts, supply chain managers, and risk officers across major economies.

Similarly, the Strait of Hormuz—a narrow maritime corridor through which 20% of the world's oil flows—remains acutely vulnerable. Escalation between Iran and Gulf states, or between Iran and the US Navy, could spike oil prices dramatically, triggering inflation, currency crises in oil-importing nations, and political instability in emerging markets. Unlike in the 1970s, today's financial system is more leveraged, more digital, and more globally integrated. A commodity shock of that magnitude would transmit instantly through derivatives, margin calls, and asset revaluations—destabilising not just energy markets, but pension funds, corporate bond portfolios, and sovereign credit ratings.

One must also consider the **economic aftershocks of military posturing**. The economic cost of NATO expansion, Chinese military drills, and proxy conflicts in Africa or the Middle East is rarely reflected in GDP figures—but it is borne in sovereign balance sheets, diverted investment, and fragile investor confidence. Nations forced to rearm or fortify trade routes incur not only fiscal costs but political ones, often at the expense of domestic welfare or structural reform. Over time, this militarisation of fiscal policy becomes self-reinforcing—defence budgets increase, productive capital is diverted, and central banks are pressured to maintain low rates despite inflationary pressures, simply to keep debt service manageable.

Geopolitical risk also expresses itself in *currency markets*, and not always in obvious ways. When the US asserts dominance through sanctions, the perceived safety of the dollar rises in the short term. But over the medium to long term, it forces even allied countries to reconsider the prudence of holding dollar reserves or settling trade in a politically volatile currency. The trend is incremental, but real: central banks are reducing their exposure to US Treasuries, increasing gold holdings, and exploring sovereign digital currencies that allow for more discrete and programmable capital controls.

This financial nationalism is a rational response to a world in which **diplomacy is increasingly transactional**. If access to the financial system is contingent on political loyalty, then maintaining autonomy requires building escape routes—alternative payment rails, bilateral trade agreements, commodity-backed instruments. These strategies are not revolutionary. They are defensive. And they reflect a growing awareness that *geopolitical stress does not just cause currency failure—it often reveals fragilities that were already in place.*

The Eurozone crisis offers another instructive example. Though triggered by fiscal imbalances in Greece, it was exacerbated by political indecision, North–South divides, and structural design flaws in the euro itself—specifically, the lack of a fiscal union to accompany the monetary one. The crisis revealed how quickly solidarity disintegrates under stress, and how cross-border financial commitments can become politically toxic. Even today, despite new fiscal frameworks, the union remains vulnerable to asymmetric shocks—whether they originate from migration, energy supply, or external conflicts.

The broader lesson is that **geopolitical events are not external to economic systems—they are endogenous to their function and failure**. Financial infrastructure is embedded in geopolitical hierarchies. Access to liquidity, security guarantees, trade routes, and technological sovereignty are all governed by shifting alliances, national interests, and diplomatic leverage. When the geopolitical ground shifts, the financial edifice tilts—sometimes slowly, sometimes suddenly.

This chapter will dissect these fault lines in more detail—mapping the high-risk zones, decoding the transmission channels, and evaluating the systemic implications. It will not predict wars, but it will demonstrate that financial preparedness in the 21st century cannot be decoupled from geopolitical awareness. Because *in a globally entangled world, collapse often begins far from where it ends—and by the time it reaches your doorstep, it's already too late to reroute exposure.*

Geopolitical fault lines are not just about missiles and borders. They are about pipelines, satellites, data flows, port leases, and treaties. They are about the durability of assumptions and the fragility of systems built on the illusion of cooperation. And they are about recognising that economic collapse does not always announce itself with market data—it sometimes begins with a diplomatic insult, a misfired drone, or a quietly rewritten trade agreement.

To prepare intelligently is not to react to headlines, but to read the tectonics beneath them. That's what this section aims to do. Not offer predictions, but *equip the reader with the insight required to interpret geopolitical noise as financial signal*—and to act accordingly.

Chaos as a Business Model

Collapse is not always a tragedy for everyone involved. For certain institutions, sectors, and power structures, systemic failure is not a threat—it is a windfall. The unsettling truth is that while ordinary citizens brace for loss during crises, there are those who benefit not in spite of the chaos, but *because* of it. This reality is not new, nor is it accidental. In fact, it is a predictable and often deliberate feature of how modern political economies allocate risk, capital, and influence. *Chaos, in many cases, has become a business model.*

To understand this, we must dispense with the naïve assumption that systemic stability is the default goal of all actors within a society. Stability is desirable for some, certainly—but for others, instability offers asymmetric opportunity. It reshuffles power hierarchies, justifies exceptional policy measures, unlocks public funding streams, and enables corporate consolidation at fire-sale prices. In short, *when the system breaks, someone profits*—and often, those actors are positioned ahead of the collapse, not behind it.

Consider the 2008 global financial crisis. While millions lost homes, jobs, and retirement savings, several hedge funds—most notably

Paulson & Co.—earned billions by betting against the housing market. More revealing, however, was how quickly financial institutions that had caused the crisis were bailed out, recapitalised, and in some cases, emerged larger and more profitable than before. Goldman Sachs, JPMorgan Chase, and Bank of America were among the recipients of emergency support, only to post record profits within a few years. The pain was socialised. The profit was privatised.

This pattern extends beyond banking. Defence contractors have long been accused of thriving on geopolitical instability, but the mechanism by which they profit is more subtle than arms sales alone. Conflict zones generate enduring demand for surveillance, cybersecurity, intelligence outsourcing, and drone technologies—products whose cost-effectiveness is difficult to audit, and whose supply chains are deeply embedded in the state apparatus. Companies like Lockheed Martin, Raytheon, and Northrop Grumman have seen their market capitalisations soar following military escalations, particularly when accompanied by fears of long-term regional instability. War, even in potential form, creates a durable revenue stream.

Similarly, private security firms expand their reach during periods of civil unrest, economic collapse, or weakened state authority. In South Africa, Venezuela, Iraq, and parts of Eastern Europe, local elites, multinationals, and even NGOs have increasingly turned to private forces to secure facilities, protect assets, and manage protests. These firms are not necessarily destabilising actors, but their profitability correlates directly with the erosion of public trust in state capacity. The greater the chaos, the more in demand their services become.

Then there is the burgeoning disaster capitalism sector—a term popularised by Naomi Klein to describe the monetisation of public trauma. Natural disasters, pandemics, and infrastructure failures have become commercial opportunities for a growing set of industries: private equity firms acquiring distressed real estate, tech companies offering "resilience platforms," pharmaceutical giants securing emergency procurement contracts, and educational firms replacing public schooling with digital content during shutdowns. COVID-19 exposed this playbook at scale. Companies like Zoom, Amazon, and Moderna experienced exponential growth, while smaller businesses collapsed under the weight of lockdown restrictions. The state response was not neutral—it often amplified existing inequalities and created new monopolies under the banner of crisis management.

What's critical to understand is that *these outcomes are not incidental.* The legal, financial, and regulatory frameworks of most advanced economies are not designed to eliminate rent-seeking during collapse—they facilitate it. Emergency legislation often weakens procurement oversight, waives antitrust scrutiny, and expands executive power. Public-private partnerships emerge under compressed timelines with limited transparency. Institutional investors with liquidity step in to acquire distressed assets while retail investors are frozen out of illiquid markets. The wealth transfer is legal, rapid, and often permanent.

Insurance, traditionally seen as a stabilising force, plays a complex role in this landscape. On one hand, it mitigates individual exposure. On the other, it creates large pools of predictable capital that can be speculatively reallocated. Reinsurance markets, catastrophe bonds, and credit default swaps are mechanisms by which financial firms profit from volatility itself. In some cases, underwriters of disaster insurance have been found to *undervalue* risk in boom periods to increase market share, only to retreat or raise premiums dramatically post-collapse—leaving communities exposed when they are most vulnerable.

Even policy-making is not immune. Governments often face perverse incentives during downturns. Crises enable the expansion of surveillance regimes, the introduction of centralised digital currencies, and the rollback of privacy protections under the guise of public safety. What begins as emergency response becomes long-term infrastructure. The temptation to *not let a crisis go to waste* is not rhetorical; it is operational doctrine in many administrative circles.

This leads to an unsettling question: if powerful institutions benefit from collapse, how sincerely invested are they in preventing it? The answer is not binary. Most actors do not orchestrate crises—they position themselves to exploit them. They invest in lobbying, narrative control, and policy access to ensure that when systems falter, they're first in line for the upside. The paradox is that they have the resources to influence outcomes before collapse—but often choose not to deploy them until after collapse, when terms are more favourable.

There is, of course, a moral cost to this dynamic. The normalisation of profit through collapse erodes social cohesion, deepens inequality, and undermines public faith in institutional legitimacy. When citizens observe that bailouts go to the well-connected, that emergency powers are seldom rolled back, and that volatility consistently benefits a narrow set of actors, they begin to disengage—not just from markets, but from governance itself. This disengagement creates a feedback loop: apathy weakens oversight, which enables further exploitation, which increases polarisation, which makes systemic reform even harder.

This is not to say that every business profiting from crisis is acting maliciously. Some innovations—resilient infrastructure, decentralised finance, off-grid energy systems—genuinely enhance societal antifragility. The distinction lies in *intent and impact.* Is the business model predicated on extracting value from breakdown, or on building systems that reduce the likelihood or severity of future collapse?

Understanding this distinction is vital for anyone seeking financial sovereignty. It shifts the focus from prediction to positioning. Instead of asking "When will the next crisis occur?" the better question is: *Who will benefit from it, and how can I avoid being on the wrong side of that equation?* This requires more than diversification. It demands clarity—about incentives, institutional behaviour, and systemic vulnerability.

This chapter will map the key sectors and strategies that monetise collapse. It will examine how profit is extracted legally during crisis, which industries are structurally geared for upside volatility, and how policy frameworks create conditions for rent-seeking. It will also explore how individuals can interpret crisis signals not only as threats, but as signals of shifting value—and how to align financial strategies with systems that reward resilience over dependency.

The uncomfortable truth is that chaos is not always a failure of the system. For some, it *is* the system. To navigate such a world, one must see clearly where power flows in moments of disruption—and ensure that they are not merely collateral in someone else's business model.

Chapter 3
Escaping the Matrix – Redefining Wealth

For most of modern history, wealth has been synonymous with accumulation. Assets, capital, real estate, prestige—these have long served as the cornerstones of what it means to be "well-off." The definitions were static, almost architectural: how much you owned, how much money you could make while seemingly doing nothing, how thoroughly your financial presence was embedded within the established systems. And for a time, that worked. The institutions were stable, the frameworks coherent, and the rules—at least in appearance—reliable across generations. But that era is slipping. The scaffolding, once so solid, now groans under the pressure of mounting debt, ecological limits, fraying political consensus, and accelerating technological disruption. As it does, the very metrics we've used to measure wealth begin to feel curiously out of step with the times.

This chapter does not reject wealth. It proposes something more unsettling—and ultimately more liberating: a redefinition. To "exit the matrix," in this context, is not to disappear off-grid or embrace a life of radical simplicity. It is to see clearly—perhaps for the first time—what the prevailing definition of wealth has cost you, who it truly serves, and how little resilience it offers when the music stops. It is to reimagine wealth not as the accumulation of static things, but as a dynamic configuration of capabilities that do not collapse when systems stutter, borders shut, or markets convulse.

One of the most seductive illusions of the old model is passive income. For years, it has been held up as the pinnacle of financial independence—the dream of earning while sleeping, of building systems that generate money without further effort. Rental properties, dividend portfolios, licensing deals, digital royalties—these are the sacred pillars. And yet, this dream rests on a dangerously fragile assumption: continuity. Passive income only functions if the structures it relies on remain intact. Rental yields assume stable tenants, enforceable contracts, and an uncorrupted currency. Dividends presuppose robust supply chains, healthy credit markets, and geopolitical calm. Even royalties can be frozen, taxed, restructured, or rendered obsolete by a mere tweak in platform policy.

Let's be clear—passive income is not divorced from labour. It is tethered, quite precariously, to systems you do not control.

This isn't to dismiss it entirely. Rather, the point is sharper: passivity, in a volatile age, is increasingly a risk. The more removed you are from the levers of your own income, the more vulnerable you become to sudden discontinuities. You cannot adapt what you do not understand. And you certainly can't respond to threats inside systems you've mistaken for certainties.

Hence, the shift: not from wealth to poverty, but from redundancy to resilience. It's a crucial distinction. Redundancy—though it sounds like a hedge—is often an illusion of safety. Having multiple versions of the same thing (three bank accounts, five revenue streams from the same industry, two passports from cooperative nations) may look like diversification, but it's often just repetition within a single paradigm. When that paradigm falters—when inflation spikes, when regulatory borders harden, when a financial regime turns predatory—your "diversification" reveals itself for what it truly is: a fragile cluster of same-bet dependencies.

Resilience, by contrast, is a different beast entirely. It moves across systems, not within them. It is the ability to flex, to reconfigure, to act when others are stuck. A resilient person doesn't simply own things—they understand how to relocate, how to liquidate, how to recontextualise value across shifting terrains. They don't cling to credentials; they cultivate actual skill. They build networks that function in chaos, not just in cocktail hours. And perhaps most importantly, they develop sovereignty over their most finite resources: time, energy, and attention—resources that, in moments of upheaval, prove more valuable than any bank balance.

This is where the legacy wealth model—income, assets, and status—begins to dissolve, making room for a sturdier triad: value sovereignty, mobility equity, and system agnosticism.

Value sovereignty begins with control: control over how your value is created, stored, and exchanged. It's the capacity to participate economically without surrendering that participation to fragile mediators—whether they be employers, platforms, fiat currencies, or infrastructural monopolies. It could mean holding hard assets outside traditional banking, or developing skills that remain valuable even in censored, automated, or politically charged environments. It's less about how much you earn, and more about how independently you earn it—and how portable that value remains across contexts.

Mobility equity is not simply the right to move. It's the meaningful capacity to do so with your economic self intact. A second passport is useless if it leads to countries in collapse. Remote work means little if your clients, payment processors, and digital identity all reside in the same geopolitical bloc. True mobility equity allows you to extract value in different environments because your assets, your identity, and your skillset can travel with you—intact, secure, and legible across jurisdictions. It's not just about where you can go. It's about how much of your life comes with you when you leave.

Then there is system agnosticism. This is the mindset—and more crucially, the infrastructure—that allows you to function across multiple systems without undue reliance on any one of them. Not cynicism. Not withdrawal. But the ability to participate strategically, without building your life around the assumption that any given system will protect you. You might bank nationally, but prepare internationally. You might use centralised platforms, while building decentralised alternatives in parallel. You are not a true believer in institutions—you are a pragmatic user of them. And when one begins to fail, you do not freeze. You move.

These three elements share more than just utility. They share a kind of philosophical posture. They are antifragile—structured not merely to survive shocks, but to thrive through them. The traditional model, by contrast, is acutely fragile. It demands consistency, calm, and continual expansion. Take any of those away, and it begins to fray.

The new model—the one we'll explore here—isn't about gambling on collapse, nor is it some romantic prepper fantasy. It is about refusing to outsource your stability. It's about owning your inputs. It's about refusing to bet your future on systems you do not understand and cannot influence.

In the chapters ahead, we'll dig deeper. We'll unpack how the financial freedom narrative has been hijacked—twisted into a marketing loop that binds you to consumerism and platform addiction. We'll explore why passive income deserves more scrutiny than reverence. We'll examine the difference between looking diversified and actually being resilient. And we'll map a path toward a financial identity that doesn't crumble when the backdrop changes—but adjusts, repositions, and carries on.

Because make no mistake: the systems around us are becoming more erratic, not less. And in that kind of world, wealth isn't about how much you've amassed. It's about what you can still do—what you can still access, still protect, still rebuild—when the defaults vanish.

This chapter is your invitation to think more clearly, act more deliberately, and build a model of wealth that does not break when the winds change—but bends, holds, and endures.

What Is True Wealth?

Wealth has long been measured in absolutes: the size of one's bank balance, the square footage of property owned, the market value of a share portfolio. These metrics are easily quantified, neatly ranked, and endlessly compared. They feed the illusion that wealth is something objective, universal, and transferable across all environments. But this framework, while intuitively satisfying, breaks down under stress. *When systems destabilise, the distinction between money and true wealth becomes painfully clear.*

A person with millions in a frozen bank account, or a luxury apartment in a city under lockdown, is not wealthy in any meaningful sense. They are *exposed.* Their resources, though numerically impressive, are contingent—on functioning markets, open borders, legal clarity, technological infrastructure, and institutional goodwill. Strip any of these away, and the digits on a screen cease to confer power. *Wealth, if it cannot be used when and where you need it, is not wealth. It is theatre.*

This chapter begins by confronting that illusion. Because to prepare intelligently for systemic volatility, one must first redefine what is worth accumulating. This is not a call for anti-capitalism or aesthetic minimalism. It is an argument for *functional wealth*: value that holds under pressure, adapts to context, and enhances autonomy rather than dependency. That redefinition requires a shift in mindset—from static accumulation to dynamic capability. From net worth to *effective capacity.*

True wealth, in this context, is better understood through four interlocking pillars: access, adaptability, mobility, and sovereignty.

Access is the foundation. It refers to the immediate *availability* of value—not just its nominal existence. Can you reach your capital during a bank freeze? Can you use your assets across jurisdictions? Can you make purchases, move money, or deploy skills without bureaucratic interference? Access is not about quantity—it's about *utility*. During economic collapse, a mechanic with access to tools, parts, and barter networks often fares better than an investor whose assets are trapped in halted exchanges. Access also includes social capital: who will take your call, lend support, share intelligence, or offer exit infrastructure when conditions deteriorate? Liquid capital matters. But *liquid relationships* often matter more.

Adaptability is the next critical layer. It is your capacity to *respond to change without dependence on a single environment or narrative.* Someone whose career, identity, and income are tied to a specific job title in a stable market may feel secure—until the industry automates, outsources, or implodes. Adaptability means not only having multiple income streams, but being able to *pivot those streams under duress.* It means acquiring knowledge that compounds, skills that translate, and habits that are system-agnostic. It is easier to build these muscles before crisis hits—but they remain learnable even in decline. The key is recognising that the ability to adapt is more valuable than any single asset that seems safe today.

Mobility extends beyond travel. It is about *frictionless transition between systems.* Can you move your business to a different jurisdiction? Can you shift your income across currencies, platforms, and client bases? Can you operate from multiple geographies without being exposed to a single government's capital controls or tax seizures? Owning a passport is not mobility if your income, legal identity, or dependencies are locked in a country with collapsing institutions. Real mobility means *preparing for movement before it is urgent.* It is infrastructural: backup data, secondary residencies, decentralised income, portable assets. But it is also psychological: the ability to detach from status markers, sunk costs, and inherited narratives about permanence.

Sovereignty is the culmination. It is not isolation or self-sufficiency—it is *strategic independence.* It means that your capacity to make choices—about where to live, how to earn, what to spend on, or whom to associate with—is not hostage to any single system. Sovereignty includes financial independence, but goes beyond it. It includes cognitive clarity, operational discretion, and the refusal to outsource responsibility for your own positioning. A sovereign individual does not need to ask permission to act. They may still operate within states, markets, and networks—but they do so *deliberately*, not by default.

This redefinition of wealth becomes more than theoretical during actual crisis. Consider recent historical examples. In Argentina's 2001 financial collapse, middle-class professionals who held pesos in domestic accounts saw their savings wiped out almost overnight. Those who retained *access* to US dollars—whether through offshore accounts or family abroad—preserved purchasing power. In Venezuela, during its prolonged currency hyperinflation, adaptability became wealth: barbers, mechanics, and software freelancers who could operate in informal or online markets often out-earned former high-salaried professionals. During the 2022 war in Ukraine, thousands of entrepreneurs and remote workers used mobility—via second passports or prior digital arrangements—to relocate, often within days, and continue their economic lives. The same cannot be said for those who depended on local infrastructure or state-backed income.

What these cases reveal is that *resilience is rarely evenly distributed.* Traditional wealth markers—degrees, salaries, property ownership—do not map neatly onto survival. What endures is not accumulation, but *capacity*. The ability to navigate disruption, maintain agency, and sustain optionality. The goal, then, is not to dismiss money, but to stop mistaking *financial exposure* for security.

This reframing also demands a rethinking of *lifestyle design.* In systems geared towards debt-fuelled consumption, many are lured into the trap of visible wealth: expensive homes, branded credentials, luxury travel. These purchases signal status, but they do not confer resilience. In fact, they often lock individuals into fragile dependencies: mortgages tied to fiat currencies, reputations tied to centralised platforms, income streams tied to employers with ideological agendas. True wealth design asks harder questions. *What do I control? What can I move? What can I rebuild?*

Importantly, this redefinition is not purely defensive. It also enables *expansion under constraint.* Those who hold the new forms of wealth—access, adaptability, mobility, and sovereignty—are positioned not just to survive collapse, but to build in its wake. They can spot arbitrage opportunities, launch new ventures, and form new alliances while others are frozen in fear or grief. This is not opportunism in the cynical sense. It is *functional leadership under uncertainty.* And it is only possible when one's economic foundation is not tethered to a dying model.

This chapter will provide a deeper examination of each pillar. It will show how to build them, how to measure them, and how to protect them—not as luxuries, but as necessities. It will also offer case studies from individuals, families, and decentralised communities who are already living this new model—not through ideology, but through practical recognition of how fragile the conventional idea of wealth has become.

Because the world is not getting simpler, calmer, or more predictable. And in that environment, *wealth must be more than stored value.* It must be *deployable capacity.* This is not a motivational abstraction. It is a strategic necessity. The people who understand that distinction—who shift from passive accumulation to active sovereignty—will not only endure the volatility ahead. They will define what comes after.

The End of Passive Income

Few concepts have achieved such universal appeal among modern investors, self-help authors, and financial influencers as *passive income*. It is sold as the ultimate aspiration—money that flows while you sleep, work, travel, or do nothing at all. Rental yields, dividend stocks, royalties, affiliate marketing, and algorithmically traded portfolios are presented as steps on the path to financial independence, with the implied promise that detachment from labour equals freedom. But beneath the seductive simplicity of this model lies a critical oversight: *passive income is never truly passive in volatile systems*. When the structures supporting it become unstable, what once felt like freedom can quickly become a liability.

To be clear, the critique here is not of income-producing assets. Earning money without trading time hour-for-hour is a rational goal. The flaw lies in assuming that *reliability is intrinsic to passivity*. In truth, every form of passive income is embedded within—and ultimately dependent upon—a broader framework of political, economic, legal, and technological stability. When those frameworks wobble, the passivity disappears, and with it, the income.

Take real estate, perhaps the most commonly championed source of passive income. Landlords are encouraged to build portfolios of rental properties, collect monthly payments, and let appreciation work quietly in the background. Yet this model is underpinned by several fragile assumptions: that tenants will pay on time; that the currency in which they pay will retain value; that property rights will be enforced; and that the state won't impose rent freezes, eviction bans, or punitive taxation. In 2020, during the early months of the COVID-19 pandemic, many governments around the world enacted emergency measures that effectively suspended landlord income. In cities like Berlin, San Francisco, and London, eviction moratoria meant that owners were legally obliged to house tenants without receiving payment, often for months. In South Africa, property owners faced judicial delays stretching beyond a year to reclaim occupancy. The system didn't break—it re-prioritised who it served.

Dividend stocks, another favourite of the passive income model, carry similar exposure. Investors are told to hold shares in stable companies, harvest quarterly payouts, and benefit from long-term appreciation. But dividends are discretionary, not contractual. They can be slashed or suspended the moment a company faces pressure. During the 2008 financial crisis, banks that had been considered dividend aristocrats—such as Citigroup and Bank of America—halted payments entirely. Even more recently, in 2020, firms across aviation, energy, and hospitality sectors suspended dividends overnight to conserve cash. Those holding shares for income saw their streams vanish without recourse. What looked like reliability turned out to be institutional fragility.

Royalties—whether from books, music, patents, or licensing agreements—offer a third example. They appear structurally independent: you create once, then earn indefinitely. But royalty income depends on enforceable contracts, functioning platforms, and market relevance. If a streaming platform changes its terms, if a distributor goes bankrupt, or if legal jurisdictions are compromised, the flow stops. More subtly, technological change can erode the very relevance of what's being monetised. A patented technology may become obsolete; a course or e-book may be delisted under new content standards; a licensing arrangement may lose value as the market shifts. Royalties are not durable income—they are contingent on systems that you do not control.

At a deeper level, passive income models tend to produce a false sense of security. They encourage a hands-off relationship with value creation, leading individuals to *outsource resilience to systems they barely understand.* The investor may know how to rebalance a portfolio, but not what to do when a platform is frozen, when dividends are nationalised, or when capital controls prevent withdrawals. In such moments, what matters is not *how much* you have, but *how sovereign* your income really is.

This is where the distinction between passive and *independent* income becomes critical. The former is income that flows without active effort but relies heavily on external systems. The latter is income that may require active engagement but is *portable, adaptable, and under your control.* A freelance skillset, for example, is not passive—but it can be deployed across jurisdictions. A small enterprise with local redundancy and global supply chains is not passive—but it is structurally antifragile. A decentralised revenue stream—whether crypto-based or peer-to-peer—is not passive, but it can bypass institutional chokepoints. In volatile times, it is *control*, not detachment, that defines the quality of income.

This reframing also demands a shift in mindset. The desire for passivity is often rooted not in financial strategy, but in psychological fatigue—an understandable yearning for rest, predictability, and detachment from precarious labour markets. But in an age of polycrisis—economic, geopolitical, technological, ecological—detachment is often the most dangerous posture. When disruption becomes the norm, the safest income is that which you can *adjust, redeploy, or reconfigure.* Not income you hope will keep coming while you're not looking.

The passive income narrative also conceals its own ideological assumptions. It tends to valorise ownership over contribution. The investor earns without engaging. The landlord profits regardless of the tenant's condition. The shareholder benefits even as a company lays off thousands. In calm times, these dynamics are rationalised as the reward for capital risk. In unstable times, they become focal points for social backlash. Political narratives shift. Regulations tighten. Tax codes change. Suddenly, what once felt like reward becomes exposure. And those who built their strategy around invisibility find themselves unprepared for scrutiny.

None of this is to suggest that passive income is inherently immoral or impractical. There are situations where it is entirely appropriate—particularly when used as one layer in a diversified, strategically agile portfolio. But it must be understood for what it is: *conditional value.* It is income that depends not just on the quality of your assets, but on the resilience of the system that processes them. In the same way that holding gold means nothing if you can't access it, passive income means little if the infrastructure around it is failing.

This chapter will examine how to reconfigure income strategies for volatility. It will outline ways to assess the systemic fragility behind "passive" streams. It will explore how to shift from dependency to autonomy—by acquiring skills, building modular business models, embracing location-independent structures, and diversifying across platforms and jurisdictions. It will also probe the deeper cultural and psychological reasons why the dream of effortless income has become so pervasive—and why, paradoxically, it may be one of the most disempowering narratives in modern finance.

Ultimately, the goal is not to abandon the pursuit of efficient income. It is to replace *passivity* with *sovereignty.* Because when the next crisis hits—and it will—those who can still generate, move, and adapt their income will not be asking which of their revenue streams survived. They'll be *deciding where and how they want to live.* That is the real dividend worth earning.

Redundancy vs. Resilience

When most people first confront the fragility of modern systems—whether financial, political, technological, or ecological—the instinctive response is to duplicate what they already have. A second passport. A second bank account. A backup generator. A diversified investment portfolio. In popular survival discourse, this approach is often lauded as "redundancy," the idea being that having more of the same across multiple channels provides safety. But the deeper truth, rarely interrogated, is this: *redundancy is not resilience.* It is an insurance model—one that works only until the same systemic logic underpins every option you've duplicated.

To understand the limits of redundancy, we must start with the assumptions behind it. Redundancy presumes that systems fail randomly, that failures are isolated, and that multiple points of access will increase your chances of remaining operational. This might make sense in a mechanical context—having two engines on a plane is clearly safer than one. But in complex, interconnected human systems, failures are often *correlated*. They are not isolated malfunctions; they are cascading breakdowns where interdependency turns duplication into illusion. When banks freeze withdrawals in one country, correspondent banking systems often transmit those restrictions across borders. When a government imposes capital controls, having an account in a second institution within the same jurisdiction offers little protection. If every option you've lined up draws from the same well, then redundancy simply delays exposure—it does not eliminate it.

This is where resilience must be distinguished, both conceptually and practically. Resilience does not mean having more of the same. *It means being able to adapt when the rules, infrastructure, or assumptions change*. Resilience is not a copy; it is a shift. It's the ability to remain functional under radically altered conditions—not because you planned for every scenario, but because you have internal capacity to improvise, navigate, and rebuild.

Consider a simple example: two individuals preparing for economic volatility. One opens multiple bank accounts, purchases extended insurance plans, and buys stocks in multiple sectors across different exchanges. The other invests in learning how to code, speak a second language, build online services, and conduct cross-border transactions using decentralised tools. The first has created *redundancy*. The second has cultivated *resilience*. When a financial crisis disrupts traditional banking systems, the first may find all accounts frozen under uniform regulatory action. The second may already be transacting in peer-to-peer networks, earning income from foreign clients, and navigating platforms outside the reach of legacy institutions. The systems may collapse, but the second person remains economically functional.

One of the reasons redundancy remains a popular strategy is psychological. It gives the appearance of control. It allows individuals to stay within their comfort zone—accumulating more of what they already understand—rather than confronting the uncomfortable task of changing the way they engage with the world. But resilience, by its nature, requires transformation. It involves *learning*, not just purchasing. It often means *discomfort*, as new skills are acquired and old paradigms relinquished. Most importantly, it involves *agency*. Resilience cannot be bought off the shelf. It must be earned through deliberate investment in your own capacity to operate across diverse conditions.

A particularly dangerous area where redundancy masquerades as safety is in the digital sphere. People are told to store backups of critical documents across multiple cloud platforms. They create redundant logins, mirror folders, even encrypt their data twice. But if those systems are centralised, monitored, or subject to government oversight, all copies are simultaneously vulnerable. True digital resilience requires understanding how to operate in decentralised environments, where encryption, peer-to-peer hosting, and jurisdictional diversity can offer functional continuity even in hostile conditions. The difference is not in how many platforms you use, but in *how independently you can function when mainstream infrastructure is degraded.*

Redundancy also fails when the nature of threat is *qualitative*, not just quantitative. During hyperinflation events—such as in Zimbabwe (2007–2008), Venezuela (2016–2019), or more recently, Lebanon—citizens who had multiple bank accounts, diverse domestic assets, or real estate portfolios were still exposed. Their entire economic universe operated within a currency system whose value collapsed. Duplicating within that frame did not protect them. Meanwhile, those who held offshore assets, barterable skills, or crypto-literate knowledge were far better positioned. Their resilience did not come from spreading bets; it came from operating across *different systems entirely.*

This introduces the concept of *antifragility*, as proposed by Nassim Nicholas Taleb. Whereas fragile things break under stress and resilient things endure stress, *antifragile* entities *gain* from disorder. They don't just withstand volatility—they use it. Resilience begins to approach antifragility when systems are designed not only to survive shocks but to evolve through them. For individuals, this might mean building value models that improve under crisis: a consultancy that helps clients navigate regulatory uncertainty; a digital skillset that becomes more valuable as institutions falter; a network of barter relationships that thrives in cash shortages. These models don't fear chaos—they anticipate it as part of their operating logic.

Another critical axis where redundancy diverges from resilience is *autonomy*. Redundant systems often remain tethered to the same provider networks, legal jurisdictions, or service agreements. Resilient systems aim for *sovereignty*. They minimise dependence on any single point of failure. This might mean growing your own food, but it could equally mean understanding open-source technology, developing local supply chain alternatives, or building a remote business with international clients. Autonomy is the common denominator of resilience—it allows you to *choose your inputs* even when the mainstream system stops offering them.

It's important, however, not to swing into binary thinking. Redundancy can be useful, even necessary, as part of a broader resilience strategy—*but only when it's layered on top of sovereign capability*. For example, having multiple water filters is helpful only if you understand how to purify water in general. Holding gold in different vaults across continents is smart only if you know how to access, transport, or exchange that gold when borders close or internet systems fail. Without foundational autonomy, redundancy becomes decorative. It reassures but does not protect.

The coming chapters will explore concrete ways to build anti-fragile wealth—systems that are not just diversified, but *decentralised in spirit, adaptable in design, and sovereign in execution.* We'll look at case studies where people relied on institutional redundancy and still lost everything, and others where modest but well-calibrated resilience enabled continuity and reinvention. We'll interrogate what it means to be financially sovereign, how to measure autonomy, and why resilience is increasingly becoming the new definition of security in an age of rolling disruption.

In times of calm, redundancy can lull us into believing we are safe. But history shows us that when the unexpected arrives—and it always does—it is not the number of systems you have that determines survival. It is the nature of those systems, and your capacity to move, think, and act within or beyond them. *Resilience is not the duplication of control—it is the design of freedom.*

The Wealth Triangle of the Future

For centuries, wealth has been measured by static accumulation: coins in vaults, numbers on spreadsheets, deeds to property. We've been taught to equate prosperity with possession and security with permanence. But the world that shaped those assumptions is disintegrating. Economic systems are undergoing structural convulsions; geographic borders are becoming financial barriers; currencies are losing their neutrality as geopolitical weapons. In this new terrain, traditional markers of wealth not only falter—they often expose their owners to greater risk. The future will not belong to the richest, but to the *most sovereign.*

In such a context, enduring wealth must be redefined—not as a stockpile of fragile symbols, but as a dynamic architecture built for movement, insulation, and independence. That architecture can be understood as a triangle—*value sovereignty*, *mobility equity*, and *system agnosticism.* These are not buzzwords. They are the three load-bearing pillars of antifragile prosperity in a world where centralised control is tightening and institutional credibility is decaying. Together, they form a framework through which the reader can examine not just what they own, but how, where, and *why* they hold value in the first place.

Value Sovereignty refers to the ability to generate, store, and transact value outside of dependent systems. It demands a shift from reliance on institutions—banks, employers, even governments—to a posture of personal or decentralised command. In practical terms, this might mean holding assets in hard money like gold or crypto, conducting business through peer-to-peer or jurisdictionally diverse platforms, or developing monetisable skills that bypass formal credentialism. But it also includes a psychological dimension: *trusting one's own capacity to produce and exchange value under uncertain conditions.*

Consider, for example, an individual whose livelihood depends on a single employer, a local currency, and a domestic bank account. This person may appear "wealthy" in conventional terms, but they are entirely exposed to institutional collapse. Now contrast that with someone who earns in multiple currencies, stores wealth in a combination of physical and digital decentralised assets, and transacts through distributed networks. Even with less nominal wealth, the latter possesses *value sovereignty*: they are not trapped in a single system's failure modes. They can pivot, hedge, and reconstitute their economic function in the face of disruption.

The second axis, **Mobility Equity**, is perhaps the least discussed but most urgently needed attribute of modern wealth. It refers to the *capacity to move oneself, one's capital, and one's livelihood across jurisdictions* without friction or dependence. While traditional wealth focuses on accumulation, mobility equity focuses on *fluidity*. It poses questions that most financial advisors never ask: Could you extract and relocate your assets within 48 hours if your country imposed capital controls? Could you earn income from multiple geographic sources without being stranded by political events in any one? Could your family, your business, your identity function elsewhere—legally, logistically, and psychologically?

History is unequivocal on this point. In every major financial collapse—whether Argentina's banking freeze in 2001, Cyprus's bail-in of depositors in 2013, or Russia's currency implosion post-sanctions—those who could *move* survived. Those who could not, regardless of how diversified their portfolios were within the collapsing system, were wiped out. *Mobility equity is not about being a nomad; it's about not being cornered.* It involves strategic choices: maintaining multiple residencies, earning location-independent income, holding transportable stores of value, and cultivating legal identities that maximise freedom of movement.

Critically, mobility equity is not purely logistical. It is also cultural and psychological. It requires a mindset flexible enough to embrace ambiguity, bureaucracies foreign enough to navigate uncertainty, and social capital diverse enough to function across multiple value systems. In this regard, investing in mobility is as much about building one's *resilience psychology* as it is about acquiring passports or portable assets.

Finally, we arrive at **System Agnosticism**, the third point of the triangle. This principle asserts that true wealth is not tethered to any single system's continuity. It is not predicated on the dollar's dominance, the EU's cohesion, the longevity of the stock market, or the reliability of pension schemes. Instead, system-agnostic wealth is structured to *function across multiple paradigms*—and survive the collapse of any single one.

This requires a dual perspective: one eye on current rules, and one on the changing architecture beneath them. A system-agnostic investor, for instance, understands that fiat currency may still function, but also prepares for its potential delegitimisation. They use current financial platforms, but with escape routes embedded—cold wallets for crypto, offshore legal entities, self-custodied stores of value. They participate in markets, but with the clarity that markets are not moral entities—they are political constructs, vulnerable to narrative shifts, regulatory coercion, and sudden liquidity evaporations.

System agnosticism also extends to ideology. One of the most dangerous blind spots in finance is belief in permanence—whether in a political party, a nation-state, or a macroeconomic theory. System-agnostic wealth builders don't seek ideological purity. They seek *adaptive neutrality*. They refuse to moralise the marketplace. They are less interested in whether a system is "right" and more interested in whether it is *functioning, durable, and optionally replaceable.*

Together, these three elements—value sovereignty, mobility equity, and system agnosticism—constitute what this book proposes as *the Wealth Triangle of the Future.* Each supports the others. Sovereignty without mobility is brittle. Mobility without system agnosticism is naive. Agnosticism without sovereignty is passive. Like any well-designed structure, the triangle's strength is in its balance.

Importantly, this framework is not only theoretical—it offers diagnostic utility. A reader can now audit their current financial life against these three dimensions. Do you control your value generation, or is it intermediated by fragile institutions? Can you relocate your income, assets, and identity quickly and legally, or are you geographically and politically trapped? Are your assumptions about wealth conditional on the stability of a particular state, currency, or ideology—or have you diversified across paradigms?

This model also invites proactive design. Instead of simply chasing yield, status, or diversification, the new investor asks: *How do I construct wealth that can move, morph, and multiply under stress?* This is not paranoia; it is strategic clarity. In an age of programmable money, data weaponisation, and volatile geopolitics, old formulas no longer apply. Security no longer comes from static abundance. It comes from structural intelligence.

To be clear, the Wealth Triangle does not advocate disengagement from society or financial institutions. It advocates *non-dependence.* It promotes engagement without captivity. Participation without exposure. It's a posture of strategic sovereignty—not isolation, but insulation.

This chapter will break down each point of the triangle in detail, offering concrete tools, case studies, and mental models. You'll explore how to build portable value, how to diversify across systems—not just within them—and how to recalibrate your understanding of wealth as the world tilts toward instability. If traditional finance taught you how to preserve capital, *escape finance* will teach you how to preserve *freedom.* That begins with reengineering wealth not as a number, but as an infrastructure of autonomy. And that, ultimately, is the only wealth worth having.

Chapter 4
Sovereign Thinking – The Inner Escape

No matter how elegantly engineered your financial plan, how diverse your holdings, or how swiftly your capital can move across borders—none of it counts for much if your thinking remains in chains. Time and again, throughout history's most instructive collapses, it is not the unbalanced ledger or the failed investment that signals the beginning of the end—it is the psyche, buckling under pressure. When institutions falter and the noise of certainty begins to fade, the rarest and most valuable form of capital is cognitive sovereignty: the ability to see clearly, choose freely, and act with precision, even as the world comes unstitched. And that clarity, that independence of thought, isn't forged in the fire of crisis. It is cultivated in the quiet before the storm.

This chapter invites us to consider what it truly means to be mentally sovereign in a world that thrives on psychological dependence. From early schooling to career ladders, from social media algorithms to government safety nets, most people are conditioned to equate stability with compliance, identity with role, and safety with proximity to institutions. Questioning that internal scaffolding—those inherited definitions of safety and success—rarely enters the picture. And in moments of disruption, those unquestioned assumptions become traps. If escape finance is to mean anything deeper than clever positioning, it must start with this: a break from the mental frameworks that quietly tether us to fragility.

Let us begin, then, with an internal realignment—a shift from scarcity to sufficiency. On the surface, these might sound like questions of resource distribution, but beneath that, they are perceptual frames. Scarcity whispers that there is never enough: not enough time, money, security, opportunity. It makes hoarders of us, convinces us that urgency is a virtue, and that the safest place is inside the crowd. Sufficiency, in contrast, isn't some blissful ignorance of threat—it's the practiced discernment of knowing what is truly enough, and acting from calm, not panic.

This mindset—more than your job title, your earnings, or your holdings—will determine how you respond when things go sideways. Time and again, studies in behavioural economics confirm the same truth: under pressure, people don't merely behave irrationally—they revert. They default to old stories of not-enoughness, even when alternative paths remain open. They sell low. They cling to crumbling institutions because they confuse familiarity with safety. They hesitate, they stall, they freeze. Not because they lack resources, but because they can't imagine acting without permission.

And so, we must acknowledge a hard truth: financial literacy, while essential, is no panacea. Without a recalibrated mindset, even the most elegantly constructed strategy will collapse under emotional strain. That's why the focus here shifts—not toward spreadsheets or tax shelters—but toward identity, perception, and imagination. We're not asking, "What do you own?" but "Who are you when the system stops pretending it can save you?"

Which brings us to the next turning point: the construction of an anti-fragile self. While the phrase may have a theoretical ring, its implications are deeply practical. Many people have built their sense of self atop institutions: the prestige of their role, the brand of their employer, the social cues that affirm their relevance. These identities thrive in predictable environments. But let those systems falter—and they do, with increasing frequency—and the collapse is not merely financial. It's existential. We saw this in the global financial crisis. We saw it in lockdowns and mass layoffs. What crumbled wasn't always a bank balance—it was people's sense of who they were without their job title, without the applause, without the structure.

The anti-fragile self, by contrast, is built not on status but on function. It is the cultivated ability to assess, respond, and adapt in real time. It's not an affirmation but an orientation—grounded in experience, but not confined by it. This kind of identity does not demand perfect foresight, only pattern recognition. It is elastic. And it's constructed not through words, but through exposure: to constraint, to ambiguity, to situations that force one to think originally rather than rely on institutional instruction.

It may require you to rewrite your personal narrative entirely. Perhaps your job isn't who you are—it's simply one application of your broader capacity to solve problems, lead, or create. Perhaps your family's stability isn't rooted in fixed pensions, but in its collective skills, fluid decision-making, and shared courage under pressure. Perhaps your legacy lies not in the wealth you bequeath, but in the adaptability you model. And perhaps, to prepare for rupture, you need to practise—not catastrophising, but running drills in identity. Who would you become if tomorrow, the frameworks you rely on were no longer reliable?

Which leads us, finally, to what may be the most subversive idea in this chapter: the Sovereign Imagination. This is not a call to fantasy. It is a call to strategic creativity—the kind that sees possibility in constraint, and finds options where the blueprint runs out. Sovereign thinking is not content to identify risk. It seeks to move within and around it. It treats imagination not as a luxury, but as a survival skill.

We are not talking about abstract hope. We're talking about trained mental elasticity. The kind that dares to ask: If your income disappeared tomorrow, what value could you still create? If your passport became a target, not a protection, where else could you move with leverage? If your data trail turned against you, how would you re-establish identity without exposure? These are not doomsday fantasies. They are drills in cognitive mobility—mental preparedness for a world that is not getting simpler.

And in that reframe lies a kind of quiet revolution. Because imagination doesn't merely help you escape collapse. It allows you to design your life through it. What if crisis didn't just represent loss—but freedom? The opportunity to walk away from inherited expectations and reconfigure your life around autonomy, agency, and dignity? What if your worth was not pegged to monthly earnings but to your capacity to say "no"—to decline offers, institutions, and compromises that no longer align with your values?

This chapter does not offer reassurance. It offers lucidity. The clarity required to build a self that can withstand, and even transcend, the systems it once depended on.

Sovereign Thinking, then, is where strategy meets philosophy. It demands more of you than asset allocation—it demands an internal reckoning. Who are you when the external scaffolding disappears? What remains when the social proof, the salary, and the routine are stripped away? For those willing to wrestle with these questions, the reward is profound. Not just resilience, but transformation. The unshakable understanding that real freedom is not handed down. It is taken back.

The chapters that follow are not feel-good manifestos. They are mirrors. They ask you to confront the beliefs that shaped your instincts, the inherited fears that still whisper in your decision-making, the familiar scripts you've never quite questioned. And then, they point to a new vantage—one where escape isn't retreat, but authorship. Where each choice you make with clarity and courage becomes not just a move away from dependency, but a movement toward becoming unconfiscatable—not merely in assets, but in thought, in identity, and in will.

Breaking Cognitive Captivity

There is no greater prison than the one we do not realise we inhabit. And in the context of modern finance, that prison is not material—it is mental. The most effective form of control in any society is not force, but belief. Not surveillance, but assumption. It is not the laws that keep people compliant, but the deeply internalised scripts they have absorbed about what is possible, permissible, or prudent. *Breaking cognitive captivity* is not about rebellion in the streets; it is about emancipation in the mind. This subchapter investigates how invisible frameworks—cultural, educational, financial—conspire to keep individuals psychologically tethered to fragile systems, even when those systems show every sign of decline. Understanding these mental scripts is the first step toward building sovereign resilience.

From childhood, most people are taught that stability lies in conformity. Go to school, get a good job, save for retirement, buy a house, trust the banks. These axioms are repeated with such regularity that they rarely receive scrutiny. But these scripts are not truths. They are behavioural programmes coded into us by institutions with a vested interest in our predictability. School systems reward obedience, not creativity. Employers value compliance more than initiative. Financial institutions benefit from customers who leave their money in low-interest accounts, accept inflation as normal, and never ask how money is created in the first place. In this context, *normal* is not synonymous with safe. It is simply the default position of those who have not yet questioned the framework.

One of the most powerful psychological mechanisms that reinforce this captivity is what behavioural economists call **status quo bias**—the cognitive tendency to prefer existing conditions over change, even when alternatives are demonstrably superior. This bias is particularly potent in financial decision-making. Consider how many people remain in high-fee pension schemes out of inertia, or how long it took for the general public to accept alternatives like digital currencies. The default assumption is: if the system hasn't failed me yet, it won't. This belief persists even in the face of overwhelming historical data showing that systems *do* fail—periodically, catastrophically, and without warning.

Equally paralysing is the **illusion of comprehension**—the mistaken belief that because one understands how to function within a system, they understand the system itself. Many professionals know how to file taxes or contribute to their pension, but lack even a rudimentary understanding of how fiat currency is created, how central banks influence liquidity, or how government debt indirectly taxes future purchasing power. This is not a personal failing; it is by design. Financial systems operate with a kind of deliberate opacity. Complexity is not merely a feature—it is a moat. The more obscure the mechanism, the less likely the average individual is to question its legitimacy or sustainability.

This opacity creates space for **authoritative narratives** to dominate the public imagination. These narratives are often delivered through state institutions, media outlets, and academic consensus, and they take the form of what philosopher Michel Foucault might describe as *discursive truths*—statements repeated so often by figures of authority that they become self-reinforcing. "The central bank is here to protect you." "Inflation is a necessary part of a growing economy." "A diversified portfolio will shield you from crisis." These are not empirical facts; they are consensus slogans, designed less to describe reality than to shape it.

Yet perhaps the most insidious script of all is the **morality of work and wealth**. In many societies, especially Western capitalist democracies, wealth is seen not just as a financial state but a moral one. Wealthy people are assumed to be hardworking, disciplined, and deserving. Those who struggle financially are often viewed—explicitly or implicitly—as irresponsible or lazy. This narrative serves a double purpose: it validates the existing distribution of resources, and it discourages critical engagement with the underlying economic mechanisms that produce inequality. When people internalise the idea that their financial outcomes are solely a result of their effort, they are far less likely to question the structural forces—monetary policy, debt instruments, taxation—that shape those outcomes.

Breaking out of this cognitive captivity requires more than intellectual understanding. It demands *disidentification.* The system does not merely shape your money; it shapes your identity. When someone says, "I am a homeowner," "I work for a multinational," or "I'm saving for retirement," they are not simply describing actions—they are describing selves. Each label implies a set of financial behaviours and dependencies. Each comes with scripts: how to behave, what to want, what to fear. To become sovereign, one must learn to hold those identities lightly, to regard them as temporary tools rather than fixed truths.

There is historical precedent for this kind of psychological detachment. Consider the philosophical stance of the Stoics, who taught that control is largely internal, and that anything governed by external systems—status, currency, citizenship—should not be the foundation of peace or power. Or look to postcolonial thinkers like Frantz Fanon, who showed how systemic domination relies as much on mental submission as material coercion. Or examine the strategies of dissidents in authoritarian regimes who develop parallel economies, encrypted communication channels, and informal educational systems—acts of resistance born from the realisation that institutional legitimacy is often more illusion than substance.

Modern individuals, even those living in relatively free societies, face a subtler but equally formidable version of this challenge. We are not told what to think, but we are told what to value. Economic growth is good. Stability is security. Risk is recklessness. Liquidity is power. These ideas, repeated across advertising, politics, education, and even entertainment, create a psychic map of reality—a map that systematically excludes non-conforming values like frugality, decentralisation, or self-sufficiency. As a result, people find it psychologically difficult to make financially rational decisions in chaotic environments. They cling to failing systems not because they believe in them, but because they have never been taught how to function without them.

To break free of this mental enclosure is not to discard systems entirely, but to *see them clearly*. And clarity often begins with discomfort. It is uncomfortable to realise that your pension fund may not deliver what it promises. That your home equity may be trapped if credit markets freeze. That your degree or professional title may become irrelevant in an AI-mediated economy. But this discomfort is not an endpoint—it is an invitation. Once the comforting scripts have been disrupted, new questions can be asked: *What do I actually own? What skills are truly portable? Who would I be if my bank closed tomorrow?* These are not doomsday queries. They are sovereignty exercises.

Ultimately, breaking cognitive captivity is about reclaiming authorship over your financial worldview. Not outsourcing your sense of safety to institutions. Not deferring responsibility to advisors or policy-makers. It is about building the intellectual, emotional, and psychological capacity to see systems as tools, not truths—and to walk away from them when they no longer serve you. This is not paranoia. It is preparedness. And in an age where financial architecture is increasingly precarious, that preparedness may prove more valuable than any asset on a balance sheet.

Scarcity vs. Sufficiency Mindset

Panic rarely makes good financial decisions. Yet panic is the default state of mind for millions of people whenever systems wobble. Whether it's a market crash, a job loss, or a supply chain disruption, the typical psychological reaction is not curiosity or strategy—it's contraction. When people perceive scarcity, they behave accordingly: they hoard, they withdraw, they defer action, or overreact. But what if scarcity is not a condition, but a perspective? What if the more profound driver of economic fragility at the personal level is not income, assets, or job security—but mindset? This is not a rhetorical flourish. Research across disciplines—from behavioural economics to neuroscience to anthropology—shows that the way we *think* about money, risk, and survival often matters more than the money itself. In this subchapter, we explore the practical and psychological split between a *scarcity mindset* and a *sufficiency mindset*, and why that distinction may determine whether someone thrives or collapses when volatility strikes.

A scarcity mindset is not simply an awareness of limited resources. It is the persistent belief that there will never be enough—of time, money, food, opportunity, safety. This belief is not always conscious, but it manifests behaviourally: a tendency to over-prepare for low-probability threats, to fixate on loss rather than potential, and to frame decisions through fear rather than agency. The scarcity mindset is not exclusive to those in poverty. High-net-worth individuals can be afflicted by it too, often evidenced in compulsive accumulation, obsession with control, or the inability to slow down. As psychologist Lynne Twist observed in *The Soul of Money*, people can have millions and still be dominated by a sense of insufficiency. They do not own their wealth—their fear does.

Contrast this with the sufficiency mindset. Sufficiency is not naïve optimism or detachment from material needs. It is a calibrated orientation toward enoughness—based not on spreadsheet targets or retirement calculators, but on clarity, adaptability, and perspective. A sufficiency mindset asks: *What do I actually need to operate well, stay free, and contribute meaningfully?* It resists both deprivation and excess. It recognises that wealth is not merely stored in accounts but in relationships, flexibility, health, skills, and access. Where scarcity reacts, sufficiency responds. Where scarcity fears, sufficiency calculates. Where scarcity hoards, sufficiency designs.

Neuroscientific studies have demonstrated that perceived scarcity narrows cognitive bandwidth. In experiments by Sendhil Mullainathan and Eldar Shafir, participants who believed themselves to be financially constrained performed significantly worse on problem-solving tasks, regardless of actual income levels. Scarcity hijacked their attention, creating a kind of mental tunnel vision that undermined good judgment. This has implications far beyond laboratory experiments. In real life, this same effect explains why financially stressed individuals may make short-term decisions—like high-interest borrowing, panic selling, or under-investment in their health—that deepen their vulnerability over time.

A sufficiency mindset, by contrast, widens the lens. It enables strategic patience, long-term planning, and creative thinking. But sufficiency must be cultivated. It does not emerge passively in crisis. For example, during the early days of the COVID-19 pandemic, some people immediately moved into solution mode: building mutual aid networks, sourcing food locally, switching to telework, bartering services. Others were paralysed, waiting for institutions to rescue them or simply spiralling into despair. The difference was not access to resources—it was orientation. The former group operated from sufficiency. The latter from scarcity.

It is also important to recognise that scarcity is often *engineered.* Financial systems, marketing narratives, and political rhetoric all exploit perceived lack to manipulate behaviour. Consumers are told daily that they are behind—behind in savings, in productivity, in lifestyle. The solution offered? Spend more. Work harder. Subscribe. Sacrifice. This is not information; it's programming. The sufficiency mindset begins, therefore, with psychological deprogramming. It challenges the default assumptions: that growth is always good, that more is always better, that risk must be outsourced, and that security is something sold rather than developed internally.

One useful tool for making this shift is scenario-based thinking. Rather than fearing what might go wrong in abstract terms, sufficiency thinkers map plausible stress events—currency devaluation, job loss, internet outages—and build *practical redundancy* around them. Not in a doomsday fashion, but as a form of life design. They ask: If I lost my income tomorrow, could I produce value another way? If my bank froze withdrawals, do I have access to alternatives? If prices spike, can I adapt consumption? These questions may look similar to those asked in a scarcity frame, but the emotional posture is different. Scarcity clings. Sufficiency reconfigures.

The sufficiency mindset also invites deeper inquiry into the emotional meaning of wealth. For many, money is not just a tool; it is a proxy for control, status, or self-worth. In times of crisis, this conflation becomes dangerous. If your sense of identity is tightly coupled to your financial situation, then volatility becomes existential. But if your identity is rooted in values, competence, and community, then financial turbulence is just that—turbulence, not collapse. Sufficiency thinkers practice *psychological decoupling* from the systems they inhabit. They use money, but do not worship it. They engage with the market, but are not defined by its fluctuations.

This decoupling is essential for resilience. In many traditional cultures, value was understood less as accumulation and more as continuity. A person was wealthy if they had strong kinship ties, practical knowledge, and reputation. Their economic ecosystem was not abstract but relational. While modern life demands engagement with formal economies, the sufficiency mindset retrieves some of this older wisdom. It prioritises *adaptability over abundance*, *usefulness over appearance*, and *context over comparison*. These are not romantic ideals; they are pragmatic anchors in a world where volatility is becoming the norm, not the exception.

Moreover, sufficiency allows for *selective disengagement* from toxic systems. Individuals who view their financial agency as internal are more willing to experiment with alternative economic models: local currencies, peer-to-peer services, digital barter, off-grid production. These aren't ideological acts—they are logical outcomes of a worldview that refuses to depend blindly on centralised systems that have already demonstrated fragility. Sufficiency thinkers understand that decentralisation is not just a technical feature; it is a psychological posture. It says: I trust my network, my skill set, and my judgment more than I trust institutions that have no accountability to me.

This shift in mindset has real-world economic outcomes. People who act from sufficiency tend to build leaner, more adaptable enterprises. They invest in skills that are portable across geographies and sectors. They design lifestyles that are not vulnerable to a single point of failure. They are slower to panic, quicker to pivot, and more likely to collaborate. This is not because they are richer—it is because they are freer.

To adopt a sufficiency mindset in the midst of systemic uncertainty is not delusional. It is evolutionary. Those who survive are rarely the strongest or the wealthiest. They are the most attuned. Sufficiency is not about lowering standards or rejecting ambition. It is about understanding the difference between *what is desirable* and *what is necessary*, and orienting your financial decisions accordingly. It is about knowing that you are already in possession of more than you think—and that clarity, not capital, is the foundation of true financial sovereignty.

Designing an Anti-Fragile Identity – Building Selfhood Rooted in Resourcefulness, Not External Validation

In every era of economic disruption, political upheaval, or cultural transformation, there emerges a silent sorting of individuals—not by income, education, or even experience, but by internal architecture. Some fracture. Others freeze. A rare few adapt—not by reverting to old strategies but by evolving entirely new ways of thinking and being. What distinguishes this third group is not luck or preparation alone. It is identity: not who they are on paper, but how they think of themselves when systems break down. And in a world increasingly defined by volatility, the most critical asset one can possess is not a credential, portfolio, or passport—it is an *anti-fragile self.*

Anti-fragility, a concept popularised by Nassim Nicholas Taleb, refers to systems that grow stronger under stress. Unlike something that is merely resilient (able to resist shock), the anti-fragile thrives on disorder, learns from pressure, and transforms through uncertainty. It is adaptive by design. But Taleb's insight extends far beyond finance or logistics. Human identity—our beliefs about who we are and what we can do—is either brittle, resilient, or anti-fragile. The difference determines whether we respond to adversity with paralysis, resistance, or evolution.

At the heart of an anti-fragile identity is *resourcefulness over reputation.* In fragile systems, identity is often externally anchored. People define themselves through job titles, brands they wear, degrees they hold, or the social validation they accrue. These markers can confer prestige in times of stability, but in disruption, they become liabilities. When the role disappears, when the institution falters, when the audience vanishes—so does the identity. The anti-fragile individual, by contrast, invests in capacities over optics. They ask: *What can I create, contribute, or solve when the usual tools are unavailable?*

This internalisation of value is not theoretical. It shows up in real-world choices. Consider the distinction between someone who sees themselves as "a consultant at a top firm" versus "a strategic thinker who solves complex problems." The former is brittle: their confidence is linked to an employer, a title, and an industry context. The latter is adaptive: their sense of worth is based on a transferable function, not a fixed form. In periods of mass layoffs, economic decline, or relocation, it is the latter who pivots swiftly. Their identity does not shatter—it reconfigures.

Crucially, anti-fragile identity is not built reactively; it is *designed intentionally*. This design begins with one core question: *Am I defining myself by what I can control or by what I can lose?* Fragile identities are contingent: on income levels, follower counts, third-party validation. Anti-fragile identities are sovereign: they are constructed through skills, philosophies, experiences, and principles that cannot be revoked. They derive confidence not from being right but from the capacity to revise, reframe, and relearn.

This mindset shift requires deep unlearning. Most institutional systems—from schools to corporations—do not reward anti-fragility. They reward conformity, hierarchy, and predictability. Success is defined by how well you fit, not how effectively you adapt. But fitting in is not the same as being equipped. In fact, over-identification with external labels can inhibit growth. A lawyer who sees themselves *only* as a legal professional may struggle to translate their abilities into other contexts. A lawyer who sees themselves as "a disciplined analyst of systems and human conflict" can reposition that identity across multiple fields.

To cultivate an anti-fragile identity, individuals must detach from the illusion of static selfhood. There is no permanent "you" waiting to be discovered. There is only the version of you that is most effective in the current and emerging environment. This is not psychological shapeshifting—it is strategic evolution. Identity becomes a toolkit, not a cage. The question is no longer *Who am I?* in abstract terms, but *Who am I under pressure?* and *What version of myself do I deploy to meet this moment?*

This brings us to a core discipline of anti-fragile identity: *deliberate exposure to calibrated adversity*. People who grow under stress are not necessarily fearless. They are familiar with discomfort. They have built callouses through practice—through small experiments, role changes, financial constraints, and creative risk. Rather than avoiding friction, they integrate it into their development cycle. They build confidence not from outcomes alone but from the *process of surviving iteration.* Every small failure becomes an inoculation against collapse.

It is also worth noting that anti-fragile identity does not depend on independence alone. It is not the myth of the lone genius or rugged individual. Rather, it is anchored in *interdependent sovereignty*—the ability to build and leverage networks without being owned by them. Anti-fragile individuals cultivate *peer relationships* over *power dependencies.* They form alliances that are mutual, not extractive. Their sense of self remains intact even as they collaborate, shift roles, or enter unfamiliar arenas. This balance—between self-trust and shared resilience—is what gives their identity strength without rigidity.

In contrast, identities driven by external validation tend to collapse under scrutiny or change. When one's self-worth is built on being liked, admired, or approved of, it becomes brittle to rejection, criticism, or loss of visibility. This is especially relevant in digital economies, where personal branding has become a form of commodification. The need to perform oneself—online, at work, in social circles—can override the deeper imperative to *develop oneself.* Anti-fragile individuals resist this performative drift. They remain *more committed to evolution than applause.*

From a psychological perspective, this orientation aligns with what Carol Dweck describes as a "growth mindset," but it goes further. The anti-fragile individual does not just believe they can improve—they deliberately position themselves in volatile, complex, or ambiguous settings where growth is not optional but required. They treat the unknown not as a threat but as a proving ground. Their identity is shaped by engagement, not protection.

Historical examples reinforce this point. Consider figures like Leonardo da Vinci, who refused to be boxed into one profession, constantly acquiring new skills and frameworks. Or more contemporarily, someone like Elon Musk, who traverses industries not because he's fearless, but because his sense of competence is modular, not locked to one domain. Whether or not one agrees with their methods, the lesson is clear: adaptability begins with *how you define yourself.*

For practical implementation, readers should consider conducting a "resilience audit" of their current identity. Ask:

What roles, titles, or labels do I rely on to feel valid?

Which parts of my self-image would dissolve if the system I rely on collapses?

What skills, qualities, or principles remain constant, regardless of external validation?

Where can I expose myself—safely and regularly—to ambiguity or discomfort, and observe how I respond?

The goal is not to eliminate structure but to *rebuild identity on a foundation of inner optionality.* When this internal core is strong, setbacks become recalibrations, not reckonings.

Ultimately, designing an anti-fragile identity is a form of economic and psychological sovereignty. It shifts the locus of control from fragile systems to the individual's adaptive capacity. It reframes instability as feedback, not failure. And it equips people not just to survive change, but to become the kind of person for whom *change is an advantage.*

In a world defined by acceleration, disruption, and uncertainty, there may be no greater currency than this: *the ability to evolve while staying rooted in who you choose to be.* That is the architecture of anti-fragile identity. Not built for show, but built to endure.

The Sovereign Imagination – Exercises to Spark Creative, Scenario-Based Thinking and Develop Inner Agility

The single greatest resource in times of systemic upheaval is not a cache of assets, a government guarantee, or even a contingency plan. It is *imagination*—not the whimsical fantasy of childhood, but its adult counterpart: a disciplined, sovereign faculty for thinking in alternate futures and acting with psychological independence. When institutions wobble and external structures degrade, the ability to mentally simulate outcomes, reposition the self, and design action within uncertainty becomes indispensable. *The sovereign imagination is not escapism. It is strategic foresight combined with internal agility.*

Mainstream education systems train for compliance, not imagination. Bureaucracies reward linear thinking, not exploratory cognition. And conventional financial advice—even when dressed up in modern language—presumes stability, not rupture. This creates a society of adults who are economically literate yet creatively disabled: intelligent individuals trained to navigate a map that no longer reflects the terrain. To survive—and lead—amid volatility, one must shift from map-following to *world-building.* That shift begins with imagination.

But not just any imagination. Sovereign imagination is grounded in autonomy. It is not outsourced to trends, algorithms, or ideology. It is not dependent on collective reassurance. It is *owned.* It does not simply seek escape from reality—it interrogates reality, deconstructs assumptions, and crafts adaptive alternatives. It is how individuals reclaim authorship of their lives in a world increasingly engineered to induce psychological dependency.

The practical question, then, is not "How do I imagine more?" but *How do I imagine better?* How do I make imagination an instrument of strategic clarity—not a place of idle speculation?

This requires two pivots: from passive consumption to active scenario-building, and from wishful thinking to *stress-testing of belief.* Below are three frameworks and accompanying exercises designed to spark sovereign imagination and expand the reader's adaptive range.

1. The Scenario Inversion Method – Flip What You Take for Granted

Most people's cognitive defaults are unchallenged until collapse arrives. Sovereign thinkers invert this process. They *pre-challenge* their assumptions by systematically asking: *What if the opposite of what I believe were true—and how would I operate then?*

Consider the following prompts:

What if the central bank lost control of inflation for a decade?

What if the currency you're paid in experienced a 70% devaluation?

What if access to traditional banking was suspended for 30 days?

What if your profession disappeared overnight—what transferable value remains?

Each prompt is not a forecast but a *provocation.* It activates a form of mental simulation akin to strategic war-gaming. The aim is not to cause anxiety but to build flexibility. The mind that has already rehearsed a breakdown is less fragile when the system genuinely fractures.

This is not paranoia—it is *prepared creativity.* Most individuals operate under an illusion of permanence. Scenario inversion strips this illusion and reveals that *systems are scaffolding, not guarantees.* When the scaffolding falls, imagination builds the next structure.

2. The 72-Hour Autonomy Drill – Rehearse Psychological and Practical Independence

Physical preparation without psychological rehearsal is performative. Sovereign imagination is *tested under compression.* This exercise introduces time-bound constraint to simulate loss of external supports. It is as much about mental calibration as logistical readiness.

The challenge is this: Imagine all institutions freeze for 72 hours. No internet, no power, no financial transactions, no outside communication. Ask:

How would I feed, hydrate, and shelter myself—immediately?

What decisions would I need to make without expert guidance?

Who would I be in the absence of systems confirming my identity or status?

What aspects of myself would become more useful, and which irrelevant?

This drill forces a confrontation with personal capability and fragility. It shifts the locus of control inward. One begins to see which aspects of life are propped up by habit and convenience rather than *design*. Sovereign imagination does not fantasise about collapse—it uses its *simulation as discipline*.

3. The Value Reorientation Exercise – Define Worth Without Institutions

Most people conflate value with valuation: job title, income, market price, social media influence. These are proxies. They are interpreted through collective filters, and often controlled by platforms or authorities. When sovereign systems falter, institutional metrics become unreliable. What remains is *intrinsic utility*.

To reorient value:

List ten capacities you have that produce real utility without needing permission, platforms, or infrastructure.

Then ask: how would these capacities function in a small community? In a black market? In a self-contained digital ecosystem?

Next: define five values that would still feel valid even in the absence of witnesses, documentation, or approval.

This is not philosophical abstraction. It's *economic recalibration.* When the external valuation of things collapses, *internal valuation becomes the new currency.* Those with a sovereign imagination can operate fluidly between systems because their value is not system-dependent.

The Philosophical Core: Uncertainty as Terrain, Not Threat

Sovereign imagination emerges most vividly in individuals who have made peace with uncertainty—not as a temporary inconvenience but as *the native environment of the modern world.* The traditional mindset seeks clarity before action. The sovereign mindset *acts to create clarity.*

This subtle inversion underlies the agility we associate with pioneers, polymaths, and survivors. They do not freeze waiting for the conditions to make sense. They act, observe, and adapt in feedback loops. Their imagination is a sensory organ for change, not just a place of retreat.

The discomfort most people feel with ambiguity is not due to a lack of capacity, but a *lack of permission.* The world trains people to defer. To wait for green lights. Sovereign imagination revokes the need for permission. It gives individuals the right to hypothesise, test, and iterate. This is not recklessness. It is *creative sovereignty.*

Contrasting the Fragile and the Imaginative Mind

Let us juxtapose the mind guided by institutional programming versus sovereign imagination.

The fragile mind asks: *What do I do if X happens?*

The sovereign mind asks: *What system am I assuming must remain intact—and what if it doesn't?*

The fragile mind seeks comfort in consensus.

The sovereign mind seeks signal in contradiction.

The fragile mind views collapse as chaos.

The sovereign mind views collapse as code to decipher and terrain to explore.

This is not an appeal to cynicism or survivalism. It is a call to *ownership of cognition.* A society of sovereign imaginations is not one that descends into fragmentation. It is one that builds anew—not from coercion, but from authorship.

Sovereign Imagination as Civic and Personal Responsibility

In volatile times, the ability to model alternatives is not optional—it is foundational. Imagination is no longer the domain of artists or entrepreneurs alone. It is a civic skill, a survival mechanism, and a moral responsibility.

To imagine sovereignly is to refuse inherited limitations. It is to sketch pathways where no institution currently leads. It is to see possibility where the system sees threat. It is to think for oneself—not merely in opposition to others, but in deep fidelity to truth.

As individuals develop this faculty—through deliberate exercises, philosophical reframing, and critical unlearning—they move from consumer to creator, from follower to forerunner. They become the architects of inner and outer sovereignty.

And in a world built on brittle dependencies, *there may be no greater power than that.*

Chapter 5
Exit Points – Knowing When and How to Leave

History doesn't always shout its turning points from rooftops. More often, it murmurs them—subtle at first, then unmistakable in retrospect. In those moments, the people who moved early weren't merely lucky; they were intentional. They didn't have secret data or privileged warnings. What they had was clarity of perception, the courage to trust it, and the discipline to act while others paused. Exit, in this light, is not an act of desperation. It is a stance—a strategic posture assumed before the ground beneath begins to crack.

Many cling to the comforting fiction of the "last-minute escape"—a romantic notion that one can observe events unfold calmly, assess all variables, and decide at the final moment, as though systems unwind politely, with fair warning. They do not. Borders can shut overnight. Banks can freeze without precedent. Bandwidth throttles, communication fails, and what was once accessible becomes sealed off in hours. Whether in the chaos of Venezuela's economic implosion, Syria's rapid fragmentation, the abrupt disintegration of the USSR, or the more recent digital runs on banks—waiting cost not just money, but dignity, agency, and choice. Preparedness, then, is not hysteria. It is the sober discipline of recognising when the conditions no longer support your sovereignty.

This chapter isn't fuelled by fear. Its engine is discernment. You won't find a bulleted list of emergency provisions or breathless calls to bunker down. What you will find are the frameworks—the mental architecture—necessary to detect the inflection points in your financial, political, or cultural environments. And once they appear, to move—not in panic, but with precision.

The idea of "leaving" needs to be reimagined. We're not always talking about a physical escape. Sometimes, certainly, it is geographic—moving capital, securing jurisdictional alternatives, stepping bodily into a new legal environment. But just as often, the exit is digital: reallocating assets into decentralised ecosystems, or shifting your work and income beyond any single point of control. And at its deepest, it is psychological—decoupling your sense of identity from institutions already in free fall. In truth, exit is less about relocation and more about orientation.

Permanence, in our world, is a seductive illusion. We are encouraged to believe that the systems surrounding us are elastic, that they bend but never break. That central banks can always intervene. That legal norms will hold. That "this" can't happen "here." But complexity doesn't mean durability—it often means fragility in disguise. Highly interdependent systems don't unwind slowly; they cascade. One critical node fails, and the rest collapses in silence, then all at once. And the more embedded you are in that web, the harder it is to extract yourself before it tightens.

To navigate this reality, we introduce a strategic lens: the Red Zone, Grey Zone, Green Zone framework. Think of it not as a survivalist's map, but as a clarity tool. Red Zones are structurally unsound and ethically compromised—you don't linger, you exit. Grey Zones are murky, unstable; they require contingency, optionality, and constant recalibration. Green Zones offer relative opportunity, but they too demand vigilance. This model isn't just about location—it's about how intelligently positioned you are to adapt when the status quo no longer holds.

From here, we'll explore two archetypes of departure: the Soft Exit and the Hard Exit. A Soft Exit is gradual, strategic, and layered—acquiring second residencies, diversifying across currencies and jurisdictions, building a digital footprint that's mobile and resilient. It's an intentional hedge against volatility. A Hard Exit, by contrast, is abrupt, reactive—evacuation, capital flight, emergency liquidation. The tragedy is that most Hard Exits were once Soft Exits deferred too long. This chapter's aim is to shorten that delay—so your next move is one of choice, not necessity.

We will turn to real case studies. Consider the Cypriot families who watched their life savings vanish during the 2013 bail-ins. Or the Argentine entrepreneurs who learned to thrive within informal economies because the formal ones had imploded. Or investors who thought their portfolios were diversified until capital controls, inflation, or sanctions rendered them unusable. These stories are not distant cautionary tales—they are contemporary casework, live files still unfolding.

The common thread through all of them? Exit readiness isn't about predicting collapse. It's about acknowledging the plausible and preparing for it. You don't need to know the precise moment the system cracks. You only need to grasp that it might—and to structure your life in a way that prioritises mobility over blind trust in bureaucratic continuity. Sovereign thinking begins where passive dependence ends.

But even among the capable, a question remains: why do so many stay too long? Why do intelligent, well-educated, well-resourced individuals delay decisive action until they're boxed in? Part of it is emotional—a longing for normalcy, a hope that the tide will turn. But part of it is cultural. We are taught that to stay is virtuous. That loyalty—to a country, an institution, a bank—is somehow nobler than mobility. This is sentiment masquerading as ethics. Sovereignty demands better discernment. Blind loyalty is not honourable—it is exposure, repackaged as virtue.

This chapter proposes a new decision-making discipline—one rooted in signal recognition, not sentimentality. You'll learn to audit your exposure across multiple domains: not just your finances, but your legal infrastructure, your digital dependencies, your social capital. You'll be asked to consider friction—the cost of exiting now versus the trauma of waiting too long. And you'll learn how to develop optionality, so that when the moment demands action, you have not only the will—but the means.

Exit is not a singular leap; it's a process. It may begin with small movements—transferring a portion of your wealth into a decentralised wallet, securing an alternate passport, building relationships in parallel geographies. Over time, it might grow into something larger: a physical relocation, a structural change in how you earn, live, and contribute. But the catalyst is always the same: awareness, sharpened and acted upon before the window narrows.

This chapter doesn't prescribe. It doesn't command. It offers a compass—something subtler and more durable. It will not tell you what to do. It will help you learn what to look for, and when. It is a guide to exiting with intelligence, on your own terms, before your terms are taken from you.

To exit well is not to abandon, but to preserve. Not to flee, but to navigate with grace. It is the quiet art of remaining whole, even when the world around you begins to fracture. That, in the end, is what we are here to study.

Reading the Early Signs of Collapse – Subtle Indicators of Systemic Breakdown

Collapse never announces itself with sirens or fireworks. It does not come with official warnings or real-time clarity. It creeps in through the seams of the familiar—*subtle distortions in how systems behave, how leaders communicate, and how ordinary people cope*. By the time a state newspaper prints the word "crisis", the real crisis has already matured. The purpose of this chapter is not to stoke fear but to sharpen *perception*. Collapse has a signature, and history has given us the pattern more than once.

It is not enough to monitor GDP, central bank minutes, or election cycles. Those are *rear-view metrics*, often massaged to maintain confidence. If you want to see collapse before it is named, *you must become a pattern recogniser*—fluent in the unspoken, attuned to weak signals, and capable of integrating social, financial, and institutional data at a behavioural level. This chapter explores those signals—disparate on the surface, but diagnostic in combination.

Let us begin where most people never look: language.

1. Semantic Decay: When Words Cease to Mean

One of the earliest signs of institutional decay is *linguistic inflation.* When governments or corporations begin using language to manage perception rather than describe reality, you are no longer being informed—you are being conditioned. This manifests as vague promises, contradictory statistics, or redefined terms. In the late Soviet Union, food shortages were framed as "supply realignment"; in Zimbabwe, 89% unemployment was dubbed "informal economic dynamism". The function of public communication shifts from *clarity* to *containment.*

In modern democracies, the same tactic persists—more polished, but no less dangerous. "Temporary liquidity event" replaces "bank run." "Transitory inflation" extends over years. "Targeted kinetic action" conceals active war. The public's trust is slowly eroded, not by a single lie, but by a thousand euphemisms. *When a society's leadership can no longer describe its problems clearly, it cannot solve them.* This is not a rhetorical defect—it is a signal.

2. Institutional Rigidity: When Systems Resist Self-Correction

Healthy systems adapt. Collapsing systems double down. A government that responds to dissent with censorship, to economic volatility with capital controls, or to policy failure with more bureaucracy is not reforming—it is entrenching. This kind of rigidity is a leading indicator of breakdown.

The Weimar Republic, in its terminal years, could not arrest its own hyperinflation without destroying the regime's political credibility—so it didn't. Lebanon's central bank continued unsustainable monetary policy long after insolvency was clear. When institutions cannot act without destabilising themselves, collapse is no longer theoretical. It is *programmed.*

You will observe this in how regulations multiply without corresponding efficacy, how emergency powers become normalised, and how the law is selectively applied to insulate insiders. The common denominator is fragility masquerading as control.

3. Elite Hedging: Watch What the Powerful Do—Not What They Say

Perhaps the most reliable leading indicator is *elite behaviour.* When those closest to power begin shielding themselves from the very systems they administer, take note. Private security firms, offshore banking, dual citizenships, secondary passports, and family relocations are not theoretical exercises—they are *insurance against the system they helped build.*

In the months leading up to Argentina's 2001 debt crisis, capital flight reached historic highs—largely led by politicians and their associates. During Greece's 2015 banking freeze, MPs quietly moved assets abroad while urging calm and patriotism. These are not ethical lapses. They are tells. *When trust breaks inside the power structure, the public is already too late.*

Track where decision-makers are sending their children for education, where they are buying real estate, and whether their own compensation is indexed to inflation. *These are the breadcrumbs of their expectations.*

4. Informal Workarounds: The Rise of Parallel Structures

When formal systems fail, informal ones rise—not by design, but by necessity. The growth of black markets, barter systems, community currencies, VPN usage, or mutual aid networks all indicate a vacuum of trust. In Venezuela, hyperinflation led to "peso towns" where Colombian currency replaced the bolivar. In Myanmar, after the 2021 military coup, underground banking surged as citizens rejected official institutions. In post-crisis Detroit, parts of the city relied more on Bitcoin than cash due to banking deserts.

When people create alternatives to core services—food, energy, education, security—you are witnessing system exit at the behavioural level. It's not revolution. It's resignation.

The more these workarounds are criminalised or denounced by the state, the more likely they are to be necessary. Remember: the legitimacy of a system lies not in its laws but in its ability to provide real, usable value.

5. Narrative Fracture: Competing Realities and Cultural Splintering

No society can function without some shared understanding of reality. When that consensus dissolves, coordination becomes impossible. A warning sign of collapse is not simply political polarisation—it is *epistemic divergence*. When groups can no longer agree on *what is happening*, let alone what to do, collapse moves from economic risk to civilizational risk.

The United States in the 2020s illustrates this vividly. Competing news ecosystems, conspiracy echo chambers, and factionalised science have created parallel Americas—each with its own facts, heroes, and villains. The result is not merely disagreement, but paralysis.

When consensus dies, so does legitimacy. And without legitimacy, governments can only govern through force or fraud. *The society may remain standing, but it no longer functions.* Its collapse is underway—first in the mind, then in the street.

6. Strategic Incoherence: When Short-Termism Replaces Statecraft

Another early warning sign is the abandonment of long-range thinking. As fiscal deficits balloon and public debt expands, you'll see policy reduced to performative gestures and reactive legislation. Monetary policy becomes politicised. National energy strategies contradict environmental goals. Immigration laws fluctuate with headlines. What connects these is a loss of long-horizon logic.

Sound governance requires *sacrifice today for stability tomorrow.* Collapsing systems reverse this: they consume credibility, liquidity, and public trust to survive each additional quarter. Eventually, they are left with no assets except coercion.

7. Acceleration Events: Normalising the Unthinkable

Collapse is not a slow fade—it is often catalysed by sharp shocks. A banking freeze. A cyberattack. A political assassination. A foreign war. These *acceleration events* do not cause collapse—they *reveal* it. Their function is diagnostic: *how a society responds tells you everything about how prepared it was.*

When COVID-19 emerged, nations differed starkly. Singapore activated civil defence protocols, maintained medical credibility, and coordinated coherently. Others hoarded, blamed, censored, or collapsed. These differences were not about the virus—they were about *resilience.*

Every collapse has a trigger. But triggers only matter when the structure is already brittle.

Integrating the Signals: Collapse as a Composite Diagnosis

Collapse is never about a single datapoint. It is an *accumulation of contradictions*. No one can predict the precise date or mode. But like a seasoned physician, you can diagnose the syndrome before the crisis becomes irreversible. This demands *pattern recognition, not prediction.*

When language becomes vague, institutions rigid, elites disengaged, workarounds necessary, narratives fractured, and governance incoherent—*you are no longer dealing with volatility*. You are witnessing systemic disintegration in real time.

What Can You Do With This Knowledge?

Recognising the early signs does not mean abandoning your country, hoarding gold, or becoming fatalistic. It means reallocating your attention, your assets, and your allegiance. *Collapse-aware individuals act differently*. They:

Stop outsourcing risk assessment to governments and media

Diversify across geography, jurisdiction, and currency

Build redundancy in skills, not just savings

Invest in networks of mutual aid and trusted community

Think in *scenarios*, not predictions

Ultimately, the value of recognising early signs is not in beating the crowd or escaping unscathed. It is in *retaining agency*. Systems may fail. But your capacity to respond—to relocate, retool, reframe—is what sovereign resilience looks like.

This chapter is a warning system. Use it not to panic, but to prepare. Because by the time collapse is declared, *you are no longer observing it—you are inside it.*

The Myth of the Last-Minute Escape – Why Delay Often Destroys Wealth and Freedom

In every historical collapse, there is one group who never believed the worst would happen—until it did. They weren't the least informed or the least capable. In fact, they were often educated, resourceful, and well-connected. What they lacked wasn't information. It was *urgency*. This chapter is about *them*—and about why betting on a last-minute escape is almost always a fatal miscalculation.

The most dangerous assumption in times of growing instability is that you will know exactly when to act. That there will be a clear signal, a final alarm bell, a final opportunity to exit just before the window closes. This belief—comforting, persistent, and deadly—is the myth of the last-minute escape.

It is a myth that has cost people their savings, their safety, and in many cases, their lives. Because collapses are rarely clean, linear, or well-telegraphed. They are ambiguous. They unfold in phases. They seduce with moments of normalcy and calm before slamming the door shut.

This subchapter dismantles that myth—not through abstract warnings, but by examining real case studies where delay became disaster. And by drawing insights into why *now* is always a better moment to prepare than later.

The Failure of the Final Signal: Case Studies in Collapse

The tragedy of delayed departure is not new. From Weimar Germany to 1970s Chile, from Sarajevo to Kyiv, from Kabul to Caracas, the timeline is shockingly familiar: denial, normalisation, hesitation, entrapment.

Consider the case of Iran in 1979. As tensions rose, many Iranian professionals and families—particularly in Tehran—hesitated to leave. They believed that the Shah's regime would survive or that order would be restored. Those who waited until after the regime fell found that their assets were frozen, bank withdrawals capped, passports invalidated, and commercial flights grounded. Overnight, their mobility disappeared. *Wealth meant nothing when it couldn't cross a border.*

In Venezuela, many middle-class citizens knew inflation was worsening well before it spiralled into hyperinflation. But they stayed, believing the bolivar would rebound or that "things would return to normal." By the time many sought to exit, border controls, currency collapse, and travel restrictions rendered their savings meaningless. One former lawyer now sells soap in Colombia. His assets? Worth less than a one-way bus ticket.

Even in Europe, history repeats. In 1991, as Yugoslavia fractured, many in Sarajevo postponed evacuation because they believed the city's cosmopolitanism—its history of interethnic harmony—would shield it. But within months, sniper alleys and food queues replaced neighbourhood cafés. *The price of waiting was being trapped in a siege without end.*

These examples are not anomalies. They are a pattern.

Psychological Inertia: Why People Wait Too Long

Why do intelligent people—often with the means to leave—delay action even as collapse gathers momentum?

The answers lie less in logic than in psychology:

Normalcy Bias – This is the tendency to assume that because things have been stable, they will remain so. It filters out contradictory evidence and frames warning signs as anomalies rather than indicators of systemic change. People cling to routines not because they are blind, but because disruption feels unbearable until it is unavoidable.

Social Anchoring – People do not want to be the first to act. They look to peers, neighbours, and local authorities for cues. If no one else is panicking, they don't want to appear alarmist. *Consensus becomes a trap.*

Sunk Cost Fallacy – Those who have invested decades in building a life—homeownership, careers, social status—struggle to walk away. The more that's been built, the harder it is to cut losses, even when collapse is imminent.

State Messaging – Governments almost never signal collapse in real-time. They downplay unrest, massage inflation data, and criminalise pessimism. Delay is not just a psychological trap—it is institutionally reinforced.

Recognising these dynamics isn't enough. You must learn to override them. Because systems *never* give you permission to leave. They only give you chances—until they don't.

When the Gates Close: The Mechanics of Entrapment

Let's make this tangible. What does it actually mean to miss the window of escape?

Capital Controls – Your bank limits international transfers. Wire requests are delayed, "under review," or outright denied. What was once liquid becomes trapped in your domestic currency—subject to devaluation, seizure, or freezing.

Travel Restrictions – Airports are shut. Visas are suspended. Borders are militarised. A journey that was possible last week becomes logistically impossible today.

Document Expiry – Passports are no longer renewed. Foreign embassies close. Exit stamps become politicised. Your legal ability to cross borders evaporates.

Asset Nationalisation – Properties are seized. Businesses are expropriated. Holdings in pension funds or equities are devalued by decree or inflated into worthlessness.

Media Blackouts and Censorship – Information flow collapses. Real-time updates become inaccessible. Your ability to assess conditions, coordinate with family, or respond in time is erased.

This is not hypothetical. Every item on this list has occurred repeatedly across collapsing states in the last 30 years. If you wait until the worst is undeniable, you will likely face these barriers head-on. And by then, *your options will no longer be choices. They will be reactions.*

A Different Philosophy of Escape: Early, Quiet, Optional

Contrast this with the logic of *early optionality*. Those who fare best in systemic crises rarely make dramatic exits. They make quiet ones—long before they're necessary.

A family in Hong Kong relocated to Lisbon in 2019—not because they predicted mass arrests, but because they read the signs and acted before emotion took over. Their peers waited, hoping the security law wouldn't pass. It did. By then, exit visas were harder to obtain and student placements dried up.

An American engineer quietly opened a bank account and acquired residency rights in Panama in 2016—not because he expected total collapse, but because he understood *optionality beats prediction*. Today, he has a fallback, while his peers debate the next election cycle.

The principle is simple: *The best exit is the one you don't yet need—but already have.*

What Escape Actually Looks Like

Too often, "escape" is romanticised as a singular, decisive act. But strategic exits are rarely theatrical. They are incremental, calculated, and often reversible.

Financial Exit – Diversifying assets offshore, securing international banking access, holding physical or decentralised stores of value.

Legal Exit – Acquiring a second residency or citizenship. Establishing the right to stay, work, or travel elsewhere—before needing to exercise it.

Physical Exit – Relocating gradually. Perhaps a "test move" first. Renting, not buying. Establishing familiarity and building networks before urgency hits.

Psychological Exit – Detaching identity from national belonging. Reframing home as a set of values and relationships, not coordinates on a map.

Those who understand this framework don't wait for the news to confirm what their instincts already suspect. They act with stealth, not noise. With foresight, not fear.

Why This Matters Now

We are living in an age where multiple systems—monetary, ecological, geopolitical—are under strain. The belief that "it won't happen here" is no longer credible. Yet the myth of the last-minute escape persists, often reinforced by media spectacles of dramatic evacuations and heroic last stands.

But real preparedness doesn't begin with adrenaline. It begins with *mental unhooking*. With examining the stories we tell ourselves about normalcy, permanence, and timing.

There is no perfect moment to leave. Only windows. And windows are best used while they're open—not when they are closing.

So ask yourself:

If borders closed next month, could you leave?

If your currency devalued 80%, would you have access to capital?

If your city fell into unrest, would you have a soft place to land?

If the answer to any of these is "no," then the time to act is not later. It's now.

Not in panic. But in clarity.

Not all at once. But step by step.

Because the only real escape is the one you've already made when the alarm finally rings.

Red Zone, Grey Zone, Green Zone Framework – A Decision-Making Model to Help Readers Assess Environment and Readiness

There is a kind of quiet violence in waiting too long to act. It is not the sudden rupture of crisis, but the slow erosion of choice. The difference between a proactive escape and a desperate evacuation often lies not in resources, but in clarity. One of the most important and underdeveloped muscles in modern life is the ability to assess one's environment with intellectual honesty—particularly under deteriorating conditions. The *Red Zone, Grey Zone, Green Zone* framework is not a theoretical construct; it is a pragmatic lens for decision-making in unstable times. It is a tool designed to protect sovereignty, preserve mobility, and time exits with intelligence rather than panic.

To grasp the gravity of this framework, we must first acknowledge an uncomfortable truth: systems do not tend to collapse all at once. They rot in stages. The warning signs are often visible long before the headlines confirm them. Financial instability, social unrest, institutional dysfunction—these tend to build cumulatively. Yet many people delay their response because they lack a mental model to interpret these signals and categorise their own readiness. This delay is not born of laziness, but of cognitive overload, social denial, and institutional reassurance.

The *Red-Grey-Green* model breaks this paralysis by giving form to the formless. Each zone offers a diagnostic map: a way to read both external conditions and internal capacity with discipline. Understanding what zone you're in—objectively, not emotionally—can mean the difference between preservation and dispossession.

Green Zone: Stability with Optionality

In the Green Zone, the fundamentals still hold. The currency system is intact, rule of law is functional, civil liberties are respected, and basic infrastructure operates predictably. Markets behave with a degree of rationality. There may be political disagreements or minor economic disruptions, but they are buffered by legitimate institutions and procedural corrections. In this environment, the focus is not on panic or exit—but on preparation.

This is the *window of strategic optionality*. Individuals in Green Zones should be building systems that make them resilient in case conditions degrade. This includes obtaining secondary citizenships, diversifying assets internationally, establishing mobile income streams, and acquiring transferable skills. Importantly, Green Zones offer the luxury of time—decisions can be made calmly, with due diligence, rather than in haste.

But the danger of the Green Zone is complacency. It is easy to believe that what is normal is also permanent. Yet history offers countless examples—Argentina in 1999, Lebanon in 2018, Ukraine pre-2014—where apparent stability masked deep fragility. *The Green Zone is the last phase where voluntary exits are cheap, legally simple, and psychologically unburdened.*

To stay in the Green Zone too long without preparing for a shift is to mistake current comfort for future security.

Grey Zone: Volatility with Shrinking Margins

The Grey Zone is defined by systemic ambiguity. The signs of decay are no longer debatable: capital controls begin to tighten, inflation becomes sticky, infrastructure becomes unreliable, and political polarisation escalates beyond normal debate. The media begins to fragment between state narratives and underground counter-narratives. Institutions lose public trust. Crime may rise—not just in volume but in brazenness. People begin to whisper what they used to say out loud.

In the Grey Zone, normal life may continue for many—but under increasing strain. The cost of delay becomes real, though not yet absolute. Currency devaluation may wipe out savings. Travel restrictions may quietly be imposed. Tax codes become more aggressive. Surveillance tightens. You may still have the legal right to leave, but practically, each day adds friction: depleting liquidity, deteriorating public services, and a shrinking window to transfer assets or emigrate smoothly.

The defining characteristic of the Grey Zone is emotional dissonance. People know something is wrong but remain socially anchored. Families are divided—some warning of collapse, others accusing them of paranoia. Governments tend to increase their rhetoric of stability while quietly enacting crisis measures.

It is within the Grey Zone that the most costly decisions are made—not because people lack information, but because they fail to act on it. Every structural exit becomes harder: moving money, changing schools, changing countries. What was a low-cost decision in the Green Zone becomes an expensive and complex manoeuvre. Timing is everything—and hesitation can metastasise into entrapment.

Red Zone: Crisis and Constraint

In the Red Zone, the mask falls. Collapse is no longer abstract—it is operational. Banks freeze withdrawals. Supermarkets run out of stock. Basic services fail. Protests turn into riots. Borders close. Property rights become ambiguous, often suspended. Surveillance reaches its apex. Exit becomes a matter of urgency, but it is now logistically restricted and politically penalised. The cost of departure is no longer just financial—it is physical, emotional, and potentially existential.

At this stage, you do not manage your exit—you survive it. People leave with what they can carry, not what they've accumulated. Paper wealth becomes worthless. Travel becomes a game of evasion, not administration. Decision-making compresses into fight-or-flight. For many, the Red Zone is the point of no return—psychologically and economically. You are no longer playing chess; you are escaping fire.

What is striking in historical case studies—from the fall of Saigon to the Venezuelan exodus—is not that collapse happened, but how many people were surprised by its finality. *There are no second chances in the Red Zone.* You leave early or you do not leave at all. The exit window closes, and with it, the illusion that you had time.

Using the Framework: Internal and External Mapping

The power of this model lies in its dual assessment: *environmental conditions* (what zone you're in) and *personal readiness* (how prepared you are to move zones). Two people in the same country may be in different readiness zones based on mobility, capital fluidity, social ties, psychological flexibility, and legal status.

This is not a binary question of whether you should flee or stay. It's a continuous calibration of exit-readiness. Ask yourself:

If your bank froze withdrawals for 72 hours, would you be able to operate?

If your passport became restricted, do you have a Plan B?

If political unrest erupted locally, how quickly could you relocate—temporarily or permanently?

Are your income streams geographically tied or mobile?

Could your children's education continue if you moved across borders?

These are not just logistical questions—they are identity questions. The person who plans for disruption is not paranoid, but pragmatic. The capacity to respond to volatility is not rooted in fear, but in agency.

Lessons from the Field: Pattern Recognition from Collapsed Societies

Historical collapses often follow similar arcs: a long phase of denial, a brief phase of disorder, and a prolonged phase of adaptation. Those who exit early are often derided as alarmist—until they are proven right. Those who delay until conditions are "obviously" bad often lose the ability to act.

In Rhodesia (now Zimbabwe), the currency devaluation and land reform policies of the 1990s came after decades of warning signs. Those who stayed until 2002 faced not just loss of land and income, but legal limbo. In Greece during the 2015 capital controls, middle-class families found themselves unable to access pensions or transfer savings abroad. In post-invasion Iraq, professionals with warning signs chose to remain—losing not just assets, but lives.

Collapse rarely announces itself politely. It accumulates in invisible queues, sudden shortages, frozen accounts, and unrecognisable rules.

Final Reflection: Exit as a Mindset, Not a Moment

To exit is not merely to relocate—it is to reclaim authorship over your trajectory. The *Red-Grey-Green* framework is not a moral judgment on where one lives, but a pragmatic method to assess how much room for manoeuvre remains. In unstable environments, *the earlier you prepare, the more optionality you preserve.* Wealth without mobility becomes a cage. Intelligence without preparation becomes regret.

Sovereign individuals do not wait for certainty. They observe, interpret, and act before consensus catches up. They measure risk not by headlines, but by the narrowing of options. The goal is not to live in fear—but to remain free by refusing to become strategically blind.

Collapse, like entropy, is always in motion. But so is awareness. And awareness—paired with timing—is the most underrated form of capital you will ever possess.

The Soft Exit vs. the Hard Exit – Differentiates Between Gradual and Urgent Relocation Strategies

Most people think of leaving as a single decision, a definitive break, a crossing of borders both literal and psychological. In reality, exit is rarely that neat. It is not just a logistical manoeuvre but a strategic shift—executed in stages or under pressure, shaped by the surrounding volatility and personal readiness. The myth of the one-size-fits-all relocation strategy has left many vulnerable to false confidence or paralysing delay. In unstable environments, understanding the difference between a *soft exit* and a *hard exit* is not simply academic—it's a survival imperative.

A *soft exit* is a slow pivot, executed while time is still on your side. A *hard exit* is a rapid disengagement, often forced by circumstance. Both are forms of strategic withdrawal—but only one preserves optionality, agency, and wealth with minimum trauma. The other is an emergency brake pulled too late.

Understanding which one applies to you—and preparing for both—is no longer a fringe concern. It's a central pillar of 21st-century resilience.

Soft Exit: The Art of Optionality

A soft exit is, above all, a proactive posture. It is the relocation equivalent of compounding interest—gradual, often invisible at first, but ultimately transformative in its impact. It begins not with a suitcase but with a shift in asset allocation, legal status, and mental framing.

At its core, the soft exit reflects a mindset of sovereignty over reaction. You do not wait for headlines to validate your instincts. You read institutional decay, capital flow restrictions, and social fragmentation as indicators—not disruptions. And you respond while the cost of exit is still low, both financially and emotionally.

What does this look like in practice?

Acquiring a second passport or residency before it becomes difficult or expensive.

Moving part of your capital offshore—legally and securely—before capital controls are introduced.

Building portable income streams so you're not geographically tethered to one regime or economy.

Enrolling children in international or bilingual education systems that prepare them for cross-border continuity.

Establishing relational networks in multiple jurisdictions to avoid total dependence on a single societal system.

In this sense, the soft exit is not one decision but a portfolio of micro-decisions. You might still live in your home country. You may still pay taxes there and maintain a career. But you are no longer exposed to systemic failure as your single point of failure. *You have de-risked your life across jurisdictions without burning bridges.*

The soft exit is characterised by *control.* You pick the timeline. You research the legal frameworks. You choose whether to commit or just create the option to do so later. It's the exit of the quietly prepared—not the loudly panicked.

Hard Exit: When the Window Slams Shut

The hard exit is the opposite of the above. It happens under duress, not design. One day you have mobility, access, and options. The next, borders are closed, bank accounts are frozen, or public safety has deteriorated to the point where leaving is no longer a choice—it is a race against collapse.

Hard exits are defined by *reactivity*. They are undertaken under intense psychological stress, without the benefit of planning or clean separation. You move not because you want to, but because staying has become untenable.

This is the exit of war refugees, of political dissidents, of middle-class families who waited too long and suddenly find themselves in lines at airports, carrying not portfolios but backpacks. It is the exit of those who mistook temporary stability for structural permanence—and paid for that illusion in lost time, capital, and safety.

We see this pattern again and again:

During the fall of Saigon in 1975, families who had the foresight to leave a year earlier exited with assets, credentials, and dignity. Those who waited were airlifted in panic—if they escaped at all.

In Venezuela, many middle-class professionals continued to believe in institutional recovery until inflation rendered their savings worthless. The early movers relocated to neighbouring countries and restarted careers. Late movers struggled to feed their families or lost legal pathways to emigrate.

In Ukraine in 2022, those with prior contingency plans—dual citizenships, international bank accounts, connections abroad—left before the first missile. Those who hesitated often faced months of chaotic displacement, red tape, or conscription.

Hard exits extract a brutal tax: emotional dislocation, asset loss, interrupted education, legal uncertainty, and often years of rebuilding. While sometimes unavoidable, they are rarely inevitable. They become necessary only when the soft exit has been neglected or denied.

Why Most People Miss the Exit Window

Few rational people would choose a hard exit over a soft one. Yet in practice, most delay action until it's too late. Why?

Social Anchoring – Humans are tribal. If no one else is leaving, most won't either—even if the indicators are clear. This psychological inertia leads people to ignore their own risk assessments in favour of group validation.

Institutional Reassurance – Governments rarely announce collapse. They promise stability until the day the ATM stops working. Citizens who rely on official narratives are often lulled into a false sense of continuity.

Emotional Denial – Leaving one's home, culture, and professional identity is painful. It requires confronting uncertainty. The brain will manufacture justifications to delay this discomfort—until it's no longer a choice.

Asset Illiquidity – People are often entangled in illiquid assets: property, local business interests, or family commitments. They delay exit because they can't or won't disentangle in time.

By the time they are ready to move, *the cost of leaving has multiplied—sometimes exponentially*.

Designing a Soft Exit Strategy: From Theory to Execution

A soft exit is not synonymous with expatriation. It may mean staying rooted while creating parallel systems of resilience. Think in terms of:

Jurisdictional diversification: Where do you have legal rights, economic access, and physical safety if your home country fails you?

Capital flexibility: How easily can you move and access your money? Are you dependent on one banking system, one currency, one tax regime?

Skill and credential mobility: Are your qualifications and professional reputation recognised internationally? Can you consult, freelance, or earn abroad?

Digital autonomy: Are you capable of operating online across borders? Or are you locked into a national infrastructure that can surveil, censor, or cut you off?

Family contingency: If you have dependents, do they have documents, language ability, or educational continuity to make a move less disruptive?

None of these require immediate action. But they demand strategic attention. *The goal is not to run. It's to prepare—so that if you must move, it is by choice and not by desperation.*

Contrasting Philosophies: Pragmatism vs. Purity

Some thinkers promote the ideal of "planting multiple flags"—a life completely unbound by any nation-state. Others argue for deep local resilience, rooted in strong communities. The truth is less ideological. Exit strategies are contextual. What matters is optionality.

The soft exit is the domain of the pragmatist: someone who is not running from, but hedging against. The hard exit is often the domain of the idealist—someone who believed too long in a system's reformability. When reform collapses into repression, their timeline disappears.

This is not about fear. It's about foresight. *Fear paralyses; foresight plans.*

Closing Insight: Exit as Sovereign Capacity

To prepare for exit is not to abandon one's country. It is to refuse captivity to one geography, one currency, or one legal system. True sovereignty means you can leave when you need to—physically, financially, psychologically.

Those who understand the distinction between a soft exit and a hard one do not wait for crisis to dictate terms. They negotiate with reality early, quietly, and thoroughly. And when the moment comes to move, they are not just survivors. They are architects of their own continuity.

Let others debate collapse. You should plan your route through it.

Chapter 6
Off-Grid Wealth – Assets Beyond the System

The assets most people cling to—salaries, pensions, equities, property—rest on a quiet but profound wager: that tomorrow will look much like today. That banks will open their doors on Monday, that the pound will still spend, that governments won't reach for the extraordinary, and that digital systems will hum along, as they always have. These are not small assumptions. They are foundational. And, for a time—especially across the developed world—they've held.

Yet beneath the surface of this apparent stability lies a more delicate truth. As our systems have become more interconnected, our exposure has multiplied. What we call "wealth"—when accrued through traditional means like retirement funds, investment accounts, or even mobile payments—often offers more illusion than insulation. These instruments, touted as safeguards, are embedded in permission-based frameworks that can be paused, reshaped, or revoked without warning. And when they are, the lesson arrives too late: the value of what you own is inextricably tied to how freely you can access, move, or exchange it.

This chapter turns toward a different conception—one less dependent on polished platforms or institutional trust. We explore the notion of off-grid wealth. Not in the caricatured sense of hiding in a woodland cabin with tins and bullion, but in the clear-headed, strategic sense of building wealth that is sovereign, resilient, mobile, and quiet. Wealth that doesn't beg permission to function. That lives with you, not under lock and key in someone else's vault—digital or otherwise.

This isn't a conversation the mainstream financial world is prepared to have. Traditional institutions don't teach portability.

They don't know how to value skills as currency, or to reckon with the subtle strength of discretion. But if your concern is autonomy—not merely accumulation—these are the metrics that matter most.

To that end, we introduce the Asset Portability Index, a tool not of theory but of use. It measures what can travel—across borders, across networks, across moments of rupture. It forces the question: if everything you relied on froze tomorrow—networks, exchanges, even airports—what could you carry? What would be useful? What could be traded for shelter, for transit, for safety? And what, for all its balance-sheet heft, would be stuck behind a password, or worse, a decree?

We then turn to something even more foundational: embodied knowledge. Skills. The kind of capital you don't store in accounts but in your hands, your mind, your voice. What can you fix, teach, create, or interpret that holds value regardless of location, regime, or exchange rate? This, what we call "skill-currency," doesn't appear on financial statements. But in fractured systems, it often outperforms every other form of wealth. And it cannot be expropriated by fiat.

From there, we move into the digital domain—not as evangelists of crypto-anarchy, but as pragmatists. Reducing your digital footprint is no longer a fringe pursuit. It's strategic. From privacy-conscious ways of storing value, to securing communication channels, to rethinking digital dependencies—we explore how to make discretion not a paranoid retreat, but a default setting. Visibility, in fragile times, is often vulnerability.

It's worth underscoring: off-grid wealth isn't about isolation. It's about detachment from fragility. There's a distinction. This is not a doctrine of exit, but a doctrine of agency. It equips you not to run, but to act—under pressure, under duress, and without having to ask anyone for permission. Whether your home is in a stable democracy, a rapidly changing state, or somewhere in between, the central question remains: how much of your wealth can operate independently of institutional grace?

Many will never ask that question—until the moment they must. You are here because you prefer to ask it now.

The tools we'll explore are not the stuff of cinematic collapse. They are practical instruments for pragmatic people who understand that no institution—however modern, however well-designed—is immune to entropy. History is littered with systems that seemed indestructible—until, abruptly, they weren't. By the time confidence vanishes, it's too late to scramble. Options aren't drawn up in crisis. They're in place—or they're not.

This chapter won't bother with doomsday timelines or collapse predictions. What it will do is reduce your dependence. Not so you can thrive in ruins—but so that you aren't flattened by their arrival. Whether you're considering offshoring capital, building location-independent income, or reducing your reliance on surveillance-heavy infrastructure, the guidance ahead is not reactionary. It is preparatory. You're not being asked to flee. You're being shown how to remain mobile, if flight becomes necessary. Not to disconnect from the world—but to be capable of re-entering it on your own terms.

And, in that process, we return to something older, deeper. True wealth—real, enduring wealth—is not just held. It is enacted. Through competence. Through freedom of movement. Through the ability to walk away without the whole of your life caving in behind you. Those who understand this do not merely survive volatility. They absorb it. They reorient around it.

This chapter doesn't deal in prescriptions. But it will unsettle your assumptions. It will invite you to rethink what it means to be "wealthy" in a world that increasingly trades stability for speed. It will ask what remains yours when the lights flicker, when the rules shift, when the systems ask you to wait—for access, for approval, for explanation.

And most of all, it will offer this: the quiet but radical proposition that the only wealth which truly endures is that which remains in your hands—when the rest of the grid goes dark.

Gold, Crypto, and the Non-Fiat Future

The notion that money is synonymous with national currency is a modern illusion. Fiat currencies—those issued by governments without intrinsic value—are relatively recent inventions in the arc of financial history. For the vast majority of human civilisation, value was stored in tangible, decentralised mediums: precious metals, livestock, land, salt, shells. These assets did not require a central authority to validate them. They had worth because they were scarce, portable, divisible, and universally recognised. And when regimes collapsed, empires fractured, or wars ignited, these alternative stores of value often outlasted the institutions that once scorned them.

Today, as sovereign debt spirals, central banks engage in aggressive monetary manipulation, and geopolitical fault lines crack wider each year, an increasing number of serious thinkers are asking: *What comes after fiat?* This question is not philosophical. It is profoundly practical. If the currency you use is inflated into worthlessness or frozen due to capital controls, what can you fall back on? What can you carry across borders, exchange under duress, or hold without exposure to state confiscation or digital surveillance?

This chapter probes the real-world mechanics of post-fiat wealth. It does not romanticise gold, evangelise crypto, or reject the utility of cash. Instead, it interrogates each alternative store of value with clear criteria: *resilience, portability, privacy, liquidity, and sovereignty.*

Because in times of breakdown, you do not need ideological purity—you need functional assets.

Gold: The Oldest Rebel Asset

For all its mystique, gold remains a brutally pragmatic hedge. Unlike stocks, bonds, or real estate, gold is no one's liability. It is not an IOU. It cannot be printed, hacked, or inflated. It does not rely on internet access, central bank solvency, or legal recognition to retain value. And in every major currency collapse of the last century—from Weimar Germany to Zimbabwe to Argentina—gold did not just preserve wealth. It restored it.

Yet, gold is not without trade-offs. It is heavy, difficult to conceal in large quantities, and subject to customs declaration when crossing borders. Physical storage introduces logistical and security challenges. Centralised gold ETFs, while convenient, reintroduce counterparty risk—negating the very reason to own gold in the first place. Sovereign gold confiscation, as seen in the United States under Executive Order 6102 (1933), is not a relic of the past. In fragile regimes, it is a repeatable pattern.

Still, *when held in secure, private custody and outside the formal banking system*, gold functions as a last-resort currency. Its purchasing power endures across centuries not because of cultural nostalgia, but because *it cannot be willed into existence by political decree.*

Crypto: The New Sovereign Infrastructure

Cryptocurrencies introduced a paradigm shift: value that is natively digital, globally transferable, censorship-resistant, and mathematically scarce. Bitcoin, the most battle-tested of them, is not a tech experiment—it is a monetary protocol. And its relevance is not limited to idealistic libertarians or Silicon Valley engineers. In authoritarian regimes, it is a survival tool. In failing economies, it is an exit ramp.

Consider Nigeria, where peer-to-peer crypto adoption has surged amidst currency devaluation and banking restrictions. Or Ukraine and Russia, where citizens used stablecoins and Bitcoin to move capital out of collapsing systems. In countries like Turkey and Argentina, local savers treat crypto less as a speculative asset and more as a practical hedge against the volatility of their national currencies.

But crypto is not monolithic. There are important distinctions. Bitcoin prioritises security and decentralisation but remains slow and energy-intensive. Ethereum enables programmable assets but is more complex and evolving. Stablecoins like USDC or USDT peg to fiat but rely on centralised issuers and regulatory goodwill—making them vulnerable to censorship. Privacy coins like Monero or Zcash attempt to obscure transaction data, but they face liquidity and regulatory headwinds.

Perhaps the most strategic way to think about crypto is not as a bet on a specific coin, but as *a modular architecture for post-fiat finance.* It offers self-custody, pseudonymity, and portability across borders without intermediaries. But it also demands competence: lost keys mean lost funds. Smart contract vulnerabilities can lead to asset drains. And jurisdictional crackdowns—from China to the EU—are not theoretical.

Still, *in terms of sovereignty per byte, crypto remains unmatched.* No other asset allows an individual to memorise a 12-word seed phrase and walk across a border with millions in value, undetectable and unconfiscatable.

Comparative Fragility: Fiat's Eroding Trust

Central banks have not been passive observers. They've responded to rising interest in alternatives by tightening regulation, accelerating Central Bank Digital Currency (CBDC) development, and increasing surveillance of financial flows. But these responses reflect a deeper fragility. Fiat systems are predicated on trust—trust in monetary policy, in legal enforcement, in technological uptime. When that trust decays, even slowly, people shift from passive saving to *strategic exit.*

Quantitative easing and negative interest rates have distorted market signals. Sovereign bonds—once considered risk-free—now carry hidden inflationary tax. Cash in bank accounts can be frozen, surveilled, or devalued with the stroke of a pen. And in a world of weaponised finance—where sanctions can cut entire countries off from the SWIFT system—*money itself has become geopolitical.*

The shift away from fiat is not speculative. It is reactive. It is a rational recalibration of risk.

Hybrid Approaches: Owning Outside the Perimeter

What does this mean for the serious investor or sovereign-minded individual? It means adopting a layered strategy. A blend of physical gold for tangible security. Crypto assets for mobility and borderless transactions. Select stablecoins or tokenised assets for interim liquidity. And, above all, *custody models that reduce dependence on third parties.*

It also means treating knowledge and skill as forms of wealth. Your ability to navigate custody tools, understand cryptographic principles, or assess counterparty risk is more valuable than passive exposure to the asset class. You cannot outsource sovereignty.

And importantly, off-grid assets must not just be acquired—they must be *practised.* Know how to verify a Bitcoin transaction without an exchange. Know where and how to exchange gold discreetly. Know how to interpret capital controls in various jurisdictions. Theory without operational understanding leads to paralysis at the moment it matters most.

The Post-Fiat Ethos: Not Escape, But Optionality

This is not a call to abandon the system or retreat into some digital wilderness. It is a call to design for optionality. To hold assets that allow *exit without panic*. To preserve value through turbulence. And to understand that real freedom is not just political or psychological—it is financial.

Gold and crypto are not perfect. They are volatile, misunderstood, and often maligned. But they offer something fiat cannot: *an alternative*. They are not just tools of wealth—they are signals of preparedness. They say, quietly but firmly: *I am not trapped in this system.*

In times of calm, that may seem paranoid. In times of crisis, it may be priceless.

Asset Portability Index – Ranking Wealth by Discretion and Mobility

Wealth is not just what you own—it's what you can keep. That distinction becomes urgent in times of geopolitical crisis, financial repression, or border volatility. In stable environments, assets like property, equity portfolios, or business shares may signal prosperity. But in a deteriorating system—where exit is not theoretical but necessary—the most valuable assets are those you can move quickly, discreetly, and without institutional permission.

The core insight is this: liquidity is no longer enough. You must now consider portability and deniability.

This article presents a rigorous mental model for assessing asset classes through a rarely applied lens: *the Asset Portability Index* (API). Not just how liquid an asset is—but how fast, how quietly, and how sovereignly it can be moved across jurisdictions under duress. This is not about speculation. It is about *strategic survivability*.

Why Portability Now Matters More Than Ever

Asset portability has become an under-discussed form of risk management. In the 20th century, it was often the difference between total loss and enduring continuity. The Jewish families who escaped Nazi Germany with diamonds sewn into coats retained intergenerational wealth. Those who hesitated lost everything. During the Rwandan genocide, some were able to cross into Uganda or the DRC with only the gold they carried. Others, whose assets were tied to frozen accounts or land titles, had nothing left to claim. In Venezuela, Argentina, and Zimbabwe, entire classes were erased—not by war, but by inflation and capital controls.

In each case, the metric of "wealth" was redefined overnight. *What couldn't be moved ceased to be real.*

And yet in the present, many affluent individuals still anchor their wealth to the immovable. Property, pensions, business shares, national stocks—all elegant on a spreadsheet, but deeply exposed when physical relocation or systemic insulation becomes necessary.

That's where the Asset Portability Index comes in—not to demonise immobile assets, but to map their limitations and recalibrate assumptions.

The Five Core Criteria of Portability

To assess portability with precision, we need specific dimensions, not vague categories. A truly portable asset exhibits:

Physical Compactness – Can it be transported personally without detection or delay?

Jurisdictional Agnosticism – Does it retain value across borders, without reliance on a single nation-state?

Conversion Liquidity – Can it be exchanged into other assets, currencies, or essentials with minimal friction?

Privacy and Deniability – Can it be held without third-party awareness, records, or counterparty exposure?

Speed of Exit – How rapidly can the asset be moved when time is scarce or controls are imminent?

With this framework, we can now examine major asset classes through a brutally practical lens.

The Index: High to Low Portability

1. ***Cryptographic Assets (e.g. Bitcoin, Monero, Ethereum)***

Compactness: Maximum – entire portfolios can be stored on a memory stick or even memorised

Jurisdictional Agnosticism: Very high – value accessible from anywhere with internet

Liquidity: Growing – especially Bitcoin and Ethereum; Monero more niche

Privacy: Varies – Bitcoin is pseudonymous but traceable; Monero is private by design

Speed of Exit: Instant – no intermediary required if pre-structured

Verdict: Cryptographic assets top the portability scale. However, operational literacy is critical. Without private key management, ownership is theoretical. *This is sovereign wealth for the technically competent.*

2. ***Physical Gold (coins, small bars)***

Compactness: Moderate – a few ounces carry thousands in value

Jurisdictional Agnosticism: High – accepted universally across cultures

Liquidity: Very high – near-global buyback and exchange markets

Privacy: High – if purchased and held outside institutional systems

Speed of Exit: Moderate – physical transport requires planning

Verdict: Gold remains the pre-digital standard for portable wealth. It's discreet, recognisable, and resilient—but not borderless. Airports and customs are choke points. *Think of gold as a tangible escape valve, not a fluid currency.*

3. ***Precious Stones (diamonds, high-grade gems)***

Compactness: Extremely high – value-to-weight ratio surpasses gold

Jurisdictional Agnosticism: High – though valuation is subjective

Liquidity: Moderate – resale depends on trust and certification

Privacy: Very high – difficult to trace or tax if unregistered

Speed of Exit: High – if pre-prepared and authenticated

Verdict: Underused but potent. Gems can discreetly transfer immense value, but require prior setup with trustworthy dealers. *Useful as an elite portability hedge, not a mainstream store of value.*

4. ***Cash (foreign hard currency, typically USD, CHF, SGD)***

Compactness: High – but degrades with inflation or detection risk

Jurisdictional Agnosticism: Limited – depends on country acceptance

Liquidity: Immediate – universally exchangeable

Privacy: High – unless crossing borders with declarations required

Speed of Exit: High – until threshold laws trigger confiscation

Verdict: Physical cash is still king in short-term collapses. However, it is fragile over time. Inflation, moisture, dogs, and customs all threaten it. *Cash is a short-term escape tool, not a long-term vault.*

5. ***Equity or Bond Portfolios (domestic brokerages)***

Compactness: Digital – but tightly tied to institutions and laws

Jurisdictional Agnosticism: Low – depends on national systems

Liquidity: Moderate – high in normalcy, low during freezes or crashes

Privacy: None – fully tracked, reported, and exposed

Speed of Exit: Delayed – especially under capital controls or panic

Verdict: Despite their size, these portfolios are portable in theory but brittle in practice. They *vanish when trust vanishes. These are immobile assets masquerading as digital.*

6. ***Real Estate***

Compactness: Zero – land cannot move

Jurisdictional Agnosticism: None – depends entirely on location laws

Liquidity: Low – especially during turmoil

Privacy: Minimal – highly documented

Speed of Exit: Very low – illiquid, visible, taxable

Verdict: Real estate is a power asset during prosperity, but a deadweight during collapse. *It is not portable. It is rooted.*

Operational Portability: Planning vs. Panic

Portability is not just about what you own—it's about what you can access *under pressure.* A hard drive with a crypto wallet you can't recover is worthless. Gold buried in a location you cannot return to is not wealth—it's a liability. A diamond ring only has value if you know where and how to sell it.

Therefore, the *practical layer* of asset portability is operational:

Have local and international exit pathways

Build discreet relationships with reputable dealers (gold, gems)

Practice your crypto retrieval protocols offline

Store redundant access tools in geographically diverse places

Know the capital declaration thresholds for every border you may cross

Assets should not just be chosen—they must be rehearsed.

Psychological Portability: Reframing "Security"

Owning what you cannot move breeds dependency. This is why the wealthy in unstable countries often appear paradoxical: they have status, but not sovereignty. Their assets are impressive until they're inaccessible. In contrast, the globally mobile entrepreneur or digital nomad with a cold wallet, a second passport, and a flexible income stream often has less net worth but *more optionality.*

True wealth is not how much you can count—it's how much you can carry when it counts.

Conclusion: Toward a Post-Paper Wealth Strategy

The Asset Portability Index is not a call to abandon long-term investments. It's a lens—one that helps separate *prestige assets* from *resilient assets.* In times of peace, that distinction is invisible. In times of rupture, it becomes everything.

As states clamp down on financial autonomy, as monetary systems flirt with fragility, and as border fluidity becomes less reliable, the ability to carry wealth discreetly becomes a first-order survival skill.

Don't just diversify across sectors. Diversify across sovereignty. Own what you can move. And know how to move it.

Barterability and Skill-Currency – Why Knowledge, Not Cash, Becomes Capital in Collapse

We are conditioned to think of wealth as static and numeric—measured in account balances, property valuations, or investment yields. Yet in periods of rapid destabilisation—whether through financial collapse, natural disaster, or geopolitical chaos—these markers often lose their utility just when they are most needed. What retains value in such moments is not what one *has*, but what one can *offer*. And often, the most enduring offer is *skill*.

Barterability—the ability of something to be traded directly for value—and *skill-currency*—the conversion of knowledge or capability into essential goods or services—redefine wealth in disrupted environments. This is not a theoretical construct. It is a pattern observed across history, geographies, and crises.

From Ledger to Labour: Why Assets Stop Trading But Skills Don't

When economies function, money serves as an efficient proxy for value. But when the system around it falters—through hyperinflation, currency controls, broken trust, or institutional breakdown—money can become inert. At that point, barter returns, not as nostalgia but necessity. And unlike goods, which are finite and deplete with trade, *skills scale.* They can be offered repeatedly, upgraded constantly, and transported invisibly.

During the Argentine economic crisis of 2001, bartering clubs sprang up across cities, with professionals exchanging services like dental care, car repair, legal advice, and childcare for food, medicine, and clothing. In the Yugoslav Wars of the 1990s, doctors and electricians often retained higher practical status than factory owners or engineers—because they could *do*, not just *supervise.* In the Syrian conflict, displaced women with culinary or sewing skills built parallel, informal economies in camps and informal settlements.

The pattern is clear: *system failure doesn't erase the economy—it reshapes it.* And in that reshaping, what rises is practical value: can you fix, teach, heal, build, grow, or translate something that someone else urgently needs?

What Makes a Skill "Currency"?

Not all skills are equal under stress. A "high-status" profession in a functional economy may offer little resilience in a breakdown scenario. Conversely, modest or overlooked competencies often become essential.

A skill becomes *currency* when it satisfies three criteria:

Immediacy of Utility – It solves a problem *now* (e.g., repairing a generator, baking bread, treating an injury).

Low Substitution Risk – It is difficult or costly to replace (e.g., plumbing, emergency dental care, language mediation).

Cross-Context Demand – It remains useful across cultural, geographic, or technological contexts (e.g., teaching children, conflict negotiation, mechanical diagnosis).

This explains why, historically, professions like midwives, blacksmiths, tailors, and butchers—once viewed as "blue-collar"—held societal primacy in early and post-collapse economies. They were not reliant on institutional credentialing, expensive tools, or formal platforms. *Their value was native and transportable.*

The Modern Skill-Currency Map

In a modern, digitally-augmented but fragile world, what might constitute high-barterability skill-sets? Let's map a few illustrative categories:

Technical Infrastructure Repair: generator mechanics, solar installation, basic electronics, plumbing, and water purification.

Health and Caregiving: first aid trainers, herbal medicine practitioners, birth assistants, elderly care.

Food and Water Security: permaculture, seed-saving, fermentation, foraging, sustainable fishing or hunting.

Communications: radio operation, off-grid networking, encryption literacy, multilingual interpretation.

Education and Training: homeschooling, basic literacy instruction, trade apprenticeships, moral leadership.

These are not low-tech or high-tech—they are *resilient-tech*. And importantly, many of them *scale downward*: they remain functional even without electricity, software, or grid support.

Contrast this with more brittle specialisations: digital marketing, high-frequency trading, compliance law, or even academic research. In a functioning system, these may be elite roles. But their barter value in collapse scenarios is negligible—because they depend on layers of abstract trust, not immediate exchange.

Building Your Personal Skill-Currency Portfolio

There's a subtle but critical shift in framing required here. This is not about acquiring new hobbies. It's about consciously *investing* in skills the same way one might allocate capital: for diversity, yield, and future-proofing.

Ask yourself:

What can I offer that others need during acute disruption?

Does this skill require infrastructure that could be compromised?

Can I teach this skill to others, thereby multiplying its value?

Could I trade this skill without relying on platforms, apps, or bureaucracy?

Learning how to weld, suture, repair a bike, or teach basic arithmetic to children without internet access may not seem economically urgent in peacetime. But it becomes *optionality insurance*—an investment in adaptability that outpaces inflation or recession.

Barter-ready skills are a hedge against systemic fragility. They are also deeply empowering: the more you can do for yourself and others, the less vulnerable you become to coercion, dependency, or abandonment.

Historical and Cultural Precedents

Ancient and traditional societies understood this implicitly. In pre-modern Japan, the concept of *shokunin*—mastery of a practical trade—was considered honourable and vital. In West African market cultures, knowledge of textiles, fermentation, or herbal medicine was passed down through generations, not just for status but for survival. In medieval Europe, guild membership offered both protection and barter leverage, functioning as both trade certification and social currency.

Modernity has severed us from this ethos. Professionalisation, credentialism, and digital abstraction have replaced direct competence. Yet the pendulum swings back when systems fail. The collapse of the Soviet Union in the 1990s saw former physicists driving taxis and chefs repairing electronics—not due to personal failure, but because the value matrix changed overnight.

The Role of Social Trust in Skill-Based Economies

Barter is not merely transactional. It is deeply relational. The effectiveness of skill-currency depends on trust, reciprocity, and community embeddedness. You are not just trading "what" you can do—you are trading on *who* people believe you to be.

In times of breakdown, reputation becomes infrastructure. Word-of-mouth, observed competence, and demonstrated fairness will outpace CVs and LinkedIn profiles. Therefore, *investing in community presence is as vital as acquiring skill itself.* A competent stranger may be valuable—but a competent neighbour is priceless.

This opens a new dimension in preparedness: practicing your skills publicly, helping others visibly, and building informal economies before formal ones disappear. When collapse occurs, trust is already scarce. Having earned it *in advance* is a form of pre-banked social capital.

How to Begin: Practical Onramps for Skill Resilience

For those raised in digital, outsourced cultures, this can feel daunting. But the path forward is grounded, not abstract:

Start local: Volunteer with a repair café, medical first responder group, or food co-op. Skills gained will be contextually relevant.

Upskill deliberately: Choose one essential domain (food, power, water, health) and build from basic literacy to functional competence.

Teach others: Hosting small workshops, sharing knowledge, or trading lessons strengthens both your skill and its social proof.

Use downtime wisely: Instead of entertainment, rotate in hands-on learning—knots, knife sharpening, carpentry, or emergency planning.

These are not "prepper" hobbies. They are the foundation of a future-proof identity.

Final Insight: Wealth Without Storage

Perhaps the most powerful feature of skill-currency is this: *it cannot be confiscated.* A state can freeze your bank account, devalue your currency, seize your home, or criminalise your gold. But they cannot undo your ability to deliver a baby, repair a solar panel, purify a water source, or coordinate a supply chain.

Skill-based wealth is invisible, mobile, and infinitely renewable. It is not speculative—it is experiential. It does not depend on permission—it depends on practice. And in times of rupture, it does not merely help you *survive.* It helps you *matter.*

Digital Disappearance – Reducing Your Digital Footprint and Securing Assets in the Age of Surveillance

Most individuals today carry the equivalent of a detailed surveillance dossier in their pocket—voluntarily. Every tap, every search, every GPS ping, credit card swipe, or cloud sync creates a data trail. In an era where data is currency, *privacy is the new scarcity.* And for those preparing for instability—whether financial, geopolitical, or institutional—one imperative rises above convenience: *the ability to disappear without being erased.*

This subchapter is not about vanishing into mythic off-grid fantasies. It is about cultivating *operational invisibility*—the deliberate reduction of exposure to digital scrutiny while retaining real-world mobility, security, and optionality. It is about transforming from a data subject into a data strategist. And it starts with understanding *what is being seen*, *by whom*, and *for what purpose.*

Why Digital Visibility Becomes a Liability in Times of Instability

The danger isn't merely theoretical. During the 2021 Myanmar military coup, social media posts were used to track down dissenters. In Russia, cryptocurrency exchanges are now compelled to report suspicious activity, including foreign conversions, as the state tightens financial surveillance. In China, the Social Credit System actively punishes undesirable behaviour with restrictions on travel, credit, or access to services—based purely on digital records.

Even in ostensibly free democracies, the pandemic era saw an acceleration in centralised data gathering: health apps, QR code tracking, central bank interest in programmable currencies. When systems strain, authorities often default to control—and *digital breadcrumbs are the blueprint of control.*

For wealth preservation and personal autonomy in volatile climates, reducing digital exposure is not a lifestyle choice. It is a resilience imperative.

The Illusion of Privacy and the Architecture of Data Extraction

Digital footprints are not confined to what you *publish.* They include what is *collected*, often without explicit consent. Metadata—who you call, where you go, how long you linger on a page—is often more revealing than content itself. And it is far harder to erase.

Consider the architecture: smartphones track location persistently unless explicitly disabled. Messaging apps, even those encrypted end-to-end, often store metadata. Search engines profile behaviour for advertisers—profiles which can be subpoenaed or sold. Even when not shared publicly, every action feeds into inference algorithms that know not just what you *did*, but what you *might do next.*

The consequence? *Predictive vulnerability.* You do not need to be monitored constantly—your patterns are enough to pre-emptively flag you as a risk.

Financial Systems as Surveillance Infrastructure

The shift to digital finance has brought immense convenience—but also near-total visibility. Credit card providers, banks, and online payment platforms are fully integrated into legal, tax, and compliance systems. Most central banks now monitor large-scale transactions in real-time under AML (anti-money laundering) and CTF (counter-terrorist financing) frameworks.

This has a crucial implication: *your wealth is no longer solely your own.* It is contingent on permissioned access—revocable by policy shifts, sanctions, or institutional failure.

Consider the Canadian trucker protests in 2022. Peaceful demonstrators and donors had their bank accounts frozen—without trial, through emergency powers. In Lebanon, ordinary citizens were locked out of savings as the banking system imploded. What these cases demonstrate is simple: *digital assets are only as secure as the regime in which they are held.*

Thus, digital disappearance is not synonymous with criminality—it is synonymous with sovereignty.

Principles of Digital Disappearance

Effective digital obscurity is not achieved by cutting cords and living in the woods. It is achieved by *deliberate compartmentalisation*, *data minimisation*, and *informed substitution.* Think of it less as retreat and more as *strategic opacity*—obscuring just enough signal to avoid becoming a target, without sacrificing function.

Here are three foundational principles:

Minimise Visibility – The less data emitted, the less there is to track. This includes using privacy-respecting browsers, disabling unnecessary app permissions, and limiting cloud-based storage.

Control Points of Identification – Avoid linking identities across platforms. Use pseudonyms where legal, compartmentalise email and communication channels, and never use one identifier (e.g., phone number) across multiple services.

Localise and Decentralise Assets – Where possible, hold wealth in forms that are not visible, indexable, or seizable by a third party (e.g., self-custodied crypto, bullion, tangible barter assets).

These principles are less about technical perfection and more about behavioural adaptation.

Tactics: Practical Steps for Strategic Obscurity

While many guides offer exhaustive checklists, this chapter prioritises conceptual clarity. Below are a few practical shifts that compound meaningfully over time:

Switch to open-source privacy browsers such as Brave or Firefox hardened with extensions like uBlock Origin and NoScript. Avoid Chrome entirely; it is structurally designed for behavioural tracking.

Use encrypted communication via apps like Signal (ideally registered with a secondary number) or Matrix-based platforms. Avoid mainstream apps with dubious privacy records like WhatsApp or Messenger.

Stop using Gmail for sensitive material. Transition to ProtonMail or Tutanota for secure, jurisdictionally distinct communication.

Use a Virtual Private Network (VPN) that doesn't log data, and combine it with the Tor network when needed. Be aware: not all VPNs are equal—many cooperate with authorities.

Sanitise metadata from shared files and images using tools like ExifTool. Most images contain hidden location and device data.

Separate devices for separate functions. Consider an "air-gapped" device (never connected to the internet) for storing seed phrases or encrypted backups.

These are not hacks. They are habits—developed deliberately, with clear rationale.

Digital Asset Security: Holding Value Invisibly

Privacy is not limited to behaviour. It extends to *where and how value is stored.* In uncertain times, this may be the difference between retaining wealth and losing access entirely.

Three categories emerge:

Self-Custodied Cryptocurrency
Assets like Bitcoin and Monero (with caveats) allow for peer-to-peer storage and transfer without intermediaries. However, security is not automatic. Poor opsec (operational security) leads to asset loss or theft more often than technical failure. Cold storage (offline wallets), multisig protection, and geographic key separation are essential.

Tangible Anonymous Assets
Gold, silver, and high-value trade goods are effective—but must be stored securely and moved discreetly. Storage outside the banking system—domestic or foreign—is vital.

Encrypted Digital Vaults
Sensitive documents, records, or identity credentials should be backed up with end-to-end encryption (e.g., VeraCrypt) and stored on physically secure media. Cloud storage—no matter how private—is always a potential leak point.

The goal is not to hide wealth entirely—it is to decentralise control and minimise third-party risk.

The Psychology of Digital Dependence

Perhaps the greatest obstacle to digital disappearance is not technical—it's psychological. People have become addicted to frictionless convenience. Instant communication, biometric unlocks, cloud-sync-everything habits—they feel efficient. But they represent a profound *externalisation of control.*

Digital autonomy requires tolerating some inefficiency: longer logins, more steps, physical backups. But the trade-off is *control over your own surface area.* Every reduction in dependency increases resilience. Every act of refusal—of convenience for sovereignty—deepens your leverage.

Digital Disappearance Is Not Withdrawal—It's Adaptation

One of the most dangerous myths is that privacy is obsolete, or that it only matters if one is doing something "wrong." That is not how history—or law—works. Rights unused become rights unrecoverable. And in times of upheaval, visibility becomes liability. Visibility invites intervention, restriction, and sometimes punishment.

Digital disappearance is the proactive discipline of retaining control in an age that rewards passivity with exposure. It is not paranoia. It is preparation.

In the context of this book, where the central concern is enduring sovereignty in fragile systems, digital disappearance is not a fringe concern. It is *one of the final frontiers of personal and financial independence.*

Chapter 7
Geopolitical Arbitrage – Living Where Others Flee

Section 1: The Geography of Privilege and Peril

Once, geography was immutable. The land you were born into, the papers you carried, the language of your school anthem—all of it etched a rough outline of your future. Rights and risks were largely dictated by place. Where you lived defined what you could hope for and what you had to fear. Today, however, that certainty is slipping. Geography is no longer a sentence—it's becoming a choice. Borders blur under the weight of capital, ideas travel faster than aircraft, and states increasingly behave like service providers rather than sovereign guardians. In this shifting terrain, a new kind of competence is emerging: not how to endure collapse from within, but how to foresee it—and relocate before the ground breaks.

This chapter doesn't concern itself with cinematic escapes. You won't find tales of smuggled gold or midnight border crossings here. What it offers instead is a quieter, more deliberate approach: positioning. Strategic, considered repositioning of your identity, your financial exposure, your physical presence. It's a fresh appraisal of what "home" really means in an age where stability is more myth than guarantee.

A country, after all, is not simply a song or a symbol. It's a jurisdiction—an engine of law, of control, of enforcement. And jurisdictions, as history demonstrates, can dissolve or turn hostile with alarming speed and little notice. The peril lies in thinking the collapse will announce itself like a storm warning. It rarely does. Trust erodes in whispers. Currencies falter in weeks. When the danger becomes visible, the exits are often bottlenecked or barred entirely.

This is where the notion of geopolitical arbitrage enters—not as a scheme, but a lens. It's the ability to evaluate nations as portfolios of risk and reward, and to act accordingly. It may sound clinical, perhaps even unfeeling. But sovereignty does not thrive on sentimentality. It requires lucidity.

Over the coming pages, we'll examine three core frameworks:

- *Citizenship as a Weapon or Shield*: how affiliations and documentation can empower—or expose—you.
- *Borderless Income Streams*: what it means to earn in a way that isn't shackled to a single nation's fortunes or rules.
- *The Myth of the Safe Haven*: the dangers of placing too much trust in geography, and how to think beyond it.

This is not a manifesto for the wealthy. While some of these tools require resources, the principles underpinning them—adaptability, foresight, autonomy—belong to everyone. They are not reserved for those with multiple passports but for those willing to question inherited assumptions.

The truly strategic mind doesn't just ask, "Where could I go?" It probes deeper: "What am I exposed to?" "What am I trusting by default?" "If the state turned against me tomorrow, how fast could I sever that cord?"

You won't be handed a checklist here. But you'll be asked to think like someone whose future is no longer anchored to place, but to preparedness.

Section 2: When Citizenship Becomes a Liability

For much of the post-war West, citizenship was a birthright imbued with protection. It was an unspoken pact: the state would shield you abroad, support you at home, and at least pretend to care in between. But that compact is fraying. Increasingly, the passport in your pocket functions less like a shield and more like a barcode—useful for sorting, tracking, and, when necessary, excluding.

Take Venezuela. As the economy imploded, the government, desperate to stem capital flight and dissent, halted the issuance of new passports. Suddenly, tens of thousands of citizens were trapped—held in place not by fences, but by expired documents. Their right to flee had become a political inconvenience. Or consider Belarus and Myanmar, where dissidents have had their citizenship revoked, their accounts frozen, their exit paths erased. In such moments, a passport isn't protection. It's a tether.

And this creeping erosion isn't limited to failed or overtly authoritarian regimes. In democratic nations—Australia, the United States, the UK—citizenship is increasingly conditional. Fall afoul of tax law, express inconvenient loyalties, or find yourself misaligned with national security narratives, and you may discover just how contingent your "rights" really are. When compliance becomes the litmus test for identity, citizenship becomes a mechanism of control.

Which brings us to a sobering point: to rely wholly on a single jurisdiction is, in the current climate, to gamble your autonomy on one roll of the geopolitical dice. This is not paranoia. It is the basic principle of diversification applied to the realm of rights.

To question your citizenship strategy is not to betray your country. It is to acknowledge that faith in governance is not the same as blind loyalty. Seeking second residencies, backup passports, or alternative legal footholds isn't abandonment—it's adult risk management.

What you must ask, then, is not simply where you are from—but what your papers truly grant you. Do they open doors, or merely track your location? Do they entitle you to protection—or subject you to scrutiny? And if tomorrow brought a shift in policy, a change in leadership, a new definition of loyalty—could you still move?

The work of geopolitical arbitrage begins here: in questioning the most familiar assumptions, and doing so before they cost you options.

Section 3: Borderless Income Streams – The Foundation Beneath Mobility

A passport may clear you through customs, but it won't feed you when your job evaporates. It won't pay rent when your bank restricts withdrawals. And it certainly won't sustain purpose when your domestic market implodes. True mobility begins not with where you can go—but whether your income can come with you.

This is where many otherwise savvy actors stumble. They plot second homes, they memorise visa policies, they imagine escapes to Portugal or Panama—but their earnings remain pinned to one economy, one tax regime, one failing system. The very income that funds their escape plan is often the first casualty in a crisis.

Mobility demands more than location freedom—it demands financial unshackling.

This doesn't mean simply becoming "remote" in the Instagrammable sense. It means building income that can travel. That lives not on servers controlled by any one state, but in structures that cross borders without tripping wires. Consultancy, digital products, intellectual property, decentralised payments—whatever the vehicle, the critical variable is resilience. Can it persist across legal domains? Can it endure exchange controls? Can it sidestep sanctions without sliding into illegality?

Ask yourself: if your country froze accounts tomorrow, how would you get paid? If it tightened tax laws, could you legally pivot? If unrest shut down infrastructure, would your business hold?

The answer defines more than your wealth. It defines your agility.

The Greek debt crisis, for instance, taught this lesson harshly. Withdrawal limits, supplier failures, evaporated liquidity. But those who earned externally, who banked flexibly, who had income beyond borders—they kept operating. Not because they had more, but because they were configured differently.

In that difference lies sovereignty.

This isn't about indulgence. It's about insulation. It's the difference between watching a country burn from within—and walking through the smoke, intact.

Section 4: The Myth of the Safe Haven – Why Geography Alone Won't Save You

We are trained to believe in sanctuaries. That somewhere, perhaps in the Alps or on a quiet coast, is a nation immune to upheaval. A place where banks won't seize, governments won't overreach, and life proceeds untouched by crisis. But in this century, such havens are ghosts. No longer places, but stories we tell ourselves while the system corrodes.

Safe havens, in the modern context, are misnomers. Stability is not a feature of the land. It is a function of layers—of diversified exposure, of legal fragmentation, of financial spread. You may live in Switzerland, yes. But what happens when global pressures override national neutrality? When sanctions dictate policy? When banks comply with someone else's agenda?

Geography, today, is porous. And power flows digitally.

The true safe haven is not a plot of land but a configuration: income from one jurisdiction, legal residency in another, citizenship in a third, assets decentralised or offshore. It is not a bunker—it is a posture. One that no single authority can entirely map, claim, or control.

There is a moment—a concept—we call jurisdictional escape velocity. The point at which no one state holds enough of you to dictate terms. Few ever reach it fully. But moving toward it—inch by deliberate inch—is transformative.

Stop looking for Eden. Start building your firewall.

Section 5: The Rise of the Stateless Strategy – Living Without Anchors, Operating Without Borders

From these fragments, a broader vision begins to emerge—not a tactic, but a mode of being: the stateless strategy. Not in the traditional sense of dispossession or exile. But in the cultivated sense of strategic detachment. Of declining to be bound by institutions that promise much and deliver selectively.

To live this way is not to renounce. It is to rearrange.

Citizenship becomes a tool, not a tether. Income, a flow rather than a contract. Location, a decision—not an inheritance. You don't deny the existence of nations. You simply choose not to make any one of them your single point of failure.

This strategy is not romantic. It is rigorous. It demands literacy—in law, in finance, in logistics. It demands effort, and occasionally discomfort. But what it returns is priceless: manoeuvrability in a world where the immobile are the first to fall.

You will find no escapism here. No utopias. But you will find something more useful: frameworks for thought. Stories that reveal patterns. Questions that erode illusion. Exercises that confront fragility not with despair, but design.

Because safety, in this age, is not inherited. It is architected. And the cornerstone of that architecture is the ability to walk away, calmly, when others cannot move at all.

Flags of Freedom – Modernising the Five Flags Theory for the Digital Surveillance Era

Section 1: From Tax Havens to Surveillance Sanctuaries – The Origins and Obsolescence of the Classic Model

It began as a playbook for the ultra-wealthy, the stateless, and the quietly strategic. The original Five Flags Theory—formulated in the 1980s by internationalisation pioneers like Harry Schultz and W.G. Hill—offered an elegant blueprint: scatter your life across multiple jurisdictions, and you could sidestep taxes, borders, and bureaucratic interference with surgical precision. Live in one country, hold your passport in another, bank offshore, run your business somewhere else, and invest anywhere. It was a geopolitical arbitrage model for libertarians with Swiss bank accounts and time to study trust law.

But the world has changed—radically, irreversibly, and faster than most internationalisation theorists anticipated. Today's landscape is not defined merely by borders or flags, but by *signals*. The system no longer needs to control your body if it can track your behaviour. Biometric data, facial recognition, IP logging, cross-jurisdictional data-sharing agreements, and financial surveillance have turned what was once a decentralised strategy into a fragile illusion. Even the most geographically dispersed person can be digitally tethered to a single nation-state's reach—without ever setting foot in its borders.

The Five Flags Theory, in its original formulation, is no longer sufficient. Its assumptions were rooted in a pre-digital world—a world where borders were physical, paper trails could be burned, and asset protection was a matter of postal secrecy, not metadata encryption. The reality of 2025 demands an evolved model—one that accounts not just for geography but for *visibility*. The question is no longer simply *where* you live, bank, or work—but *how observable you are* while doing it.

In this chapter, we will modernise and re-engineer the Five Flags framework for a post-SWIFT, post-KYC, blockchain-aware, hyperconnected environment. We will examine how a flag's utility today is not only legal and financial, but increasingly algorithmic and reputational. You are being scored, ranked, profiled, and predicted—whether or not you hold dual citizenship or file taxes in Monaco. True sovereignty now hinges on something more elusive: your ability to *disappear in plain sight.*

This shift isn't theoretical. Consider the case of a dual national investor with accounts in Singapore, a second passport from St Kitts, and property in Dubai—textbook old-school flag theory. If that individual is also using Gmail, posting on LinkedIn, and holding all their capital in centralised exchanges, they are fully legible to at least five governments and two dozen data brokers. A politically neutral residence means little if one's behavioural data is triangulated in real time by AI models designed to detect tax evasion or dissident tendencies.

So what replaces the old flags? That's the heart of our inquiry. We will not discard the geographical framework entirely—location independence still matters—but we will layer it with a new dimension: *signal sovereignty*. In a digital-first surveillance state, your ability to relocate your physical body must be matched by your ability to obfuscate, redirect, or control your *informational footprint.*

To accomplish this, we'll redefine each traditional flag in light of modern constraints and emerging technologies. We'll explore:

Why a *data-neutral citizenship* may be more important than a tax-neutral one.

How asset mobility now includes encryption, not just international wire transfer logistics.

Why residency without legal or algorithmic exposure—not simply "where you live"—is the new Gold Standard.

How operating businesses anonymously through distributed systems, pseudonymous identifiers, and DAO governance can outperform legacy offshore incorporations.

And why the *new fifth flag* isn't necessarily "where you play," but *how little you can be seen doing it.*

The practical implications of this modernisation are profound. They extend beyond nomadic entrepreneurs and digital expats to include investigative journalists, political dissidents, whistle-blowers, and increasingly—ordinary citizens seeking to regain control of their autonomy in a world where freedom has become performative.

This modernised Flags of Freedom framework is not about fleeing accountability—it's about reclaiming *choice.* It's about designing your presence in the world—economic, legal, social, digital—*intentionally.* And it's about creating multiple exit points, not just from places, but from platforms, protocols, and systems that presume ownership over your life simply because you logged in once and never logged out.

In the sections that follow, we will walk through each of the revised flags—not as static categories but as dynamic strategies. You'll learn how to assess not only your tax exposure or residency options, but your signal exposure, metadata exhaust, and algorithmic legibility. We'll discuss the tools, the jurisdictions, the risks, and the blind spots. We will examine real-world case studies—of people who executed their exits well, and those who misjudged timing, visibility, or digital dependency and paid dearly for it.

Because in the end, freedom is not about leaving. It's about *not being followed.*

Section 2: Redefining the Five Flags – A Modern Framework for Digital and Jurisdictional Autonomy

The traditional Five Flags Theory was built around five core pillars: citizenship, residency, business base, asset haven, and playgrounds. Each represented a flag to be planted in a distinct jurisdiction to maximise personal freedom and minimise state control. In theory, this compartmentalisation reduced your exposure to any one nation's overreach. But that model assumed a world where jurisdictions operated independently, databases weren't connected, and sovereignty could be leveraged without surveillance.

That world is gone.

Today, these five flags must be reinterpreted—not discarded, but recoded. Each must now address a dual mandate: *jurisdictional safety* and *signal resilience.* What follows is not merely a reclassification but a reframing of how the individual interacts with power in a networked, monitored world.

1. Flag of Citizenship: From Tax Loophole to Data Liability

The first flag—citizenship—was originally about tax arbitrage. If your primary passport was from a nation that didn't tax global income, or had weak enforcement, you could live elsewhere, earn freely, and legally pay nothing. But in the age of automatic information exchange agreements (like the Common Reporting

Standard) and extra-territorial tax laws (e.g., FATCA), *citizenship is now a data liability.*

Your passport determines which governments can demand your financial records, freeze your accounts, or obligate foreign institutions to report your holdings. A powerful passport today is not only one that facilitates global mobility—it's one that minimises digital visibility.

Modern heuristic: Choose a citizenship that limits automatic data-sharing, avoids extraterritorial tax drag, and does not politicise its citizens' global behaviour.

St Kitts and Vanuatu may offer low-tax citizenships, but their passports are flagged for enhanced scrutiny by financial institutions. In contrast, countries like Portugal or Uruguay—while not tax havens—strike a better balance between global acceptance and signal neutrality.

2. Flag of Residency: Rethinking Presence in a World of Traces

Where you legally reside has implications beyond tax brackets. It influences surveillance exposure, financial scrutiny, and your day-to-day operating latitude. Traditional flag theory treated residency as a matter of cost or lifestyle. Today, *residency is a vector of digital capture.*

Residency often requires registering biometric data, participating in local banking systems, and enrolling in healthcare or ID programs—all of which become hooks into broader data ecosystems. Your presence becomes an anchor for metadata, AI-based profiling, and even predictive surveillance.

Modern heuristic: Select residencies that offer legal protection, minimal digital friction, and geopolitical stability—without forcing full spectrum integration into state systems.

Examples include Georgia, Panama, or certain autonomous regions with light-touch bureaucracy and non-citizen long-term visa programs. A low-footprint residence trumps a tax-free paradise if the former leaves fewer digital fingerprints.

3. Flag of Business Base: From Incorporation to Obfuscation

The third flag traditionally focused on *where* your business was incorporated, with the aim of reducing tax exposure and regulatory burdens. Today, the jurisdiction of incorporation remains important, but it's *how that business transacts digitally* that determines its exposure.

A Wyoming LLC may offer privacy on paper, but if it runs on Stripe, Google Workspace, and AWS, it's only nominally private. Modern business sovereignty is achieved not through paperwork, but through architectural design: pseudonymous operations, decentralised infrastructure, and jurisdictional dispersion of team members and assets.

Modern heuristic: Architect your business infrastructure for systemic resilience, not just legal minimisation. Host critical infrastructure outside Five Eyes nations. Pay attention to DNS, hosting jurisdiction, cloud stack, and financial intermediaries.

DAO-based structures, multi-signature wallets, and code-hosting on censorship-resistant platforms like IPFS or Arweave are emerging alternatives to old-world offshore shells. *System agnosticism* now matters as much as tax deferral.

4. Flag of Asset Haven: Mobility over Volume, Fungibility over Size

Traditionally, this flag meant banking and investing in jurisdictions with secrecy laws or low/no tax on capital gains. Switzerland, the Caymans, and Liechtenstein once topped the list. But in a world of digital surveillance, asset protection means *signal insulation*, not merely offshore vaults.

Assets are now traceable not only by transaction records but through behavioural signals—travel patterns, messaging content, and third-party analytics. Owning gold in Singapore means little if your insurance policy, courier records, and exit strategy are all indexed and visible.

Modern heuristic: Prioritise asset classes with high mobility, low traceability, and strong global barter potential. Think beyond volume. Think velocity.

Portable assets include cold-stored crypto (secured via air-gapped hardware), tokenised physical metals, and bearer instruments. But even these must be held with operational discretion. *Visibility, not legality, is the new risk surface.*

5. Flag of Playgrounds: Where You Spend, Without Being Tracked

This final flag—"where you play"—was once about lifestyle optimisation: choosing countries where you could spend money, enjoy freedom, and avoid regulation. Now, *playgrounds are the most surveilled environments of all.* Hotels, airports, nightlife, health spas—all are honeypots for identity exposure and data mining.

In the digital era, playgrounds must be chosen for *low metadata yield*, not just beaches and banking. Privacy-friendly jurisdictions with poor facial recognition networks, minimal telecom monitoring, and low digital infrastructure density may ironically offer *more* freedom than luxury urban centres.

Modern heuristic: Avoid countries where play is synonymous with exposure. Use disposable devices, local SIMs, and physical cash where possible. Your leisure should not compromise your sovereignty.

Section 3: From Blueprint to Action – Designing a Multi-Flag Life with Minimal Exposure

The theoretical elegance of the Five Flags model lies in its compartmentalisation—no single government has total control over your identity, assets, movements, or livelihood. But in a world where legal firewalls are penetrated by data-sharing treaties, digital surveillance, and behavioural profiling, *compartmentalisation must evolve into decentralisation.* That is, not just separating your flags geographically, but also diffusing their digital dependencies, temporal overlaps, and signal vectors.

This section explores how to *operationalise sovereignty*, offering practical strategies for individuals seeking to apply this philosophy to real life—without becoming nomadic fantasists or political dissidents. The goal is *durable autonomy*, not ideological purity.

1. Begin with a Risk Map, Not a Travel Wishlist

Most people start by asking, "Where should I move?" or "Which passport should I get?" These are premature questions. A smarter starting point is to assess your *exposure footprint*—a map of where your data, income, obligations, and dependencies currently reside.

Ask:
– Where are your assets visible to institutions?
– Where are your business records stored and subject to disclosure?
– Which countries can compel you to appear, pay, or disclose?
– Where are you biometrically registered or digitally integrated?

This is not about paranoia—it's about architectural awareness. By mapping exposure before action, you convert abstract fears into tractable design decisions.

2. Phase Your Flag Strategy by Constraint, Not Fantasy

It is tempting to fantasise about holding multiple passports, owning offshore properties, or conducting business entirely in crypto. But real-world sovereignty is built incrementally. Begin with the flag that addresses your *greatest constraint*—usually tax, asset protection, or censorship.

For example:
– If you're a US citizen running an online business, your pain point is likely *taxation and data drag.* A second citizenship and foreign incorporation may help.
– If you're a Chinese entrepreneur concerned about capital controls, *offshore asset movement* and *alternative residencies* become priority.
– If you're a journalist in a politically unstable nation, your greatest flag may be *secure communications and digital disappearance.*

This phased, problem-led approach prevents overwhelm and grounds your strategy in relevance rather than escapism.

3. Combine Legal Tools with Digital Discipline

Even with a perfect array of flags—second passport, offshore company, alternative residence—your operational sovereignty can collapse from a single point of failure: *digital leakage.* Your IP address, cloud documents, GPS metadata, messaging platforms, and even cloud keyboard logs can recreate your entire life for a surveillance actor.

Thus, digital hygiene must become part of your flag framework:
– Use open-source, encrypted tools (e.g. Signal, ProtonMail,

Matrix) for critical communication
– Split personas across secure devices: one for legal ID, one for operational autonomy
– Host infrastructure in censorship-resistant, jurisdictionally diverse environments
– Avoid SaaS platforms headquartered in Five Eyes or treaty-heavy states

Freedom is not just where you live. It's how your tools behave in the dark.

4. Design Redundancy Without Exposure

Many well-meaning sovereigns replicate their setup across multiple countries—two companies, two passports, two bank accounts—believing this constitutes resilience. But if each setup *mirrors the other*, they become mirrored liabilities. If the same email address, IP logs, legal agent, or financial intermediary connects them, *you've duplicated vulnerability, not defused it.*

Instead, create strategic asymmetries:
– Bank in countries that are *not* your business base
– Store crypto in multisig vaults with keys distributed across trusted jurisdictions
– Maintain passive residencies (e.g. Panama, Mexico) that don't require global reporting
– Segment digital identities—don't log into every system from the same device or network

You want not just multiple flags, but flags that don't know each other exist. *Information asymmetry is the cornerstone of functional sovereignty.*

5. Think Like an Architect, Not a Tourist

Many adopt the Five Flags model to "escape the system," only to end up with a new version of the same trap—endless visas, compliance confusion, digital exposure, and a pseudo-nomadic identity with no roots or leverage. Sovereignty should not be a reactive escape. It should be a deliberate structure—engineered with logic, iteration, and constraint management.

That means:
– Creating legal entities that *don't conflict* with citizenship obligations
– Building income streams that are *geographically agnostic but reputationally sound*
– Managing asset types based on *time-to-move and effort-to-convert*, not paper value
– Designing a personal infrastructure (from communications to currency) that is *detached from any single point of failure*

True sovereigns are not invisible—they are unreadable by default, and legible by choice.

Section 4: Ethical Sovereignty – Power, Privacy, and the New Moral Landscape of Flag Theory

As Flag Theory evolves from its libertarian roots into a broader framework for digital and geopolitical autonomy, a new tension arises—*the ethical weight of self-liberation in a world bound by interdependence.* The original model framed sovereignty as escape: escape from taxes, regulations, and coercive states. But in the modern context, especially among high-agency actors with mobile capital and rare skills, sovereignty becomes less about isolation and more about *how one wields freedom when others cannot.*

Put simply: *to be sovereign today is to possess asymmetric freedom in a system that punishes most for noncompliance.* That power demands reflection.

1. Sovereignty Without Solipsism

Some critics of modern Flag Theory argue that it encourages narcissistic disengagement—wealthy individuals disconnecting from the civic obligations that sustain their societies. There is merit in the concern. An individual who benefits from an educated workforce, infrastructure, rule of law, and institutional stability, only to extract wealth and declare unilateral independence, *risks becoming a parasite rather than a pioneer.*

But this critique only holds when sovereignty is framed as *pure withdrawal.* Ethical sovereignty, by contrast, is *active stewardship.* It seeks systems where consent matters, where contribution is voluntary and aligned with values, and where power can be refused without ruin. It does not ignore interdependence—it *chooses its forms deliberately.*

The sovereign doesn't abandon society. They abandon illegitimate coercion in pursuit of earned trust.

2. Privacy as a Civic Good

One of the most misunderstood aspects of modern sovereignty is digital privacy. It's often dismissed as paranoia or subterfuge. But in truth, *privacy is not concealment—it is discretion.* It protects individuals from arbitrary profiling, algorithmic punishment, and pre-criminal suspicion. It also reinforces autonomy in ways that transcend personal interest.

By opting out of surveillance capitalism—through encrypted tools, decentralised identities, and obfuscated metadata—sovereign individuals *lower the surveillance surface area for everyone.* They create demand for privacy-respecting alternatives, fund open-source infrastructure, and expand the Overton window of permissible resistance.

In a networked society, privacy is public defence.

3. Geo-Liberty Without Geo-Exploitation

Geopolitical arbitrage—living in one country, earning in another, and paying tax in neither—has become a hallmark of advanced flag strategists. Yet, when poorly executed, this approach *replicates colonial extractivism*: taking advantage of favourable labour, legal laxity, or political fragility without investing in the communities that make it possible.

Modern Flag Theory must confront this shadow. It's not enough to seek *maximum yield per flag.* One must also ask: *what am I giving back to the jurisdictions I depend on, and how am I shaping the environments I temporarily inhabit?* If sovereignty becomes synonymous with exploitation, the backlash will not be moral—it will be legal and technological.

Sustainable sovereignty requires *geo-ethical equilibrium*: *use without abuse, presence without predation.*

4. Consent as the Cornerstone of Jurisdiction

Ultimately, the ethical arc of modern Flag Theory rests on a radical idea: *jurisdiction should be by consent, not accident.* Most people live under systems they did not choose, subject to rules they cannot change, paying into institutions they cannot audit. Sovereign individuals flip that script. They choose jurisdictions as they would choose vendors—based on performance, fairness, and alignment.

But that choice must be exercised with rigour. It means:
– Paying tax where value is received, not merely avoided
– Respecting laws where rights are protected, not just exploited
– Using mobility as a lever for reform, not just evasion

The sovereign imagination, in this sense, is not anarchic. It is constitutional in the truest sense: it believes in self-determination grounded in clarity, contribution, and consent.

Citizenship as a Weapon or Shield – How Passports Become Strategic Instruments in Crisis

A passport, to the casual holder, is a travel document—a laminated artefact tucked into a drawer until summer holidays arrive. To the globally literate, however, it is *sovereign code* embedded in paper: a marker of rights, liabilities, expectations, and constraints. In moments of systemic collapse or geopolitical rupture, this simple booklet transforms. It can save you—or betray you.

The 20th century taught us that citizenship is not neutral. History is replete with examples where passports determined whether one could flee, where one could land, and whether one was treated as a refugee or a fugitive. But the 21st century adds a new layer: the weaponisation of citizenship by digital surveillance states, automated border control, and financial data-sharing regimes. *Your nationality now travels faster than you do*—through SWIFT systems, visa databases, no-fly lists, and tax treaties.

To be unstrategic about your citizenship in the modern world is to gamble with your autonomy, your capital, and your future mobility.

This chapter explores the underestimated power of citizenship as both *a shield*—offering protection, options, and extrication—and *a weapon*—used to compel, control, and even capture those who thought they were free.

The Illusion of Safe Citizenship

Many readers assume that if they were born in a politically stable, economically developed country, their citizenship is a lifelong asset. But the concept of "safe citizenship" is historically brittle. Consider the following:

During the Second World War, American citizens of Japanese descent were interned on U.S. soil despite full legal status. Their citizenship failed to shield them from state suspicion and confinement.

In 2008, Icelandic citizens watched their banks collapse. Those living abroad were suddenly treated with suspicion, denied basic services, and saw frozen assets because of international financial retaliation.

In 2016, the Indian government demonetised 86% of its currency overnight, and citizens could not exchange their own legal tender unless they were physically within the country—passport holders abroad were trapped with worthless notes.

A passport may promise protection, but it also signals *vulnerability*—to the whims of central banks, intelligence-sharing alliances, or emergency decrees.

Citizenship is not inherently good or bad. It is *conditional*, *jurisdictional*, and *revocable*.

The Weaponisation of Citizenship in the Digital Era

Modern nation-states increasingly use citizenship as a *point of leverage*. This is not always obvious, but the effects are profound. Three primary domains illustrate this:

Financial Surveillance and Taxation

Citizens of countries like the United States are taxed on their *worldwide income*, regardless of residence. The Foreign Account Tax Compliance Act (FATCA) compels foreign banks to report U.S. citizens' financial activities to the IRS. Citizenship here is not a right—it is an enforcement vector. Similarly, the Common Reporting Standard (CRS), adopted by over 100 jurisdictions, allows governments to access your offshore holdings based on your nationality or tax residency, even if you have no local ties.

Travel and Detention Risks

In conflict zones or political incidents, the perceived value or liability of a given passport can shift overnight. A Western passport might afford evacuation rights one week—and attract hostility or detention the next. During the 2006 Lebanon War, dual nationals trying to escape Beirut were subjected to triage evacuations. Some were denied assistance because their primary citizenship was in a non-intervening country.

Revocation and Exile

In the UK, Australia, and parts of Europe, citizenship revocation powers are expanding. If a citizen is deemed to be a national security risk—even without conviction—they may lose their nationality and be rendered stateless. This trend, once unimaginable in liberal democracies, reveals how easily citizenship can be reclassified from a right to a *conditional privilege*.

The sovereign individual must ask: which passport policies protect liberty, and which encode latent control?

Multi-Citizenship as a Hedge, Not a Luxury

Second citizenship is often misunderstood as a vanity project of the ultra-wealthy. In reality, it is a *foundational redundancy mechanism*—a form of geopolitical diversification. Just as you wouldn't hold all assets in one bank or currency, placing your legal identity in a single nation is a concentration risk.

Case Study: Venezuelan Collapse

In the early 2010s, Venezuela was a promising middle-income country. When hyperinflation, crime, and political chaos erupted, those with second passports—often acquired quietly through ancestral ties or Caribbean programmes—escaped early. Those without were trapped behind a dysfunctional passport system, unable to leave legally or access foreign banking.

Second citizenship does not guarantee comfort, but it provides *escape velocity*. It creates options when domestic systems fail or when your primary passport becomes politically charged.

When a Passport Becomes a Liability

Some nationalities invite scrutiny by default. Holders of Iranian, Russian, North Korean, or Afghan passports find themselves automatically subject to secondary screening, travel bans, and financial blacklists.

However, it's not only geopolitically sensitive states that present risk. Citizens of high-tax, high-surveillance Western democracies are increasingly *presumed guilty until proven compliant* in matters of tax, investment, and border crossing.

Moreover, passport privilege can *collapse in transnational crises*. During the COVID-19 pandemic, European Union citizens lost access to their own free-movement rights overnight. U.S. citizens found themselves locked out of over 180 countries. The idea of "global mobility" was revealed as a *conditional convenience*, not an inherent right.

A passport is not a travel document. It is a *political trust score*, subject to revocation, deterioration, or inflation—just like currency.

From Legal Identity to Mobility Architecture

Sovereign thinkers must move beyond static citizenship and begin to architect their *mobility stack*. This includes:

A legally secure place of residence (domicile)

A travel-efficient passport or set of passports

Jurisdictions with non-extradition clauses (for legal resilience)

Consular coverage in multiple jurisdictions

Countries that do not require asset disclosures for citizenship

This mobility stack is not merely about *escape*. It's about *negotiating life with strategic freedom*, where one can pivot between locations, legal systems, and economic networks as needed.

Ethics, Power, and Responsibility

It is tempting to see strategic citizenship as a personal optimisation game—minimise tax, maximise travel, dodge instability. But sovereignty without ethics becomes exploitation.

Smart citizens ask:

Am I contributing to the jurisdictions that protect me?

Am I hiding assets from injustice or from fair contribution?

Am I selecting passports to serve justice or to avoid it?

True sovereignty is not about avoiding accountability. It is about *choosing which accountability structures you honour*—and being able to walk away from those that abuse your trust.

Final Thought

A passport is more than a key. It is a contract. A good one shields you. A bad one tags you, taxes you, tracks you, and traps you. The difference is not just in the colour of the cover, but in the intent of the issuing state.

To become sovereign, you must learn to *read passports as power instruments*—negotiated assets, not birth entitlements. And if you're serious about enduring liberty, you must diversify them as you would your wealth.

Borderless Income Streams – How to Earn Globally Without Being Locked into One Nation's Fate

There is no such thing as economic freedom if your income is geographically captive. This truth, once the concern of only the elite or the exiled, now applies to anyone seeking financial sovereignty in a world where governments can freeze bank accounts, manipulate tax codes, or wall off their economies from the outside world. If your cashflow is anchored entirely within one nation-state, so is your fate. When your revenue stops crossing borders, so does your freedom.

The ability to earn borderlessly is no longer a luxury; it's a form of modern defence. The professional who can generate income globally retains optionality. The business owner whose clients span time zones and tax jurisdictions can walk away from dysfunction. The freelancer paid in Bitcoin, the investor holding foreign equity, the coder selling code to a DAO—each is quietly decoupling their survival from the fragility of national systems.

What was once called "location independence" now deserves a more strategic name: *income sovereignty*. This chapter unpacks how to build it—and why waiting to do so is, increasingly, a form of economic negligence.

The Fragility of Domestic Earnings

Consider the café owner in Argentina, the teacher in Turkey, or the accountant in Sri Lanka. All three may be highly skilled, well-networked, and financially prudent within their local economy. Yet when inflation spikes, capital controls tighten, or regimes turn hostile to independent business, their income collapses in real terms. They have earned, saved, and planned—but only in one currency, one language, and one legal system. When that system falters, so does their livelihood.

Even in more "developed" economies, the risk is real. During the COVID-19 lockdowns, entire sectors were rendered obsolete overnight—event organisers, gym owners, hospitality providers—while remote freelancers, digital product sellers, and software consultants grew their income faster than ever.

Earning locally in a globally unstable world is the modern equivalent of storing your wealth in a single building made of glass.

What Borderless Income Actually Means

Borderless income is not just about earning money online. It is about designing income streams that are:

Detachable from any one country's political or economic fate.

Resilient across currencies, jurisdictions, and regulatory climates.

Difficult to freeze, track, or confiscate by a single government actor.

This includes, but is not limited to:

Remote consultancy or freelance work with international clients.

Ownership of intellectual property that pays royalties globally.

Dividend-producing investments held in jurisdictions other than one's residence.

Crypto-native income such as staking, DeFi yield farming, or contributions to decentralised protocols.

Selling products or knowledge assets (courses, books, tools) in international marketplaces.

It is *not* simply about working on your laptop at the beach. The aesthetic of the "digital nomad" is far less important than the architecture of the income.

Case Studies in Income Sovereignty

Case 1: The Copywriter in Nairobi

Grace, a marketing copywriter based in Kenya, began working with US and European clients via Upwork and later moved to direct contracts. When the Kenyan shilling devalued sharply in 2023, her dollar-based income remained stable—and her local purchasing power actually increased. Because her services were borderless, her income adjusted favourably to local instability.

Case 2: The Developer in Belarus

Anton, a blockchain developer, earned cryptocurrency for his work with decentralised autonomous organisations (DAOs). When political unrest and internet shutdowns escalated in Belarus, he was able to relocate to Georgia within days. His income, wallet, and network travelled with him. No banking authorisation or employer permission was needed.

Case 3: The Educator in New Zealand

Lisa ran a tutoring centre in Auckland. When her business was forced to close during lockdowns, she digitised her curriculum and began teaching international students online. She now runs a six-figure course business, serves students in five countries, and no longer depends on local demand or regulation to maintain her revenue.

These are not fantasies; they are the *new professional middle class*. They are sovereign not because of their wealth, but because of their earnings architecture.

Design Principles of Borderless Income

Borderless income is not something you stumble into. It is built deliberately. The following principles provide a blueprint:

Service Arbitrage

Sell your labour where it's valued highest, spend where it's cheapest. For example, a British-educated UX designer can command £75/hour from US clients while living in Portugal, Poland, or Thailand at a fraction of UK costs.

Jurisdictional Separation

Where you live, where you earn, and where your money is stored should ideally be three separate locations. This makes you legally and financially harder to trap or target.

Currency Hedging via Revenue

Earning in multiple currencies reduces exposure to inflation or political devaluation. For example, earning both in USD and EUR provides natural currency hedging for those outside those regions.

Income via Intellectual Leverage

Time-bound services are harder to scale. Assets like books, software, music, and educational content scale better. They cross borders with zero marginal cost, cannot be confiscated at customs, and often remain legally protected.

Crypto-Native Revenue Models

Earning in crypto—whether through direct payments, royalties on NFTs, or staking yield—is still early, but offers censorship resistance and unparalleled portability. This is not just about Bitcoin as storage. It is about earning *natively within digital systems* that do not map neatly onto nation-states.

Challenges and Realities

Earning borderlessly is not without complexity. Governments do not easily let go of tax rights or surveillance opportunities. Compliance burdens can increase if not structured intelligently. For instance:

A US citizen abroad must still file taxes annually and potentially pay if thresholds are met.

Many freelance platforms default to domestic banking systems and may report income back to tax authorities.

Some payment processors block users from specific "high-risk" jurisdictions due to AML/KYC concerns.

But these are problems of structure—not impossibilities. The sovereign actor learns the rules, builds around them, and diversifies routes of income to remain agile.

The Ethics of Geographic Arbitrage

Critics of location-independent income often raise ethical concerns: Are you exploiting lower costs in other countries? Are you avoiding taxes unfairly? These questions deserve real engagement.

But here's the counterpoint: sovereign income is not about evasion—it's about resilience. It's about *reducing systemic exposure to jurisdictions that demand obedience without accountability*. It's about building a livelihood that can survive fiat collapses, authoritarian drift, or war-time decrees.

A sovereign citizen with global income still contributes—to the communities they live in, the clients they serve, and the networks they build. But they do so *by choice*, not by captivity.

Toward Portable Prosperity

Ultimately, borderless income is about *permissionless prosperity*. You are no longer waiting for your government to stabilise, your economy to recover, or your sector to reopen. You are not begging a bank to unfreeze your funds or an employer to sponsor your visa.

You are *earning with your mind, not just your passport*. And your income moves with you, not despite you.

If wealth is what you keep, income is what you *repeat*. And when that repetition is borderless, so too is your freedom.

The Myth of the Safe Haven – Why Security Is Not a Place but a Practice

There is a persistent illusion in the modern imagination that somewhere out there—hidden between mountains, nestled in rural farmland, or tucked into a low-tax microstate—there exists a place immune to collapse. A safe haven. A sanctuary. A country that will remain calm while others riot, solvent while others default, free while others suppress.

This belief is not merely wrong; it is dangerously disorienting. It causes paralysis when action is required. It persuades people to *wait* for the perfect refuge while their options narrow. It seduces them into thinking safety is a location to be found, rather than a system to be built.

True resilience begins by rejecting the myth that safety is static.

Why Geography Alone Cannot Guarantee Safety

Geography once offered a kind of physical buffer: oceans protected nations, mountains deterred invasion, and distance slowed contagion—biological or political. But these geographic moats are now obsolete in the face of instantaneous digital surveillance, globalised financial contagion, and algorithmically enforced compliance.

In 2022, Canadian citizens discovered this first-hand when peaceful protestors and their supporters had their bank accounts frozen by federal mandate—without court orders or criminal charges. The geography did not matter. *Their perceived financial and legal security vanished within hours.*

A European passport did not protect Cypriot citizens in 2013 when the government imposed a sudden levy on bank deposits. Nor did distance protect Australians when their international borders were sealed for nearly two years, even to their own citizens.

Safety is no longer determined by location. It is determined by *leverage, structure, timing, and awareness.*

Historical Blind Spots: Safe Havens That Weren't

Throughout history, people have fled failing systems for what they believed were permanent sanctuaries—only to discover that no place remains neutral in a geopolitical storm.

• **Pre-World War II Europe:** Many German Jews relocated to France, the Netherlands, or Belgium to escape rising antisemitism in Germany. These were liberal democracies. Within a few years, they were occupied by Nazi forces.

• **Rhodesia to South Africa:** As the political situation in Rhodesia (now Zimbabwe) deteriorated in the 1970s, white families moved south, believing South Africa offered permanence and protection. A decade later, apartheid South Africa was internationally isolated, economically sanctioned, and internally unstable.

• **Hong Kong:** Long viewed as a haven of economic freedom and rule of law, the 2019 protests and subsequent imposition of the National Security Law marked a rapid transformation. The illusion of political independence collapsed in less than a year.

These are not just historical anecdotes. They are recurring patterns. *A place is only a safe haven until it isn't.* The conditions that make a place safe—stable governance, strong institutions, social cohesion—can be revoked, rapidly and without warning.

False Comfort in Second Passports

One of the most popular expressions of the safe haven myth is the "second passport" strategy. While there is nothing inherently wrong with holding dual citizenship—indeed, it can be a powerful form of strategic mobility—the belief that a second passport guarantees escape or exemption from crisis is flawed.

A passport is a tool, not a shelter. Its value can erode, its privileges can be suspended, and its issuance can be revoked. Consider the following:

In times of war or upheaval, even "strong" passports can become liabilities. Citizens of G7 nations may find themselves targets of anti-Western sentiment or barred from certain airspaces and financial systems.

Dual citizenship can increase obligations, not reduce them. Taxation, military conscription, or surveillance may follow citizens even when they've left their country of birth.

Embassy protection is political, not absolute. A passport does not ensure safe passage in hostile territory—particularly when diplomatic relations deteriorate.

The problem is not with owning a second passport, but with thinking of it as a *permanent escape hatch.* The world does not guarantee you the right to flee, much less the right to thrive elsewhere.

The Strategic Alternative: Safety as a System, Not a Spot

Instead of fixating on a single country as a sanctuary, a more intelligent approach is to *diversify the sources of your safety*. This is the logic behind sovereign systems thinking—designing your life so that no single actor, state, or event can disrupt your autonomy.

This includes:

Jurisdictional diversification: Holding assets, residency rights, and business operations across multiple countries.

Income mobility: Ensuring your earnings are not tied to a single economy or legal jurisdiction.

Legal structuring: Using international legal entities to separate ownership from control, and to provide layers of protection against hostile local action.

Low visibility: Reducing digital footprints and paper trails that make it easy for governments or corporations to track and restrict you.

Rather than retreating to a bunker or banking on a utopia, this approach accepts that *all systems are fragile*, and therefore builds across them.

The Allure—and Danger—of Expat Echo Chambers

Many so-called "expat hubs" are marketed as havens for liberty-minded thinkers. Places like Panama, Portugal, Uruguay, Georgia, or the UAE are often listed as "top expat destinations" for their tax policies, lifestyle perks, and ease of entry.

But these hubs can become echo chambers. When everyone believes they've found the perfect safe haven, critical analysis diminishes. The early movers are often agile, savvy, and strategic. But the later wave often arrives emotionally, uncritically, and with a misplaced sense of permanence.

History teaches that *the moment too many people converge on a haven, its advantages begin to degrade.* Costs rise. Scrutiny increases. Governments respond. The community ossifies. What was once agile becomes crowded and visible. This is not paranoia. It is pattern recognition.

Mental Agility Beats Physical Refuge

The most adaptable individuals in systemic breakdowns are not those who found the best hideout—but those who saw the signs early, moved incrementally, and could mentally pivot before conditions deteriorated.

They understood that *safety is an active process of recalibration*, not a passive hope.

This agility stems from a combination of traits:

Awareness: The ability to see patterns beneath headlines.

Preparedness: Practical skills, portable wealth, and flexible relationships.

Low dependency: Few fixed costs, low visibility, minimal reliance on state systems.

Strategic exit options: Pre-defined pathways to relocate wealth, citizenship, or physical presence quickly.

If you have those, you do not need a perfect location. *You are the safe haven.*

Reframing the Idea of "Home"

Perhaps the most radical—but necessary—shift is to detach the concept of safety from sentiment. Many people confuse nostalgia, familiarity, or aesthetics with resilience. They think a place feels safe because they *want* it to be.

But emotional loyalty to a location can be economically lethal. Cities like San Francisco, Sydney, or London may offer familiarity—but they now combine high costs, aggressive taxation, and increasing authoritarian policy creep.

Meanwhile, lesser-known jurisdictions may offer better governance, lower overhead, and greater autonomy—but lack the comforting mythology of "home."

In an unstable world, *your home must be where your systems work best*, not where your memories live most vividly.

From Place to Practice

The great mistake of the 20th century was to assume that borders defined meaning and that passports defined protection. The wise actors of the 21st century will understand that *safety is not a place—it is a practice.* A continuous, evolving system of diversification, discretion, and decentralisation.

In the digital surveillance age, the most resilient are not those who stockpile passports or rush to islands. They are the ones who build quietly, move fluidly, and never confuse stability with stasis.

There is no safe haven.

But there are safer lives—built by sovereign minds.

Chapter 8
The Family Firewall – Protecting Loved Ones

SECTION 1: The Premise of Protection in a Fragmenting World

Collapse doesn't knock first. It creeps, splintering slowly through inflation spikes, erratic currencies, murmurs of failing banks next door—then, almost cruelly, it crashes in. And when that moment arrives, survival rarely belongs to the optimistic or the ideological. Nor is it gifted to the wealthy by default. It belongs to the prepared—those who've built for rupture before the first tremor struck.

Yet amid all the talk of readiness, a problematic archetype dominates: the lone wolf. The crypto-savvy drifter with offshore backups and a fast exit. The prepper in the hills. The ultra-rich hedging their bets with second passports and security details. But these visions—dramatic as they are—overlook a simple reality: most people don't want to leave their families behind. Nor should they. Real protection isn't built for the individual. It's constructed around the family unit, with all its messiness, interdependence, and obligation. And that shift changes everything.

A resilient person can outlast a crisis. A resilient family can outlive one.

This isn't a call to stockpile tins or vanish into the wilderness. It's a framework for building something quieter, and far stronger: a protective web around your loved ones. Call it a firewall if you like, but think of it as a system—one designed not only to preserve life but to protect dignity, continuity, and the calm needed to navigate disorder with purpose.

The work here is neither glamorous nor fear-driven. It is structured care. A turning of the mind towards what matters, before chaos makes that choice for you.

True protection does not seek comfort. It seeks clarity. It doesn't indulge denial—it demands discipline. And it refuses to cede the future to fear.

SECTION 2: Intergenerational Exit Thinking

There's a profound difference between crafting a getaway plan for oneself and building a system robust enough to carry multiple generations through crisis. Planning for a family exit isn't merely a logistical exercise—it's a philosophical declaration: that your legacy should not just consist of assets and heirlooms, but agency. The capacity to choose sovereignty over subjugation, wherever and whenever it becomes necessary.

So, what does it mean to leave behind more than wealth? It means cultivating literacy across generations. Can your teenager verify truth in a flood of propaganda? Can your elderly parents navigate the implications of a government-issued digital currency? If you're incapacitated, could your partner initiate the relocation strategy without your guidance? These aren't idle hypotheticals. They're skill sets. And like any skill, they must be taught, tested, and internalised.

Families that survive breakdowns are rarely those with the most impressive bug-out kits or fortified homes. They're the ones who've anticipated the unseen—who've appointed roles, formalised protocols, rehearsed difficult decisions, and ensured that information isn't hoarded but distributed. They understand that when the centre doesn't hold, clarity does.

Intergenerational preparedness is not sentimental—it's structural. It replaces wishful thinking with pre-defined thresholds for action, legal contingencies, operational roles, and portable forms of wealth and identity. And it's alive. What works for a young couple in Singapore will differ radically from what's needed by a widow in Buenos Aires or a single parent in Lagos. Exit strategies are dynamic systems—responsive to geopolitical tides, family dynamics, and emerging technologies.

Think of it as maintenance, not mastery. Something to be revised, not revered. Like security patches or estate plans, it's the audit that matters—the regular, unflinching check-in on whether the protection you've designed still fits the shape of your family's present and future.

If that resonates, we can now move into Section 3, where we shift from philosophy to infrastructure: documents, data, and the fragile architecture of proof.

SECTION 3: Securing Critical Documents and Digital Assets

In times of fracture, identity becomes contested territory. A document, once mundane, becomes a key or a lock. A passport determines your right to leave—or your right to be detained. A marriage certificate, a lease, a power of attorney—these aren't just files. They're permission slips to act, move, and protect.

But the shoebox of papers in a bedroom drawer won't suffice anymore. Nor will a USB hidden in a sock drawer. The threats are digital, the stakes immense, and the margins for error narrow.

What's needed is a layered system. A decentralised, redundant, encrypted architecture where hard copies are backed by tamper-evident scans. Where digital files are secured in multiple jurisdictions, and where every essential actor in the family—be it spouse, sibling, or child—knows not only what to access, but how.

There is no room for centralisation of knowledge. If one person holds all the keys, the entire structure is a single point of failure. So, think in terms of inheritance protocols: password vaults with staggered access permissions, multisignature wallets requiring multiple family members to act, biometric logins, emergency recovery systems. And yes, "dead man's switches"—those slightly unsettling mechanisms that trigger access if you disappear for too long.

If this sounds extreme, consider what's already true. Most families today are invisibly reliant on cloud-stored documents, online accounts, and state-managed identification systems. These are not optional luxuries—they are functional lifelines. And as such, their preservation is not just technical but existential.

You are not only storing data. You're storing continuity. The ability to reconstitute your family's rights and resources in the aftermath of disruption. And that continuity must survive both the chaos and the human error that chaos invites.

When you're ready, we can move toward the less tangible—but no less vital—dimension: mental resilience. How calm is cultivated when the world unravels.

SECTION 4: Cultivating Calm in Crisis

No vault can help you if you lose the code under pressure. And no contingency plan is useful if the person holding it crumbles when the air grows thin. Psychological resilience isn't an afterthought—it is the secret thread that holds every other preparation together.

Families that endure don't just rehearse what to do. They practise *how* to be. Under stress, children watch faces. Spouses tune into tone, not just content. The nervous system, more than the intellect, sets the tempo of response. If calm is rehearsed, it can be recalled. If not, it's often out of reach.

Ancient wisdom knew this well. Stoic thinkers, writing amidst collapsing republics and burning cities, insisted that mastery of the self was the only true sanctuary. The same holds now. Emotional literacy, shared language, and scenario-based drills are not soft practices—they are strategic ones.

Mental inoculation is the term crisis psychologists use. By gradually exposing individuals to elevated stress in controlled environments, one builds a buffer against panic. Families can do the same: simulated disruptions, role-reversal exercises, decision-making games. Each a tool in the service of collective composure.

And structure helps. When responsibilities are shared, when decision trees are visible to all, when judgement is decentralised, panic has fewer doors through which to enter. A family trained this way does not devolve into fear—it transforms into a system that can *act* even when its leader cannot.

This is the firewall that can't be encrypted or outsourced. It is the nervous system of preparedness—the calm beneath the protocol.

Next, we'll bring these strands together in Section 5—a practical architecture for turning fragility into fortification across real-world family configurations.

SECTION 5: From Fragility to Fortification — A Practical Continuum

What follows here is not a prepackaged list of actions, nor a lifestyle prescription. Rather, it's a living framework—one that meets you not in fantasy, but in the exact shape of your reality. Whether you're raising toddlers in a second-tier city, managing cross-continental eldercare, or overseeing a multigenerational household with overlapping vulnerabilities, this is where abstraction turns operational.

You'll explore how to transmit sovereignty—not just money—across generations. How to design asset protection that spans borders and decades. How to decentralise legal authority, information access, and income flow in a way that doesn't disorient, but dignify.

Above all, you'll be building not just procedures but culture. A shared rhythm of calm. A family posture that doesn't flinch at disruption but flexes around it.

This isn't about feeling invincible. That myth dissolves fast under pressure. What you're constructing instead is a form of sovereign coherence—a structure that holds under strain because it was built with strain in mind.

Protection, in this context, is not a panic response. It is not a bunker. It is a system. One measured not by how it behaves during peace, but by how it sustains when peace is no longer guaranteed.

Shall we move into the first subchapter? Or would you prefer this formatted for print, or prepped for distribution?

Financial Literacy for Collapse Conditions – Teaching Clear, Non-Fear-Based Financial Education for Families

There is a profound difference between knowing how to make money and understanding how money works—particularly when it begins to fail. In times of relative stability, traditional financial education tends to centre on budgeting, investing, credit scores, and retirement planning. These topics are relevant and often essential. Yet they assume the continued existence of a functioning financial infrastructure: banks that honour withdrawals, governments that uphold property rights, and currencies that retain value. In collapse conditions—whether triggered by war, hyperinflation, systemic banking failure, or supply chain disintegration—this foundational infrastructure begins to fracture. And when it does, families who possess only conventional financial knowledge often find themselves exposed, confused, or paralysed.

Financial literacy under collapse conditions is not an extension of mainstream financial advice. It is a separate discipline—one that blends economic realism, historical pattern recognition, psychological preparedness, and practical skills transfer. Crucially, it must be *non-fear-based* because fear distorts thinking and undermines trust within families. Instead, this form of literacy should empower. It must be taught calmly, clearly, and communally, so that each generation learns to adapt not only to market cycles but to systemic volatility.

To begin, we must first reframe what we mean by "wealth". In stable environments, wealth is often expressed in abstractions—portfolios, valuations, projections. But in unstable environments, those abstractions lose traction quickly. Wealth becomes defined by *functionality*: what can be accessed, exchanged, protected, and moved when things go wrong. Consider Venezuela's middle class during the 2010s. Families with generous pensions and properties in Caracas found themselves reliant on remittances from relatives abroad. Why? Because their "assets" were denominated in a currency that no longer held external purchasing power. Conversely, Venezuelans who understood international remittance channels, who held modest stores of hard currency or gold, or who possessed high-demand barterable skills—such as auto repair, medicine, or cooking—managed not only to survive but to help others.

This is not a call to abandon modern finance. Rather, it's a recognition that under stress, the financial map changes—and with it, the skillset must evolve. A core tenet of collapse-oriented literacy is that *money is a tool, not a guarantee*. Its usefulness is contingent on trust: trust in the issuing authority, trust in the system's continuity, trust in its convertibility. When that trust breaks, wealth must be reinterpreted through the lens of *resilience and mobility*, not accumulation.

For families, the implications are direct. Begin by teaching children and adolescents the difference between *currency* and *value*. A currency is a medium of exchange; value is what something is worth to someone in a particular context. In scarcity environments, the two diverge. An ounce of gold may be valuable on paper, but if you're cold and hungry in a refugee corridor, a bottle of clean water and a functioning lighter may be of far greater value in that moment. Teach them that financial thinking should always include *situational awareness*. Ask: what is valuable *here*, *now*, and *to whom*?

From a practical standpoint, families should familiarise themselves with multiple forms of liquidity—cash, precious metals, foreign currency, digital assets—and their trade-offs. This is not about speculative investing. It's about understanding *access and exit*. Cash is immediate but vulnerable to inflation. Gold is stable but heavy and difficult to move. Crypto offers portability but requires technical confidence and security discipline. Each has its place in a multi-layered defence strategy. Educating children and spouses in how to store, access, and understand these mediums builds confidence and distributes capability.

But technical knowledge alone is not enough. Collapse financial literacy must also include *emotional conditioning*. Historical case studies—Weimar Germany, Zimbabwe, Yugoslavia in the 1990s—consistently show that one of the most paralysing responses to financial collapse is psychological inertia. People freeze, waiting for a return to normalcy. They hesitate to make hard decisions—liquidating assets, relocating, reallocating resources—because the cost of being "wrong" feels too high. But collapse is rarely a binary switch. It unfolds incrementally, then all at once. Teaching families to recognise early warning signs, make provisional plans, and act decisively when thresholds are crossed is arguably the most valuable financial skill of all.

This brings us to intergenerational communication. Many families avoid financial conversations altogether, often out of discomfort, privacy, or misguided notions of protection. But silence breeds ignorance. Children who grow up in households where money is never discussed tend to enter adulthood ill-equipped to navigate financial uncertainty—let alone crisis. Financial literacy for collapse conditions demands radical transparency. Not in terms of exact numbers, but in shared principles and open scenario modelling. Walk children through "what if" exercises. What would we do if the ATMs stopped working for a week? If fuel prices doubled? If we needed to leave the country in 48 hours, what assets would we take, and how?

These conversations do not need to be framed as paranoia. On the contrary, they build trust and foster agency. When conducted with calm, they convey an essential message: *you are part of the solution.* Children internalise more than instruction—they absorb tone. A parent who can calmly discuss fallback plans models adaptability, not anxiety.

From a systems perspective, collapse-oriented financial education should also include knowledge of *risk jurisdictions.* Where you bank, where your digital assets are stored, where your citizenship ties are located—all influence your financial exposure. Families that diversify these risk points—by holding multiple residencies, foreign bank accounts, or decentralised assets—are not being conspiratorial. They are implementing structural redundancy. Much like an architect designs buildings to withstand earthquakes by embedding flexibility, so too must families design financial plans that remain functional under duress.

Let us also consider the importance of *non-monetary stores of value.* In disruption scenarios, formal economies contract and informal ones expand. Barter systems, favour networks, and underground exchanges become dominant. A child who can repair a drone, treat a wound, or teach mathematics holds a form of wealth that cannot be devalued by fiat collapse. Skill is a currency. Time, attention, and reputation—these too are assets. Embedding this recognition into family culture creates a more robust form of preparedness. Encourage children not just to learn, but to *teach*, to solve, to trade, and to document. These practices future-proof human capital.

Of course, collapse literacy must also account for ethics. Preparing for instability cannot become an excuse for selfishness or cynicism. Families must discuss not only how to protect themselves, but how to contribute constructively in community scenarios. Who will you help if things deteriorate? What is your code of conduct under pressure? These are not abstract questions. In times of chaos, your values—if well-articulated—become a compass when rules vanish. This is why Stoic and survival psychology principles are a worthy addition to financial education. They stabilise the inner world when the outer one destabilises. Resilience is as much about inner discipline as it is about external assets.

Lastly, the method of instruction matters. Financial literacy for collapse should not be a one-time lesson but a series of ongoing dialogues. Use global events as teaching prompts. Involve children in financial decisions, scaled to their level of understanding. Encourage questions. Treat mistakes as learning opportunities. The goal is not to create miniature preppers, but to raise competent, agile, morally grounded individuals who understand that money is a system, not a sanctuary—and that systems, like empires, can and do fail.

If conventional financial education teaches us how to thrive within the system, collapse financial literacy teaches us how to survive and adapt *beyond it*. Both are necessary. But the latter is rarely taught—because it requires confronting uncomfortable truths. It asks us to think in terms of *fragility*, *adaptability*, and *continuity*, not just profit and loss. In doing so, it offers something far more enduring than wealth: it offers clarity, autonomy, and resilience. That, ultimately, is what families must pass down. Not blind optimism, not paralysing fear—but informed, active stewardship across generations.

Let that be the new financial legacy.

Intergenerational Exit Planning – Creating Legacy Protocols for Family Safety and Continuity

There is no continuity without foresight—and no true legacy without resilience. Most family planning focuses on wealth transmission: trusts, wills, property deeds, and investment accounts. While these instruments are essential in stable systems, they are structurally dependent on functioning institutions: governments that enforce contracts, banks that honour transfers, and societies that preserve order. In times of geopolitical upheaval, economic collapse, or civil unrest, these assumptions disintegrate. What remains is not what is written in law, but what is remembered in action—what has been prepared, transmitted, and understood *before* systems fail. That is the essence of intergenerational exit planning: ensuring that future generations do not just inherit *assets*, but *agency*.

Historically, families who weathered chaos were rarely the wealthiest, but rather the most prepared. Armenians who fled the Ottoman Empire, German Jews escaping the Third Reich, Rwandans during the 1994 genocide, or Ukrainians navigating the current conflict—all offer enduring lessons. Those who survived and rebuilt did so not by chance, but through foresight, contingency plans, and intra-family coordination. These were not generic bug-out plans. They were thoughtful protocols for mobility, identity transfer, knowledge preservation, and networked resilience. *Intergenerational exit planning is not about fleeing—it is about ensuring continuity when permanence is no longer an option.*

To begin with, we must strip the word "exit" of its cinematic connotations. It is not necessarily dramatic or last-minute. Nor is it exclusively physical. Exit can mean jurisdictional repositioning, capital migration, citizenship reshuffling, or simply the ability to *withhold participation* in failing systems. Families who prepare exits plan *options*, not destinations. They focus on mobility, not fantasy. More importantly, they begin early—before the stressors become acute.

Such planning begins with clarity of *family structure*. Who is involved? Who is dependent? Who is mobile, and who is not? The answers to these questions dictate the scope of exit preparation. An intergenerational plan must account for ageing parents, dependent children, medically vulnerable members, and even extended kin. Mapping capability and constraint is the foundation of resilience. It allows for the rational distribution of resources, roles, and responsibilities across generations.

Next, families must identify and safeguard their *core assets*. These include not only financial stores (bank accounts, precious metals, crypto holdings), but *identity-critical* documentation: passports, birth and marriage certificates, medical records, titles, citizenship papers. In collapse scenarios, the ability to prove who you are—and who you are related to—can mean the difference between asylum and statelessness. Documents should be digitised, encrypted, redundantly stored, and geographically dispersed. Trusted relatives, ideally in safer jurisdictions, should hold access keys. Children approaching adulthood should be taught not only where these assets are, but *why they matter*.

Yet, documentation alone is insufficient. Families must also preserve *narrative continuity*. In many disrupted societies, lineage becomes obscured, and with it, claims to property, identity, and even protection. Holocaust survivors who lost family names often lost their claims to restitution. Syrian refugees who fled without academic credentials saw careers collapse into obscurity.

Intergenerational planning must therefore include secure record-keeping of family history, property claims, professional qualifications, and intellectual capital. These records are not sentimental; they are strategic.

One of the most neglected elements of exit planning is the *knowledge transfer of soft infrastructure*: how to operate hardware wallets; how to execute an international wire; how to apply for a second passport; how to handle a consular emergency; how to enter a black or grey market without being exploited. Parents or grandparents who have these skills often underestimate the *learning curve* for younger members. Exit resilience is not hereditary—it is taught.

This means that financial literacy, legal knowledge, and logistical competence must be deliberately transmitted across generations. Use family meetings not just for birthdays and holidays, but for scenario reviews and skill training. Rotate leadership: let younger members present contingency updates, evaluate risk exposure, or lead walk-throughs of evacuation routes. Such exercises not only build competency but normalise responsibility-sharing. When the first phone call under duress is to a teenage daughter with practical knowledge and composure, the family's future is already more secure.

A critical pillar of intergenerational exit planning is the creation of *parallel infrastructure*. This includes maintaining second residencies, offshore accounts, alternative income streams, and dual-citizenship pathways—not for tax evasion or exotic living, but for systemic insulation. A family that has a European Union passport, income from decentralised digital work, and a modest property in a neutral jurisdiction is functionally buffered against many forms of national collapse. The more independent these pillars are from one another—jurisdictionally, technologically, and institutionally—the greater the resilience.

Yet it is not enough to establish these pathways. They must be maintained. Second passports must be renewed, alternative bank accounts monitored, cross-border contacts nurtured. Like muscles, these systems atrophy without attention. *Continuity is not about plans on paper—it's about systems in motion.*

Ethically, intergenerational planning must also wrestle with dilemmas of fairness and preparedness. Should younger generations inherit hard-won mobility while their peers remain trapped by borders or poverty? Should families share access with trusted outsiders or prioritise lineage? These are not abstract questions in collapse zones. They affect real-time decisions—who gets included in the boat, the plan, the escape. Thoughtful families debate these questions *before* urgency clouds judgment. By articulating values in advance, they avoid paralysis or moral compromise later.

Psychologically, such planning must be framed as *empowering*, not fatalistic. Children who grow up rehearsing family contingency protocols can absorb either fear or capability, depending on presentation. Done well, these conversations foster clarity and maturity. Done poorly, they breed anxiety or avoidance. The tone must be that of a strategist, not a doomsayer. Explain that every era has its risks, and every responsible family prepares accordingly. Emphasise *probability management*, not paranoia. Present the plan not as a prophecy of doom, but as an expression of love, duty, and confidence in their future capability.

Finally, exit planning must be adaptive. Conditions change. Laws shift. Routes open and close. A country that is safe today may be volatile tomorrow. A bank considered reliable may be frozen overnight. Families must schedule periodic reviews—biannual or annual—to audit assumptions, test fail-safes, and refresh skillsets. Planning must become culture.

To that end, families should formalise their exit logic in writing. A *Continuity Dossier*—a living document that contains encrypted access keys, contingency playbooks, contact networks, financial accounts, citizenship options, and ethical guidance—can serve as the spine of intergenerational strategy. It need not be voluminous. What matters is clarity, distribution, and renewal.

Intergenerational exit planning is not merely a safeguard against tyranny or collapse. It is a reaffirmation of long-term thinking in an age of distraction. It teaches that families are not temporary economic units, but ongoing sovereign entities capable of adapting to changing systems without losing identity or cohesion. It reminds us that wealth is not simply what we accumulate, but what we preserve, teach, and transmit under pressure.

Families that think in decades—not quarters—are those most likely to endure. Their continuity is not an accident, nor a privilege of the elite. It is the result of deliberate planning, calm instruction, ethical clarity, and practical readiness. In uncertain times, this is not just survival. It is stewardship.

Let that be the measure of legacy.

Securing Critical Documents and Digital Assets – Best practices for storing essential items securely

In times of calm, documents are bureaucratic. In times of crisis, they are existential. A birth certificate becomes the difference between citizenship and statelessness. A title deed becomes a lifeline to shelter. A hardware wallet seed phrase can mean access to one's life savings—or total loss. If financial resilience is the structure, document security is its scaffolding: unseen but absolutely critical. Yet despite its fundamental importance, the secure storage of essential items—both physical and digital—is frequently misunderstood, poorly executed, or fatally delayed. Most people assume they'll "get around to it." Few realise that *by the time you need these assets, it's often too late to secure them.*

The false comfort of centralisation—trusting banks, cloud storage, national ID systems—belies a sobering truth: central systems are vulnerable to failure, censorship, or corruption. A collapsing regime may revoke passports, freeze bank accounts, or alter legal records. A natural disaster may destroy physical archives. A cyberattack may render entire databases inaccessible. In such environments, redundancy is not a luxury; it is a precondition for autonomy.

To prepare, one must begin with a clear inventory of what constitutes a *critical asset.* This includes, at minimum, identity documentation (passports, birth and marriage certificates, national ID cards), legal and financial records (wills, property titles, insurance policies, bank account access, loan contracts), and access credentials (passwords, recovery keys, authentication backups). Increasingly, it also includes digital assets: cryptocurrency wallets, encrypted messages, private keys, and cloud-stored media. It is not enough to *own* these assets; one must be able to *prove ownership*, *transfer control*, and *access them under pressure.*

Let's first address the conventional approach: the home filing cabinet. It remains astonishing how many people still rely on a single drawer or briefcase to hold all family documents. It may feel organised—but in any fire, flood, theft, or forced relocation, it's as vulnerable as an unlocked door. Worse still is the growing dependency on unsecured digital environments—Google Drives with no encryption, cloud logins with no two-factor authentication, and shared folders whose access is long forgotten.

The modern reality demands a layered approach, merging physical, digital, and jurisdictional strategies. Physically, documents must be stored in water-resistant, fireproof containers—preferably in more than one location. A safe deposit box in a politically neutral country is no longer the domain of oligarchs; it is increasingly the rational move for any individual holding cross-border wealth, even modestly. Digitally, all critical documents should be scanned at high resolution, encrypted using open-source standards such as GPG or VeraCrypt, and stored redundantly—on local drives, password-protected USB keys, and decentralised cloud services. Each method has strengths and trade-offs. Combined, they offer robustness.

For digital assets, the stakes are even higher. Cryptographic wealth—whether in the form of Bitcoin, Ethereum, Monero, or other decentralised currencies—requires both technical literacy and strategic forethought. Private keys or seed phrases must never exist in a single point of failure. A common but reckless mistake is to store them on a computer or smartphone exposed to the internet. Equally dangerous is the popular misconception that writing them down on a sticky note and hiding them in a drawer constitutes security.

Instead, consider the principle of *geographic key-splitting*. For example, a 24-word recovery phrase can be divided using Shamir's Secret Sharing (a cryptographic method) into three or more parts, with each part stored in a different trusted location or with different family members. This ensures that no single breach leads to total loss, and that recovery is still possible if one part is lost or compromised. For those less technically inclined, even manual split-and-store methods—e.g., writing half a seed phrase in one location and the other half elsewhere—can dramatically reduce risk, provided integrity is maintained.

But encryption alone is not enough. *Access pathways must be taught and tested.* It is not uncommon for a family's digital fortune to become irretrievable simply because one spouse, child, or trustee lacked the knowledge to unlock it. This is particularly acute when digital assets are coupled with privacy practices—pseudonyms, alias email addresses, multi-step authentications. Without clear instructions and tested walk-throughs, your secure system may outwit your own heirs.

This leads to the necessity of *contingency documentation*. Every family should maintain a plain-language instruction set—encrypted, of course—detailing how to access key accounts, reset passwords, decrypt files, or recover wallets. This "access codex" should be reviewed at least annually, and entrusted to multiple parties under defined legal and ethical conditions. Many families are now turning to services like digital inheritance platforms and decentralised dead man's switches that release credentials based on inactivity or pre-set triggers.

However, these systems, too, must be scrutinised. A digital dead man's switch hosted on a platform based in a politically unstable or surveillance-heavy jurisdiction could be intercepted or manipulated. In the same way that banks are not ideologically neutral, neither are software providers. Choosing tools built on open-source, decentralised protocols is often wiser than relying on polished proprietary platforms whose internal governance is opaque.

We must also interrogate our assumptions about trust. The old model of "give everything to your lawyer or accountant" is increasingly outdated in a world of cross-border complexity. Lawyers die. Accountants migrate. Families fracture. Trust is no longer a function of professional role—it is a function of *distributed resilience*. Relying on a single point of trust (a family head, a lawyer, a friend) introduces the very vulnerability exit planning aims to eliminate.

Instead, consider the principle of *trusted distribution*. Disperse access—never too much to one party, but never too little to leave someone powerless. Create concentric rings of access: what a spouse can reach instantly, what a sibling or child can reach under specific conditions, what an executor can access with consensus.

Do not hide critical information under the illusion of secrecy; train your family to manage it responsibly.

From a psychological standpoint, this process must be approached with *rational urgency*. That is, it should be prioritised *before* the adrenaline of collapse sets in—when minds are calm, records are intact, and institutional friction is low. Waiting until a border closes or a bank imposes withdrawal limits is not merely risky—it is often irreversible.

Education plays a role here. Many families hesitate to teach younger members about digital asset security, fearing they are too immature. But ignorance is a greater risk than immaturity. Teaching responsible stewardship of encrypted assets, multi-jurisdictional storage, and secure communication should be part of any modern financial education.

Moreover, every layer of your asset security must be tested under *scenario drills*. Create mock exercises: a simulated account freeze, a forced relocation, a communications blackout. These stress-tests reveal the true weak points—not in technology, but in coordination, memory, and readiness. The family member who panics when asked to locate a USB key is not yet ready. The teenager who forgets the password protocol after six months needs a refresher. These are not failures; they are feedback.

Security is not an event. It is a rhythm. It is sustained through review, audit, clarity, and cultural integration within the household. When document and asset security becomes a shared norm—rather than a chore assigned to the "tech-savvy one"—families transform from vulnerable dependents into resilient micro-institutions.

The ultimate goal is not merely safety. It is agency. The ability to act, decide, and relocate without waiting for permission. The power to preserve autonomy not just for oneself, but for one's descendants, in a world where control is increasingly centralised, and surveillance increasingly normalised. Properly secured, a document is not just paper. A digital asset is not just code. They are, in effect, your portable sovereignty.

And sovereignty is never accidental. It is the result of deliberate, intelligent, forward-looking design. The kind you're building now.

Cultivating Calm in Crisis – Resilience Tools Rooted in Stoicism and Survival Psychology

There is a psychological paradox at the centre of collapse preparation: the more sophisticated our tools become—satellite phones, encrypted assets, offshore redundancy—the more fragile we often remain at the human level. Panic, indecision, and emotional contagion have derailed even the most technically prepared families and institutions. *Resilience in crisis is not first a matter of equipment. It is first a matter of internal posture.* The mind, more than any cache of gear or plan, determines whether an individual acts with clarity or contributes to chaos.

Modern preparedness often over-indexes on external logistics and underinvests in internal sovereignty. But if we examine the survival outcomes of real crises—natural disasters, regime collapses, sudden wars—it becomes unmistakably clear: those who endured with dignity and resourcefulness were not simply better supplied; they were calmer. Not sedated, not detached—*calmer.* And that calm was not accidental. It was trained, habituated, and, in many cases, philosophically grounded.

Stoicism, an ancient school of Hellenistic philosophy, offers one of the most durable psychological toolkits for cultivating such calm. Popularised by figures like Marcus Aurelius, Seneca, and Epictetus—and revived in modern secular thought—it teaches that while external circumstances are unpredictable, our internal responses can be governed by discipline, reason, and choice. The Stoics were not indifferent to suffering. Rather, they believed that emotional disturbance results primarily from our interpretation of events, not the events themselves. This insight is echoed by cognitive behavioural therapy today, which traces its lineage directly to Stoic principles.

In a crisis, this distinction is more than theoretical. The person who, upon hearing that the power grid is down, instantly spirals into "we're going to die" is fundamentally less equipped than the one who pauses, breathes, and asks: *What is within my control right now?* Stoicism's core principle—*focus only on what you can control*—acts like an internal firewall against paralysis and hysteria. It teaches that composure is not passivity, but the precondition for effective action.

But this is not merely philosophical speculation. *Survival psychology*—a field that emerged from studying plane crashes, war zone behaviours, and disaster response—reaches strikingly similar conclusions. Research by experts like John Leach and Laurence Gonzales shows that survivors tend to follow a specific arc: initial denial, swift adaptation, structured action. Those who adapt most quickly share common traits: emotional regulation, realistic optimism, mental rehearsal, and internal locus of control. These traits can be nurtured. They are not genetic. They are trained—through repetition, reflection, and systems of meaning.

In fact, *meaning* itself becomes a functional survival asset. Viktor Frankl, the Austrian psychiatrist and Holocaust survivor, observed in his seminal work *Man's Search for Meaning* that those who survived the camps were often those who retained a deep sense of purpose. Not blind hope—purpose. Something to serve beyond the immediate terror. Modern military psychology backs this. Soldiers who maintain moral clarity under fire are less susceptible to trauma than those who feel their actions are incoherent with their values.

This has significant implications for families preparing for economic or geopolitical instability. Teaching your children how to operate a water filter is useful. But teaching them *why they are learning it*—framing it as stewardship, care for others, or preservation of freedom—roots the skill in an ethical backbone. When stress peaks, it is not technical skill but meaning that prevents collapse into despair.

Practically, how is calm trained?

First, through *ritualised stress exposure.* This is not the same as trauma. It's the deliberate practice of encountering difficulty in controlled conditions. Cold showers, fasting, navigation drills, communication tests—all are forms of inoculation. They normalise discomfort and build confidence that discomfort is survivable. This mirrors Stoic exercises like *premeditatio malorum*—the mental rehearsal of worst-case scenarios. Far from being morbid, this practice fosters resilience by shrinking the psychological shock of real events.

Second, through *language discipline.* Crisis amplifies language. A single shouted "we're trapped!" can destabilise a group. Therefore, cultivating non-reactive, specific communication habits within your household or team is critical. Instead of "We're out of food," say, "We have a three-day supply. Let's prioritise rationing." The Stoics were obsessed with language not because they were pedantic, but because they understood: *words shape perception, and perception determines action.*

Third, through *environmental design.* Calm is easier when one's surroundings do not scream emergency. Even in a bunker or during displacement, small rituals—tea, journaling, group reflection—can anchor individuals in agency. Psychological anchoring matters more than decor. Neuroscience confirms that predictability in routine—even micro-routines—lowers cortisol levels and preserves executive function under pressure. Every family or group should design simple, portable rituals: a shared song, a code phrase, a meal order. They become mental handrails when the world becomes disordered.

There is also value in *emotionally modelling calm.* Children, in particular, calibrate their emotional state by watching adults. If the parent panics, their anxiety multiplies. If the parent acknowledges difficulty but remains grounded, children often rise to the occasion with surprising maturity. This places a heavy but essential burden on leaders and heads of households: your composure is not personal—it is strategic.

Of course, none of this negates fear. *Fear is not the enemy. Panic is.* Fear alerts us to threat. Panic disables decision-making. The goal of cultivating calm is not to eliminate fear but to govern it. To use it as data, not destiny. In the same way a pilot respects turbulence but does not scream in the cockpit, the mentally trained individual recognises distress and continues to navigate.

Here, we must be careful to avoid the modern distortion of Stoicism as emotional suppression. The ancient Stoics did not advise eliminating feelings. They advised disciplining reactions. Seneca wrote extensively on grief. Marcus Aurelius, though emperor, wrote openly about exhaustion, injustice, and loss. Their genius was not detachment but *deliberate engagement.* They reminded themselves, daily, that external chaos was not a verdict on internal peace.

In practical preparation, families should institutionalise this mindset. Create a "calm protocol"—a pre-agreed set of actions and language used when certain triggers occur. If the internet goes down, we do X. If a protest breaks out nearby, we meet at Y. No speculation. Just actions. This mirrors elite crisis response units: clarity reduces panic. And clarity flows from forethought.

Lastly, calm requires *intellectual humility.* Many fail in crisis because they are too attached to a single plan, ideology, or prediction. They mistake the map for the terrain. But true Stoic calm is not brittle—it is adaptive. It is rooted in the assumption that uncertainty is the norm, and that *resilience is the ability to remain coherent in uncertainty.* The family that rehearses multiple evacuation routes, diversifies their assets, and keeps their identity modular is not paranoid—they are resilient.

Calm is not a natural state. It is earned. Trained. Cultivated through repeated exposure, philosophical anchoring, and deliberate structure. In an age where digital distraction erodes attention, where panic is amplified in real time, and where instability can unfold in days, cultivating calm is no longer optional. It is strategic.

And like any strategy worth its name, it begins long before it's needed.

Chapter 9
Escape Plans and Personal Protocols

When the moment to act finally arrives, the time for planning has already passed.

There comes a point in every conversation about resilience—be it financial, political, or personal—where reflection must yield to resolve. Theory, no matter how intellectually satisfying, must eventually surrender to the demands of reality. It's here, in the unglamorous realm of actual readiness, that this chapter takes its stand. If earlier sections have stirred doubts, questioned your dependencies, or opened your eyes to the quiet erosion of stability, this one asks something more difficult: that you do something about it.

This is the juncture at which strategy ceases to be an idea and becomes a choreography of deliberate, practiced movement. Quiet, perhaps even invisible from the outside, but precise: exit routes mapped, emergency bags packed, secondary accounts created, rehearsals run. Preparedness, real preparedness, is never loud. It's structured and lived. The line separating the aware from the truly ready is not drawn by knowledge alone—it is marked by rehearsal. And yet, in the noise of modern discourse, this most intimate form of resilience often goes unspoken. Why? Because it demands confrontation—confrontation with fear, with inertia, with one's obligations to others. Preparing to leave is not dramatic; it's deeply personal. It's often inconvenient. And that, ironically, is what makes it essential.

What follows is a structured passage from theory to execution—three domains of focus: evacuation, parallelism, and simulation. These are not abstract categories. They are operational fields. First, we examine the contours of personalised escape and relocation plans. This is not about adopting someone else's blueprint; it is about drafting your own—mapped to your realities: your geography, your obligations, your limitations. Where is the line you will not cross? What defines your red line? When would you go, where would you go, and what—specifically—would you take? These are not hypotheticals. They are preparatory diagnostics.

Next, we explore the notion of "shadow systems"—an unfortunate term, perhaps, but a necessary one. These refer to alternate infrastructures: parallel banking pathways, legal safe zones, and discreet communication lines. Not built for rebellion, but for resilience. Not illegal, but often neglected. Shadow systems are the practical scaffolding that permits temporary detachment—from a failing institution, a seized account, or a censored network. And while some may hear echoes of paranoia, the wise will recognise what diplomats, investigative journalists, and seasoned entrepreneurs already know: redundancy is not luxury—it's survival architecture.

Lastly, we turn to the human edge: simulation. Plans that reside in folders die at the first sign of stress. Under pressure, only what's been embodied survives. Here, we delve into the power of rehearsal: scenario drills, decision trees, and family-wide protocols that turn confusion into coordination. These simulations needn't be theatrical or dramatic. In fact, the more mundane, the better. Think like a pilot: emergency procedures aren't romantic—they're routine. Their very ordinariness is what makes them reliable when things go wrong.

This is not a manifesto for fleeing. It is not a call to disappear. It is an acknowledgment that even the best systems—governments, banks, networks, currencies—sometimes falter. That readiness is not a sign of fear, but of seriousness. Consider the examples that history hands us, often coldly: professionals in Venezuela who waited too long, clinging to status while their savings vanished. Afghan families caught in the fall of Kabul with no backup plan.

Ukrainians scrambling for the border with no access to funds. What they lacked wasn't awareness. It was execution.

And the comfortable should not be complacent. The last few years have reminded even those in the so-called safe zones: borders can close, ATMs can go dark, airports can shut without warning, and internet lines can vanish under a minister's order. These aren't dystopian fantasies. They're logged events. So ask yourself: if you had fifteen minutes to leave your home, could you? If your bank accounts were frozen overnight, how would you operate? If you lost signal and couldn't contact your family, what would you fall back on?

To ignore these questions is not peace. It's fragility dressed up as calm.

Yet even as we lean into the practical, there's a moral thread running through all of this. Preparedness must never become a fortress mindset. True readiness, rightly conceived, is not a withdrawal from others—it's a way to better serve them. The person who is not panicked can assist. The family with a plan can shelter others. Resilience, when properly stewarded, becomes an act of generosity.

Let's also be honest: no plan is eternal. You change. Your family changes. Borders shift. Technology evolves. The plan must live, evolve, and be rehearsed accordingly. It should be reviewed the way a pilot checks an aircraft—frequently, even if nothing seems wrong. Especially then.

But all of this infrastructure—legal, logistical, digital—still rests upon the most unpredictable element of all: the human psyche. Many fail not because they lacked a plan, but because they couldn't act on it. Paralysed by fear, guilt, or disbelief, they falter when resolve is required. This is where pre-commitments come in. You must know in advance: what will tip the scale for you? What's the line that, if crossed, triggers motion? And, more subtly, do you grant yourself permission to act? Because no matter how well constructed the blueprint, if the mind hesitates at the critical moment, everything falls.

Let this also be your caution: once you engage with what follows, you will not be able to retreat to comfortable ignorance. You'll see gaps you had overlooked. You'll feel the weight of postponed decisions. That's intentional. Awareness is not always pleasant—but it is always the beginning of strength. This is not the chapter for comfort. It is the chapter for competence. And competence is built—methodically, deliberately, without drama.

You've now entered what may be the most tangible, demanding, and liberating section of this book. It doesn't trade in speculative doom or preach technocratic fixes. It asks more of you. To write the plan. Build the fallback. Rehearse the break. Share the protocol. Update the variables. Face the discomfort.

Because when the system buckles—and history, not theory, assures us that some systems will—what matters is not how surprised you were.

What matters is whether you could move.

The Chaos Protocol Map – A Tiered Response Map Built on Specific Triggers

The illusion of order is not merely a feature of modern civilisation—it is its cornerstone. Behind every traffic light, tax bracket, and government-issued forecast lies an implicit belief: that tomorrow will resemble today. And yet, history demonstrates otherwise. Collapses rarely arrive unannounced; they begin with whispers, with anomalies that slip past the inattentive. For the alert, the objective is not prediction—it is preparation. And preparation demands a framework. Enter the *Chaos Protocol Map*: a tiered decision-making structure that empowers individuals and families to respond rationally, not reactively, to breakdowns in economic, political, or social systems.

This map does not offer guarantees. It offers process. Its purpose is not to amplify fear but to neutralise panic through pre-commitment to actions grounded in thoughtful thresholds. Think of it not as a manual for the apocalypse, but as a protocol for maintaining sovereignty when systems lose theirs.

The Problem with Waiting

Throughout history, delay has been the downfall of many. The comfortable German-Jewish professionals who assumed Hitler's radicalism would moderate. The affluent Venezuelan families who dismissed early signs of inflation as cyclical. The Afghan translators who trusted exit promises until the very last plane left Kabul. These stories are not abstract warnings—they are pattern recognition exercises.

People fail to act not because they are ignorant, but because they are emotionally entangled with the world they know. The Chaos Protocol Map exists to short-circuit that bias. It embeds rationality into pre-crisis thinking so that decisions made in calm carry through into chaos. The key to this system is tiering: layered responses tied to *specific, observable* triggers.

Let's examine the framework.

Tier 1: Monitoring Signals – The Era of Subtle Decay

Tier 1 begins with pattern detection, not disruption. This stage requires no immediate action but demands heightened attentiveness. The defining feature of Tier 1 is *systemic ambiguity*—indicators emerge, but clarity is absent. Like the first clouds in an otherwise clear sky, they don't justify retreat, but they demand that one stop ignoring the weather.

Examples of Tier 1 triggers might include:

Currency instability or stealth capital controls (e.g., Argentina's creeping withdrawal limits)

Sudden resignations of key government officials amid corruption accusations

Unexplained internet outages tied to political events

Shifts in property rights enforcement or banking regulations without legislative debate

At this stage, the protocols are diagnostic: review existing exit and asset plans, update residency paperwork, test the functionality of digital backups, review foreign accounts, and conduct a full family risk audit. *You are not escaping here. You are refining your capability to escape.*

It is also the moment to establish a communication hierarchy. If you have dependents, this is when you rehearse "just-in-case" check-in protocols. Quietly. Without drama. Preparation at Tier 1 is like installing a sprinkler system—not because the house is on fire, but because it could be.

Tier 2: Strategic Movement – Fractures Become Visible

By Tier 2, the system is visibly fraying. The warning signs are no longer speculative—they have materialised. The currency no longer holds value in practice. The government starts targeting specific groups with asset freezes or arbitrary detentions. Supply chains show structural disruptions. Social unrest is no longer episodic but sustained.

Common Tier 2 triggers include:

Emergency powers enacted beyond natural disasters

Escalating civil-military tensions or mobilisation

Passport controls tightening without clear cause

Confiscatory taxation or forced conversions (e.g., Lebanon's "Lollars")

This is the phase where *partial action* becomes necessary. Think: portfolio diversification becomes portfolio evacuation. Tangible steps include:

Liquidating in-country assets where feasible

Relocating family members to a stable fallback zone under the guise of education, medical care, or sabbatical

Securing alternate communications infrastructure (e.g., satellite phones, decentralised messaging apps)

Redeploying mobile capital into transportable, secure forms—gold, crypto, or legally portable fiat

Crucially, Tier 2 is not necessarily the moment to run. But it is the point of no further inaction. You may still have weeks, even months, but you no longer have the luxury of uncertainty. If you're unsure whether you've entered Tier 2, you're already late.

Tier 3: Emergency Exit – The Window Narrows

By Tier 3, institutional legitimacy is collapsing in real time. Borders may remain physically open, but the true closures are logistical: flights are unavailable, passports are voided, funds are frozen, and narratives shift from "this will pass" to "you should have left."

Tier 3 signals include:

Martial law or military-on-civilian enforcement outside declared war zones

Mass detentions of political dissidents, journalists, or protestors

Banking system "holidays" or ATM shutdowns

Diplomatic evacuations by foreign consulates

This tier is about *velocity and minimalism.* Your plan is no longer theoretical—it is the script you act out under pressure. If you're negotiating with yourself, the map failed. Exit should have already been gamed out, rehearsed, and resourced. Tier 3 is where failures of imagination become irreparable.

Those who survive Tier 3 intact are not necessarily lucky. They are prepared. They have redundant passports, rehearsed border crossings, stored travel cash outside their home currency, and assets offshore—legally and pre-positioned. They aren't acting on instinct; they're following a protocol that was designed in calmer times.

Protocols vs. Panic: Why Pre-Commitment Matters

Human behaviour under stress regresses toward the primitive. In crisis, abstraction is a liability. That's why *decision architecture* matters. The Chaos Protocol Map isn't merely a flowchart. It is a commitment device. Pre-committed actions grounded in observable, public signals are your defence against paralysis. You don't "feel" your way through collapse. You follow the map.

The map works because it:

Converts abstract risks into observable thresholds

Ties actions to triggers, not emotions

Distributes decisions across time, preventing last-minute scrambles

Helps avoid binary thinking ("Stay or go?") by offering graduated responses

Importantly, these protocols are designed to be *reversible* in Tier 1 and Tier 2. You can always step back—until you can't. The goal is not to escape needlessly, but to never be stuck *trying* to escape while others already have.

Designing Your Personal Protocol Map

The architecture of your own Chaos Protocol Map must be tailored to your geography, citizenship, profession, and family dynamics. A journalist in Hong Kong requires different Tier 2 triggers than a retiree in Lisbon. A family of five cannot react with the same velocity as a single entrepreneur.

Questions to ask when designing your protocol:

What signals would force me to act—even if it feels premature?

Where are my friction points: passports, dependents, capital controls, health needs?

What alternate jurisdictions align with my values, legal obligations, and access?

Who do I trust to act as my proxy, relay, or secondary decision-maker if I'm cut off?

This process is not merely logistical. It is philosophical. It requires clarity on what matters most: safety, sovereignty, mobility, continuity. Your responses must protect those priorities in descending order of constraint.

Beyond the Individual: Protocols for Family, Team, or Organisation

While most protocols begin with the individual, they must scale to family units, business partners, or even small communities. Clarity matters more than consensus. It is better to have a divergent but functional protocol than a democratic deadlock in crisis.

One technique is to establish *trigger-action pairs* that everyone understands. For example:

If X occurs (e.g., government shuts down international bank transfers), then Y must happen (e.g., begin flight booking via international agent using offshore card).

If Z is confirmed (e.g., national ID system goes offline), then initiate Plan C (e.g., move to border town with transport cache and standby fuel).

When everyone knows the rules in advance, panic dissolves into procedure.

Final Insight: Collapse is a Gradient, Not a Moment

Perhaps the most dangerous myth surrounding systemic collapse is that it happens *all at once.* In reality, most collapses are protracted—and survivable—for those with foresight. The map is your scaffold. Without it, you're improvising in the dark.

The Chaos Protocol Map does not predict the future. It gives you leverage against its uncertainty. It will not eliminate risk, but it can reallocate it—away from luck and toward structure, away from panic and toward protocol.

The ultimate lesson is this: *Do not wait for clarity. Wait for your trigger—and then move decisively.*

Personal Evacuation and Relocation Plans – Designing Actionable Blueprints for Escape

There is a psychological gravity that binds people to place—an almost invisible inertia powered by routine, familiarity, and identity. But systems, like bodies, can fail. And when they do, those who survive aren't the strongest or most optimistic. They are the most prepared. Yet very few people ever develop a concrete, functional evacuation and relocation plan. The common reasons range from denial to decision fatigue. But excuses are not strategies. *The absence of a plan is itself a decision—a high-risk gamble based on the continued goodwill of systems you do not control.*

This chapter is not about fear. It is about freedom of movement—freedom from naivety, from logistical chaos, and from being forced to react under pressure. A proper evacuation plan is the civilian equivalent of a parachute: boring to carry, essential when needed.

The goal of this subchapter is clear: *to help you design a realistic, tiered, and fully executable escape and relocation blueprint tailored to your actual constraints.* Not a fantasy plan, not a wish-list, and not a bunker-bound caricature—but a system rooted in geography, psychology, legal frameworks, and real-world logistics.

The Myth of Spontaneous Escape

There is a persistent cinematic myth that escape is about grabbing a go-bag and running into the night. This fantasy dissolves quickly when confronted with border controls, missing passports, disabled financial accounts, closed embassies, and dependent family members asking, "What now?" Evacuation is not an improvisation. It is an *orchestration.* It requires rehearsal, sequencing, and resource redundancy.

There are five interdependent layers in any serious personal escape plan:

Trigger Conditions

Evacuation Routes

Transport and Transit Strategy

Destination Infrastructure

Continuity of Identity and Assets

Each layer must be defined, rehearsed, and, when possible, de-risked.

1. Trigger Conditions – Defining the Threshold for Action

The first failure point in most crisis situations is hesitation. People wait too long. They rationalise away danger. They delay action, hoping for clarity. A robust evacuation plan begins by *pre-defining the triggers that compel activation.*

These triggers must be external, observable, and agreed upon in advance. Examples include:

Closure of international banking gateways

Imposition of martial law or emergency decrees without legislative oversight

Internet shutdowns coinciding with political purges

Seizure or freezing of private property under "security" pretexts

The critical insight here is this: If you wait until evacuation "feels" necessary, you are too late.

These triggers should be documented—not debated in real-time. They are the signal to move from readiness to execution.

2. Evacuation Routes – Planning for Movement Under Constraint

You don't leave *from* your home. You leave *through* your geography. That includes roads, borders, checkpoints, airports, ports, or natural terrain. Each offers different vulnerabilities.

Primary routes are conventional—international airports, expressways, official border crossings.

Secondary routes are semi-official—smaller land crossings, regional transport hubs, ferry ports.

Tertiary routes are unconventional—small boats, mountain passes, or land routes accessible only under duress.

The viability of these routes depends on your region, citizenship status, and the nature of the disruption. A well-constructed plan includes multiple pathways, tested by travel when possible. Knowing the alternate road out of your city is not a luxury—it's a necessity. In several nations, from Myanmar to Ukraine, the difference between safe escape and entrapment came down to one unblocked road.

Evacuation is geography's test of your strategic imagination.

3. Transport and Transit – Don't Assume Access

Plans built on access to personal vehicles or commercial flights are often fragile. In Tier 3 conditions (immediate crisis), fuel stations may be empty, airports flooded with people, and checkpoints politicised. You need *fallback transport modalities*.

This includes:

Pre-arranged transportation via trusted contacts or private services

Physical currency and fuel caches at known staging areas

Transit documents stored in redundant physical and digital formats

Resilience against digital restrictions (e.g., phone apps failing at border control)

Also consider *exit redundancies*:

Can you move without internet?

Without a functioning debit card?

Without luggage?

The moment you discover which resource is essential but inaccessible is the moment the plan fails. *Stress-test your assumptions ahead of time.*

4. Destination Infrastructure – Escaping to What?

An evacuation is not only a departure; it is a *transition into continuity*. What awaits you at the other end? The best-designed plans include legally viable destinations where you can re-establish identity, access finances, and find temporary or long-term safety.

There are three classes of destination to plan for:

Legal fallback: second citizenship or residency permit with guaranteed re-entry

Networked fallback: property, family, or institutional ties (e.g., a friend's business, an NGO safe house)

Transactional fallback: jurisdictions where you can enter with minimal visa requirements and rent stability short-term (e.g., Georgia, Mexico, Serbia, Panama)

Importantly, your destination must be chosen not just for safety—but for *sovereign compatibility*. Is it stable, financially liberalised, and free from political alignment with your country of origin? Safety is more than physical—it's jurisdictional.

5. Continuity of Identity and Assets – Escape Without Disappearance

Many people mistakenly plan as if they are going into hiding. But most of us will need to *resume normal life*—work, education, digital access, banking—soon after relocation. The personal evacuation blueprint must preserve continuity.

This includes:

Digital infrastructure: access to email, two-factor authentication, cryptocurrency keys, encrypted backups

Legal identity: valid passports, birth/marriage certificates, digital copies of academic and medical records

Financial continuity: accounts in stable jurisdictions, assets stored offshore, crypto wallets recoverable without the original device

This infrastructure must be tested. If you can't access your second bank account from your mobile on a VPN while travelling, you're not prepared.

Evacuation without identity is exile. Evacuation with continuity is repositioning.

Real-World Lessons: A Case Study in Timeliness

In 2021, Afghan interpreters who had collaborated with NATO forces faced an escalating risk. Many delayed applying for evacuation visas until the Taliban were at the gates of Kabul. Paperwork bottlenecks, frozen email systems, and fear of retaliation paralysed families. Those who had prepared second-country legal entry, scanned their documents, pre-booked transport, and coordinated with support networks made it out. Those who waited on promises were trapped.

What distinguished these groups? Not courage, but *readiness*. The same could be said of Jewish families who left Germany in 1936 vs. 1939. Those who evacuated early often had time to pack heirlooms, secure funds, and relocate strategically. Those who waited fled with nothing—or didn't flee at all.

Designing Your Escape Blueprint: Philosophical Groundwork

Before logistics, one must confront values. What are you unwilling to leave behind? What are you willing to compromise temporarily to preserve the long game? These questions are not sentimental. They are structural.

A family with young children and a home business will design differently than a digital nomad with dual citizenship. Some may prioritise speed; others discretion. *The key is designing with honest constraints—not hypothetical freedom.*

Begin by creating a personal or family *Evacuation Protocol Document* that includes:

Predefined triggers

Family rendezvous point

Route and backup routes

Asset grab list and access methods

Transport mode and fallback plans

Destination infrastructure readiness

Communications backup

Financial continuity strategy

Review this document at least annually. Rehearse it. Make it muscle memory.

Final Thought: Escape Is a Skill, Not a Panic Response

There is dignity in planning. There is sovereignty in foresight. Designing your personal evacuation and relocation plan is not paranoia—it is prudence. In systems where stability is assumed, contingency planning is a superpower. As the global terrain becomes less predictable, the capacity to *move* becomes as vital as the capacity to think.

An actionable escape plan does not make you a pessimist. It makes you capable.

Shadow Accounts and Parallel Systems – Legal and Effective Ways to Build Minimal-Friction Alternatives

It is often assumed—implicitly by citizens and explicitly by authorities—that an individual's financial and logistical infrastructure must exist entirely within the framework of their nation-state. Most people live, earn, store, and transact within one jurisdiction, in one currency, and under one tax authority. This alignment is rarely questioned until crisis strikes. But in an age of hyper-surveillance, political instability, weaponised finance, and abrupt border closures, this alignment ceases to be a matter of convenience and becomes a point of vulnerability.

Shadow accounts and parallel systems are not about criminal evasion or subversive disobedience—they are about legal resilience. They represent a strategic decoupling from single-point failure. When designed ethically and executed properly, they offer a sophisticated framework for maintaining mobility, continuity, and agency in an increasingly unpredictable world.

This article is not about offshoring for secrecy or tax avoidance. It is about building a *redundant architecture of access and control*—a distributed set of financial, digital, and operational tools that function even when conventional systems falter.

The Fragility of Total Dependence

One need not look far to witness the consequences of over-dependence. In 2015, when capital controls were introduced in Greece, citizens were limited to withdrawing €60 per day. Long queues formed at ATMs while banks shuttered. The following year, India's demonetisation wiped out 86% of the currency in circulation almost overnight, creating widespread chaos for individuals and small businesses. More recently, in Russia and Argentina, sudden currency devaluations rendered local bank balances half-worthless in real terms within weeks.

In these cases, individuals who had *no secondary pathways*—no foreign currency accounts, no offshore digital wallets, no access to crypto, no extraterritorial payment processors—were trapped in a liquidity bottleneck. The lesson here is not alarmist; it is actuarial. It speaks to the *need for graceful failover*, akin to how data systems use backup nodes and mirrored servers.

Shadow Accounts: Definition and Function

In the context of this framework, a "shadow account" is not illegal or secretive. It is any *legal financial or logistical structure* that exists outside the default domestic environment. These may include:

Foreign bank accounts in politically neutral jurisdictions

Offshore payment wallets (e.g., Wise, Revolut, Payoneer)

Secondary SIM cards or eSIMs registered to foreign carriers

Digital wallets for cryptocurrencies held in cold storage or via DeFi protocols

International brokerage accounts not tied to a single national ID

Cloud-based encrypted vaults for storing critical personal or business documents

These accounts *do not replace* primary systems, but complement them. They are designed to give the individual optionality—not in a utopian sense of escape, but in the practical sense of maintaining control when circumstances shift.

The question is not *"How do I hide?"* but *"How do I stay operational when others freeze?"*

Parallel Systems: Operating Beyond the Default Grid

While shadow accounts focus on storage and access, *parallel systems* speak to process and structure. They answer a deeper question: *How do I maintain functionality when the dominant system is offline, compromised, or weaponised against me?*

Consider the following examples:

Communication: Using end-to-end encrypted tools such as Signal or Session over Tor or mesh networks rather than SMS or standard email, which can be surveilled or blocked.

Income Generation: Building location-independent income through freelancing platforms, royalties, or decentralised gig networks that pay in stablecoins or foreign currencies.

Authentication and Identity: Possessing secondary forms of ID (where legal), maintaining e-residencies (e.g., Estonia), and separating identity from activity using privacy-preserving digital identities.

Storage and Collaboration: Using decentralised file storage (e.g., IPFS, Skiff) instead of Google Drive or Dropbox, especially for critical documents and intellectual property.

Business Structures: Registering LLCs or IBCs in pro-business jurisdictions (e.g., UAE, Singapore, Estonia) that allow legal remote operation, reducing dependence on local regulatory climates.

Each parallel system functions like a lifeboat tied to the main ship. You don't use it every day—but you want it seaworthy when it counts.

Legal, Ethical, and Strategic Clarity

A common question raised about such systems is: *Is this legal?* The answer lies in *how* one sets up and uses them. Owning a bank account in Singapore while living in Germany is not illegal if declared. Using a foreign payment processor to receive freelance income is not illegal if reported. The distinction lies in transparency with relevant tax authorities and compliance with local and international regulations such as FATCA, CRS, or AML requirements.

What distinguishes ethical use from grey-market misuse is intent and disclosure. The purpose is *resilience*, not concealment; *continuity*, not evasion.

It is not a loophole game. It is an architecture of optionality designed for *systemic redundancy*, not regulatory arbitrage.

Psychological Resistance to Parallel Systems

Despite the logic, many professionals—even those intellectually convinced—fail to act. Why? Because the dominant system encourages passivity through convenience and perceived stability. We are taught from birth to trust the institutions around us: banks, passports, telecom networks, health records. Taking responsibility for redundant systems introduces mental friction—*it feels like distrust.* And yet, the most successful organisations—from militaries to hedge funds—are built on redundancy.

Trust is not a plan. Trust is a luxury of calm periods. In crisis, systems—not sentiments—determine outcomes.

Psychologically, individuals may feel that creating parallel systems is too technical or expensive. But most of the essential components are not only accessible, but increasingly user-friendly: international fintech platforms, secure cloud drives, digital notarisation, encrypted communication tools, and multi-signature crypto wallets have never been easier to set up.

The real barrier is *conceptual inertia*—the assumption that what works today will work tomorrow, and that preparing for exception is paranoid rather than prudent.

Redundancy as a Personal Philosophy

Professionals diversify investment portfolios, but rarely diversify systems of access, income, and identification. This is a fatal inconsistency. In an interconnected world subject to discontinuous shocks—pandemics, sanctions, cyberattacks, border closures, censorship, capital controls—resilience demands more than a diversified asset class. It demands a *diversified architecture of life.*

This architecture must be:

Legally compliant

Technically discreet

Logistically simple

Psychologically preloaded

Meaning: it must be easy to activate, invisible to casual observation, and aligned with both the letter of the law and the spirit of personal autonomy.

To function under stress, *shadow systems must be rehearsed, not just designed.* Cold wallets should be tested. Redundant logins practiced. Access credentials shared with trusted family or fiduciaries. A dead-letter protocol—clear instructions in the event of incapacity—must exist.

Case Study: The Freelancer in Exile

Consider a Ukrainian software engineer in 2022 who held assets only in hryvnia, worked through a local agency, and had no foreign bank account or alternative payment method. When war broke out, banks paused. The engineer was locked out of savings and income. Compare this to another peer who had a Payoneer account receiving USD, a cold wallet with stablecoins, a digital mailbox in Estonia, and a second SIM tied to a neutral jurisdiction. That person kept working, kept earning, and could relocate without liquidity constraints.

The difference between collapse and continuity is often not the magnitude of crisis, but the design of systems behind the scenes.

Final Thought: Freedom is Infrastructure

In the end, the lesson is not about survivalism or secrecy—it is about *infrastructure.* Freedom is not merely a philosophical condition; it is a logistical one. *Whoever controls your payments, your documents, your communications, your access—controls your life.* To reclaim this autonomy legally and responsibly requires forethought, not panic; proactivity, not paranoia.

Shadow accounts and parallel systems are not extreme. They are prudent. They are not fringe; they are becoming best practice among those who understand that the world is no longer linear, and that optionality is not a luxury, but a necessity.

The well-prepared individual of the future will not merely be a citizen of one nation—but a self-sovereign node in a globally resilient network of trust, tools, and access.

Scenario Drills and Family Simulations – Exercises to Turn Plans into Muscle Memory

The most robust evacuation plan is useless if it cannot be recalled under pressure. The most well-stocked emergency kit, if locked away in a forgotten cupboard, becomes little more than theatre. In a real crisis, *reaction supplants cognition*, and decisions are made not in calm reflection but in split seconds governed by muscle memory and emotional conditioning. In such moments, preparation must transcend theory. This is the purpose of scenario drills and family simulations: to translate contingency into competency.

Intelligent families don't just plan—they rehearse. They do not assume cooperation; they test it. They do not trust in static protocols; they stress-test dynamic behaviours. The aim is not perfection but priming: calibrating minds and systems so that, when the unpredictable becomes reality, action is automatic.

Why Plans Fail Under Pressure

To understand the critical importance of simulation, we must first grasp the basic psychology of stress. Under acute pressure—especially in novel, high-stakes scenarios—the prefrontal cortex, responsible for rational thinking and executive function, is compromised. The brain defaults to its faster, more primitive systems: *fight, flight, or freeze*. This is not weakness; it is biology.

From airline pilots to fire captains to trauma surgeons, elite professionals know that *competence under pressure is a trained response*. It cannot be improvised. This is why simulations—not reading, not thinking, not talking—form the backbone of any high-performance response culture.

In families, where cohesion must be voluntary and no one wears a uniform, this lesson is even more vital. Children freeze. Parents over-function. Hierarchies collapse. Unless *roles are known, rehearsed, and retrievable*, chaos reigns.

The Anatomy of an Effective Scenario Drill

An effective scenario drill is not simply an alarm and a stopwatch. It is a full-cycle rehearsal that mirrors the complexity, unpredictability, and psychological load of a real event. A family's emergency protocol must account for physical readiness, decision-making clarity, emotional resilience, and team coordination.

A scenario drill must be:

Specific: A defined trigger and scenario (e.g., power outage plus external civil unrest)

Timed: Actions must occur under clock pressure

Measured: Review who did what, when, how accurately, and how calmly

Debriefed: The exercise must end with reflection and adjustment

Drills are not about creating fear; they are about creating *familiarity*. The point is not to mimic a Hollywood-level collapse, but to ensure that *key decisions are rehearsed into the nervous system.*

From Plans to Protocols to Habits

Most families, if they have any plan at all, keep it in a folder or a spreadsheet. These are often static, incomplete, and untested. A true protocol is not a document but a *living system.* And like any system, it must be updated, practised, and refined.

For example:

Knowing the evacuation route on paper is insufficient; you must *walk it* at different times of day and under different conditions.

Knowing the location of passports is insufficient; each family member must *retrieve and pack them in under 60 seconds.*

Knowing the go-bag contents is insufficient; you must *simulate living off them for 24 hours*, including with children or elderly relatives.

Memory degrades under stress. Muscle memory survives.

Psychological Calibration: Training the Mind, Not Just the Map

A common mistake in emergency planning is the overemphasis on logistics and underinvestment in psychology. In reality, *mindset is the multiplier of strategy*. A child who panics in a shelter drill is unlikely to follow commands during a real evacuation. A parent who cannot regulate their own nervous system will inadvertently increase household stress during the very event they are supposed to manage.

Here, tools from Stoicism and survival psychology become operational. Repeated exposure to controlled adversity—*cold, hunger, uncertainty, boredom, noise*—builds emotional tolerance. Role-playing difficult conversations and unpredictable reactions (e.g., a missing pet, a wounded neighbour, a corrupt official) trains *cognitive flexibility*. By simulating not only procedures but emotional conditions, we teach our families not only what to do—but who to be.

This is not "toughness training." It is *dignified self-governance under duress*.

The Family as a Decision-Making Unit

During crisis, ambiguity multiplies. Should we leave or stay? Which route is safest? Who calls whom? Without pre-defined delegation of authority, families default to hesitation or argument. Every second counts.

A clear simulation script can include:

Designated leader(s) for decision-making

Backup contacts in case of mobile service failure

Communication protocols (e.g., signal apps, walkie-talkie codes)

Check-in locations if separated

These are not militaristic impositions. They are compassionate tools to prevent panic and paralysis.

And they must be rehearsed. Once annually is insufficient. Quarterly is ideal. In high-risk areas, even monthly micro-drills are appropriate. Just as we test fire alarms, we should test *family coherence.*

Simulations That Mirror Modern Risk

Legacy survival training often focuses on wilderness skills or rural retreat scenarios. But today's collapse scenarios are more likely to be *urban, digital, financial, or legal.* Families must simulate not only wildfires and floods, but also:

Cyber outage: What happens if Google, banking, and mobile services go dark for 48 hours?

Legal surprise: What if border guards confiscate your devices and ask for passwords?

Travel lockdown: How do you extract a family member stuck in a foreign jurisdiction?

Financial freeze: How do you operate for 72 hours if banks suspend withdrawals?

Simulations must match likely risk vectors—not nostalgic fantasies. They must account for complexity, including mixed-citizenship households, elderly or disabled dependents, and modern constraints such as digital IDs or biometric checkpoints.

Teaching Without Trauma

The goal of family simulation is not to terrify children into compliance. It is to build *calm confidence through competence.* For younger family members, the approach must be developmental—using gamification, role-play, and positive reinforcement. A "blackout weekend" can become a fun challenge rather than a punishment. A "go-bag race" becomes a bonding activity, not a dystopian drill.

The tone matters: *preparedness is not paranoia—it's love in practical form.* We do not prepare because we fear collapse. We prepare so that our values and our agency *survive collapse.*

After-Action Reviews: Where Real Growth Happens

Every simulation must end with an honest debrief. What worked? What broke? Who forgot what? What emotions came up? This feedback loop is where the plan becomes personalised, and the protocol becomes *family culture.*

These reviews also foster ownership. Children and spouses begin to feel like participants, not passengers. They begin to spot gaps, suggest improvements, and build their own confidence. The simulation becomes not an imposition—but a platform for shared responsibility.

Preparedness, in the deepest sense, is not about control. It is about capacity.

Chapter 10
The New Frontier – Designing Post-Collapse Life

Collapse is so often imagined as a clean break—the lights flickering out, systems going dark, governments dissolving into either chaos or silence. Yet the truth, as told by both history and the human psyche, is rather more subtle. Collapse doesn't merely extinguish order; it redraws the scale. It compresses sprawling systems into something more human-sized, localised, and tangible. Power retracts, relationships surface, and—if we're attentive—possibilities begin to flicker at the edges. Collapse isn't solely about destruction; it's a clearing, a rare and raw moment in which the old loses its grip and something else, not yet formed, can begin.

This chapter isn't an ode to bunkers or off-grid escapism. Nor is it a call to withdraw into solitary self-sufficiency. It's about leaning into the latent opportunities that emerge once the edifices of centralised governance, monopolistic economies, and inherited legitimacy begin to crack. This is a guide not for the retreating, but for the remakers—for those who sense that surviving the future is not enough, and who are ready to begin shaping what comes next. The New Frontier is not only geographic. It is conceptual. Legal. Spiritual. It's terrain available to those willing to move beyond the conventional borders of obedience.

The nation-state, once a marvel of coordination and identity, is ageing poorly. Its core promises—security, fairness, competence—are fraying, often quite visibly. In that widening breach, new forms of order are surfacing. These aren't speculative thought experiments. They're functional, if embryonic, alternatives: decentralised governance protocols spun from blockchain consensus, floating communities exploring legal autonomy at sea, small intentional enclaves refusing the terms of mass society. The uniting thread? Not ideology, but structural pluralism. A rejection of singular authority in favour of distributed legitimacy—governance that is chosen, not imposed.

Still, before we can discuss what might emerge, we must speak clearly about what it is we're leaving. Collapse doesn't arrive with a Hollywood score. It seeps in—quiet, cumulative, and unremarkable until it's everywhere. A slow erosion of trust. Institutions failing not with drama, but with indifference. Consider Argentina in 2001—not a collapse in the cinematic sense, but a slow bleed of credibility. Lebanon's state didn't vanish; its middle class did. And in the United States? Legal recourse is often reserved for those who can afford the privilege. Medical consistency is a postcode lottery. Accountability is more aspirational than real. Collapse isn't total. It's uneven. And that unevenness makes navigating it a uniquely complex task.

But this isn't merely about navigating. It's about designing—intentionally.

First comes the matter of sovereignty. The proliferation of micro-nations, cloud republics, and decentralised states isn't science fiction anymore; it's geopolitics evolving in real time. From Estonia's e-residency to Liberland's legal provocation on a Danube island, sovereignty is shifting from flags and armies to code, capital, and coherent narrative. A sovereign entity today might be a DAO (decentralised autonomous organisation) with its own dispute resolution, treasury, and voluntary citizenry. Or a private city, governed by a bespoke charter. Or a transnational community whose members have never met in person but live by shared norms etched in code. As trust in traditional states wanes, legitimacy is being rewired—less by geography, more by functionality.

The second design space is inward. There is a spiritual architecture to escape—one that is too often ignored. Without it, the most elaborate logistical plan becomes hollow, a kind of mobile panic.

To really step away from failing systems, one must first step away from their seductions—the illusory safety of titles, the dopamine economy of digital scheduling, the hollow prestige of centralised validation. This is not an abandonment of responsibility. It's a recalibration. For some, that means letting go of professional credentials that no longer confer stability. For others, it's rediscovering time—not as an industrial resource to be managed, but as a rhythm rooted in place, relationships, and meaning. The Stoics called it ataraxia—a serene clarity untouched by the chaos of outcomes. That's not detachment. That's agency.

Indeed, the most acute symptom of societal breakdown may not be material deprivation, but existential disorientation. When institutions falter, people don't just lose access to services—they lose the scripts by which they made sense of their lives. Direction, then, becomes the design imperative: What are we orienting toward? What rituals need renewal? What patterns of control must be decentralised, and what old habits abandoned altogether?

Which brings us to the most urgent frontier: the project of rebuilding. Too often, those attuned to collapse fall into the aesthetic of escape—always watching, always warning, never creating. But disengagement is not a viable long game. It's a holding pattern. The real challenge, the generative challenge, is to begin building new orders—not just for oneself, but as templates others might inherit or adapt. Resilience that doesn't scale is just insulation.

Where to begin? Scale matters. The most enduring post-collapse systems tend to be small, but not simplistic. They are intimate enough to foster trust, yet structured enough to distribute roles—legal, economic, even spiritual. Historical precedents abound: the Amish, with their community-centred governance; the Swiss cantons, balancing autonomy with federal coherence; cooperative societies where resource cycles are embedded in shared ownership. Modern equivalents are surfacing: cohousing networks, permaculture enclaves, digital guilds that blend decentralised infrastructure with relational depth.

This is also the moment for jurisdictional entrepreneurship. In the past, map lines were redrawn by monarchs. Now, civic technologists are reimagining governance itself. They're drafting new charters, writing governance algorithms, testing alternative currencies. Not from utopian zeal, but from sober recognition that monopoly governance is brittle. These movements are plural. Some bend libertarian, others communitarian. But all share one principle: the belief that power must not calcify.

And here's the paradox: multiplicity is not chaos. It is the precondition for resilience. It allows communities to define success on their own terms. It invites economic and legal experimentation. It replaces fragility with variation. But you don't get to benefit from this renaissance as a spectator. You have to join in. The frameworks in this chapter are not for theorising—they are for applying. Legally, ethically, responsibly.

A final word, perhaps the most essential: dignity. The survivalist narrative too often reduces the human to a collection of needs—food, shelter, protection. But a life worth preserving requires something more: connection, story, music, ritual, a shared sense of what matters. Without these, we are merely surviving, not living. The future we build—if it is to be worthy of us—must attend to the aesthetic and the moral as much as the mechanical.

You're not here because you're frightened. You're here because you've decided not to be passive. You understand that resilience is more than preparation. It is design. It is participation. It is a refusal to cede one's life to the failures of inherited systems.

This chapter is a map—not out of collapse, but through it. Toward something built, chosen, and worth inheriting.

Post-System Prosperity – Imagines new micro-economies and ways to flourish beyond old systems

The concept of prosperity has long been tethered to legacy systems—national currencies, central banks, global financial institutions, formal employment structures, and regulated markets. These constructs, built during the industrial and post-industrial eras, form the scaffolding of what most consider the "normal" economic environment. Yet, their fragility has become increasingly apparent. From 2008's banking collapse to the recent global disruptions of supply chains and sovereign debt crises, the illusion of permanence has been shattered. The world is entering a new economic epoch: one that no longer guarantees continuity, predictability, or even relevance for traditional financial models.

Post-system prosperity is not a dystopian fantasy or a libertarian dreamscape. It is an emerging necessity for individuals and families seeking to remain economically viable—and even thrive—when existing institutions falter. It reframes wealth not as accumulation within a closed system, but as adaptive capability across decentralised, flexible, and often informal structures.

To navigate this shift, we must examine not only what's breaking down but also what's breaking through.

Replacing Trust with Design: The Collapse of Centralised Confidence

Every economy relies on trust. In traditional systems, that trust is conferred upon institutions: banks to protect savings, governments to honour debt, courts to enforce contracts. But when those institutions become unreliable—whether due to corruption, incompetence, or systemic overload—prosperity must be reimagined through *design*, not deference.

Post-system prosperity begins with this pivot: the conscious reallocation of reliance from hierarchical institutions to *intentional systems*. These are not lawless, but law-generative; not chaotic, but self-regulating. Communities don't wait for fiat; they create functionality through decentralised mechanisms that embed accountability and resilience. Blockchain technology is one form. Mutual credit networks, reputation-based trade systems, time banking, and autonomous cooperatives are others.

Take the example of Sardex in Sardinia, Italy—a regional mutual credit system founded during the European debt crisis. Sardex allowed businesses to trade goods and services without using euros, enabling liquidity when banks refused to lend. The currency gained such traction that thousands of firms joined, reinvigorating local commerce in the face of macroeconomic dysfunction.

This is not merely a workaround. It is a philosophical inversion: from central trust and top-down control to peer-generated economic coherence.

Sovereignty from the Bottom Up: The Rise of Network Micro-Economies

One of the defining traits of post-system prosperity is *sovereignty at scale*. This does not mean isolationism or retreat into primitive barter. Rather, it signifies the ability of individuals or networks to generate value independent of state-defined constraints—while still participating selectively in global exchange.

We see this in the emergence of *micro-economies*: cohesive networks that operate on shared values, secure infrastructure, and internal trade. These networks are increasingly built on decentralised technology stacks—tools that allow for secure communication, borderless payments, trustless contracts, and anonymous collaboration.

The digital nomad movement, while often caricatured, has pioneered aspects of this model. Consider the way tech freelancers in Southeast Asia or Latin America function within self-contained ecosystems—employing crypto for payments, DAO-like structures for coordination, and reputation-based platforms for contract resolution. Their prosperity does not depend on national GDP or labour statistics; it depends on mobility, skill liquidity, and strategic optionality.

But post-system prosperity is not limited to tech-savvy expatriates. Rural cooperatives, indigenous land trusts, and off-grid intentional communities also embody this ethic. In places like Chiapas, Mexico, and Northern Thailand, parallel systems of healthcare, agriculture, education, and even dispute resolution have arisen—not out of ideology, but necessity.

The Role of Value Anchors: Skills, Reputation, and Redundancy

If currency collapses, contracts fail, and borders harden, what persists? Not fiat. Not pension funds. Not index-linked investments.

What endures are *value anchors*—elements that retain worth because they are fungible, relevant, and hard to confiscate.

In post-system economics, three value anchors dominate:

Skills – Technical, medical, agricultural, logistical, linguistic, and psychological skills that can be applied across environments and exchanged directly for necessities or privileges.

Reputation – In decentralised economies, identity is less about documentation and more about trust pathways. Reputation becomes a portable asset—your track record in a distributed ledger, peer-reviewed system, or community trust pool can unlock access, credit, and security.

Redundancy – Not just in supply chains, but in systems of income, mobility, and storage. Individuals who operate on multi-vector frameworks—multiple passports, currencies, income sources, and social circles—become antifragile. They thrive on volatility, not despite it.

The future of wealth is not how much you own within one system, but how fluidly you can adapt between them.

Why Collapse Doesn't Mean Retreat: Regeneration as Strategy

Prosperity, in this context, does not mean survivalism or permanent defence. In fact, the most forward-thinking strategies are not about retreat but *regeneration.* They ask: How do we shape something better—not just for ourselves, but for others—after collapse has discredited the old structures?

This spirit underpins movements like permaculture, which is not merely a method of organic farming, but a broader design philosophy: create abundance through sustainable cycles, build systems where waste becomes input, and increase the resilience of every node.

In a financial context, this could mean establishing community land banks, member-owned credit unions, decentralised autonomous organisations (DAOs) with voting equity, or energy cooperatives. These structures are already emerging—not hypotheticals, but functioning models.

Rebuild, don't just resist.

Contrasting Visions: Exit vs Integration

Not all post-system strategies agree. There is a clear philosophical divergence between two schools of thought:

Exit Paradigm – Favoured by crypto-libertarians, off-grid preppers, and digital nomads. Focuses on withdrawal from failing systems and self-sovereignty at the individual or family level.

Integration Paradigm – Advocated by regenerative economists, civic technologists, and pluralistic thinkers. Emphasises rebuilding alongside disruption, integrating decentralised tools into community frameworks.

Both have merit. What matters is clarity. Are you optimising for mobility or rootedness? Privacy or interdependence? Control or cohesion?

The most resilient actors borrow from both. They maintain exit capacity *and* invest in collaborative infrastructure. They build shadow systems not to hoard, but to serve as parallel lifeboats when legacy systems capsize.

From Strategy to Ethos: Redefining Prosperity

Ultimately, post-system prosperity is a redefinition of wealth. Not a downgrade, but a reimagining. Not austerity, but *agency*.

It asks: What would abundance look like if measured not in money, but in momentum, trust, adaptability, purpose?

This question is not abstract. It is operational. A family that has redundancy in shelter, food, education, communications, and income—across multiple jurisdictions and systems—is wealthy, even if not "rich." An individual who can exit one framework and enter another without friction is free. A community that generates its own power, governs its own affairs, and resolves disputes without courts is sovereign.

This is not utopia. It is blueprint.

Final Reflection

Post-system prosperity is neither an act of rebellion nor a concession to chaos. It is a moral and strategic response to the failures of centralised modernity. Where trust in institutions collapses, ingenuity must rise. Where legacy structures decay, new patterns must be designed—not only to endure, but to improve.

The future belongs not to the wealthiest, but to the most adaptable. Not to the compliant, but to the constructive. And not to those who cling to what was—but to those who build what could be.

The Rise of Micro-Nations and Decentralised States

Part I – Sovereignty Beyond the Flag

A nation-state, as conventionally defined, is a territory governed by a central authority, recognised by its peers, and embedded in the global order. That definition, forged in the aftermath of the Peace of Westphalia in 1648 and expanded through centuries of colonial ambition and bureaucratic standardisation, has now come under strain. The contours of sovereignty are blurring. Legitimacy is no longer guaranteed by geography. Authority is no longer monopolised by the state. And for a growing number of visionaries, dissidents, technologists, and pragmatists, the very idea of what constitutes a functioning "country" is ripe for reinvention.

The rise of *micro-nations* and *decentralised states* is not a fringe curiosity—it is a serious response to the faltering promises of modern governance. As global institutions fumble over crises—economic instability, ecological degradation, digital overreach, and cultural fracturing—new models of sovereignty are not only being imagined but enacted. Some are legal experiments. Others are ideological laboratories. A few are audacious scams. But together, they signal a larger shift: the decline of the nation-state's monopoly on legitimacy, and the ascent of plural, modular, networked sovereignties.

We are witnessing a slow, deliberate unbundling of the state.

Post-Nationalism and the Failure of Scale

The 20th century was the high-water mark of centralisation. The welfare state, the command economy, the military-industrial complex—these were all expressions of scale as virtue. Bigger was safer. Bigger was more stable. Bigger delivered efficiency, uniformity, and control.

But in the 21st century, scale has begun to implode under its own weight. Bureaucratic states struggle to respond to nimble threats. Regulatory complexity chokes innovation. Citizens find themselves governed by machinery that neither understands nor represents them. And more critically, the tools once monopolised by governments—communication, encryption, currency, identity, diplomacy—are now in the hands of individuals and networks.

A 15-year-old with a VPN and a crypto wallet arguably possesses more economic sovereignty than a citizen in a debt-ridden, inflation-addled nation with capital controls. The tools of autonomy have been democratised. But where should that autonomy go?

This question lies at the heart of the rise of micro-nations and decentralised states.

Micronations: Satire, Symbolism, and Strategic Fiction

Micronations are often dismissed as comic curiosities: self-declared kingdoms in suburban gardens, floating libertarian projects at sea, or monarchies made of manifestos. Some, like the *Principality of Sealand*—a World War II anti-aircraft platform off the British coast—exist in legal grey zones, tantalisingly outside the reach of conventional jurisdiction. Others, such as the *Republic of Molossia* in Nevada or the *Empire of Atlantium* in Australia, blend performance art with genuine constitutional play.

Yet behind their theatre lies something potent: the assertion of alternative sovereignty. Micronations ask not whether they can become countries in the UN's eyes, but whether they can offer models, critiques, or containers for autonomy on a smaller, more agile scale. They play with the machinery of governance—laws, flags, currencies, rituals—not as gimmicks, but as prototypes.

A micronation is less a place than a statement: *What if governance could be voluntary? What if identity was consensual?*

Network States and Digital Polities

If micronations emerge from territory, *network states* emerge from community. Popularised by technologist and former Coinbase CTO Balaji Srinivasan, the "network state" is a concept for a digitally-native polity: one that begins as a moral community online, then aggregates capital, reputation, and coordination, ultimately acquiring physical territory or diplomatic recognition.

The premise is simple, yet radical: *A state is not defined by land, but by aligned people.* In a world where community can be built faster than infrastructure, the nation becomes portable. The network replaces the nation as the primary substrate for collective identity and action.

One emerging example is *Praxis*, a self-described "city of the future" being developed by a global community of techno-optimists seeking to build physical communities from shared digital values. While sceptics critique the feasibility or ideological tenor of such projects, the underlying trend is clear: decentralised identity, transnational coordination, and the collapsing costs of institutional tooling have created the preconditions for post-geographic governance.

In effect, a *decentralised state* is one in which governance is distributed, portable, and voluntary—and sovereignty is a matter of code and consensus, not conquest.

Case Studies in Experimental Sovereignty (Preview of Part II)

In the next section of this article, we will explore the following active and planned models that illustrate the rise of decentralised sovereignty:

Liberland – A self-proclaimed libertarian microstate on disputed land between Croatia and Serbia, using blockchain for governance.

Prospera (Honduras) – A semi-autonomous "charter city" attracting technologists and investors seeking legal and economic experimentation.

Zomia – A stateless highland region in Southeast Asia whose people have historically resisted integration into nation-states, offering a living anthropology of decentralised life.

Radical Markets-inspired DAOs – Platforms that use market-based governance to allocate public goods and adjudicate disputes without borders.

These projects are neither uniformly successful nor universally respected. But their significance lies in their function as *experiments*: testbeds for governance innovation, models for modular sovereignty, and harbingers of the post-national condition.

Part II – Case Studies and Strategic Implications

If Part I outlined the theory—why traditional sovereignty is fragmenting and how post-geographic polities are emerging—then Part II examines the fieldwork: *Where is this happening, and what can we learn from the frontier experiments now in motion?* These cases are not aspirational in theory alone. They are real, unfolding scenarios, each with its own tensions, failures, and revelations.

1. Liberland – Blockchain Libertarianism on Disputed Soil

In 2015, a Czech politician and economist, Vít Jedlička, claimed a 7 km^2 parcel of uninhabited land between Croatia and Serbia and declared it the *Free Republic of Liberland.* Its constitution champions individual liberty, voluntary taxation, and a radically limited state. But Liberland's innovation lies not in its physical claim—largely symbolic and contested—but in its attempt to build a state architecture rooted in blockchain infrastructure.

From digital IDs to decentralised arbitration, Liberland attempts to realise a libertarian state with minimal human bureaucracy. It uses cryptocurrency as its preferred medium of exchange and positions itself as a stateless services provider—*more a protocol than a place.*

However, Liberland reveals a key friction in this space: *you can start a government on code, but you still need borders, recognition, or resilience against physical coercion.* The project's current stasis, largely confined to digital expression and ideological celebration, underscores the limits of land-based secession without sufficient geopolitical leverage.

2. Prospera – Charter Cities as Legal Startups

In Honduras, the *Prospera* ZEDE (Zone for Employment and Economic Development) represents a radically different model: a charter city sanctioned by host nation law, but allowed to operate under its own legal and regulatory framework. With backing from Silicon Valley and libertarian think tanks, Prospera invites entrepreneurs to build in a jurisdiction designed from scratch—leaner laws, competitive governance, and strong investor protections.

It functions like a sovereign startup hub: governments-as-a-service, but franchised within an existing state. Critics argue it enables corporate colonialism or undermines democratic control. Advocates counter that it introduces *regulatory competition*—allowing citizens to "vote with their feet" within zones that outcompete failed states.

The Prospera model teaches that sovereignty need not be absolute. *Partial autonomy—granted or leased—can be a platform for institutional experimentation.* In a global system increasingly sceptical of centralised bureaucracy, this "legal special economic zone" approach may prove more scalable than full secessionist micro-nations.

3. Zomia – Statelessness as Civilisation

Contrary to modern assumptions, statelessness is not always chaos. The highlands of Southeast Asia—known as *Zomia*—are home to over 100 million people, many of whom have historically lived beyond the reach of formal states. Their governance is decentralised, oral, kinship-based, and often anarchic by design. James C. Scott, in his seminal work *The Art of Not Being Governed*, argued that these communities have actively resisted state formation for centuries, valuing autonomy over "progress."

Zomia represents the inverse of the network state: not a digital frontier, but an *anthropological memory of decentralised living.* It reminds us that states are not evolutionary inevitabilities, but contingent historical arrangements. And it proves that resilient, cooperative order is possible *without flags, armies, or central banks.*

The strategic insight here is clear: *the technologies of decentralisation may be new, but the ethos is ancient.* The past may offer blueprints for a post-collapse future.

4. Blockchain-Based DAOs – Governance Without Geography

Perhaps the most potent new sovereignty model is also the least visible. *Decentralised Autonomous Organisations* (DAOs), built on blockchain platforms like Ethereum, now manage billions in assets, execute smart contracts, and allow thousands of members to coordinate without ever meeting in person.

DAOs are code-based governance systems where rules are enforced by software, not states. Their members span countries. Their decisions are made through tokens. Their assets are cryptographic, not territorial. Some act as investment funds (e.g., MetaCartel), others as service collectives, and some experiment with justice and adjudication. What unites them is the principle of *non-coercive, programmable order.*

DAOs challenge a core assumption of political science: that power requires place. They suggest that *governance can become platform-based*—modular, forkable, and consensus-driven. In this paradigm, sovereignty is no longer a matter of land—it's a function of code integrity, reputation, and user participation.

But DAOs also reveal risks: plutocracy through token capture, opaque voting dynamics, and brittle consensus models. Their lesson is not that software can replace the state, but that *institutional design is now open-source*—and subject to iteration.

Strategic Implications: The Unbundling of Sovereignty

What unites these diverse examples—Liberland, Prospera, Zomia, DAOs—is not a common ideology but a shared impulse: *to disaggregate sovereignty into modular components.* Each challenges the monopoly of the nation-state, not through brute force, but through strategic circumvention, legal innovation, or network substitution.

If we examine sovereignty as a stack of functions—identity issuance, currency provision, dispute resolution, security, territory—we see that each is now being unbundled:

Identity is now decentralised via self-sovereign ID and cryptographic signatures

Currency is borderless via Bitcoin and stablecoins

Dispute resolution is being explored via online arbitration and smart contracts

Territory is negotiated through leased jurisdictions or floating platforms

Security is becoming privatised and protocol-driven

This disaggregation offers a profound strategic shift for individuals seeking resilience in a fragmenting world: *You no longer need to rely on a single state to provide every critical function of your life.* You can now assemble your own sovereignty stack—a personalised protocol of freedom, mobility, and security.

Part III – Ethical Reflections and the Future of Plural Sovereignty

If micro-nations and decentralised states promise freedom, flexibility, and escape from institutional sclerosis, they also raise deeper, more uncomfortable questions: *Who gets to opt out? Who gets left behind? What is the moral legitimacy of sovereignty without solidarity?*

The unbundling of state functions—while seductive for those with means, mobility, or technical skill—risks creating a two-tier world: one where the agile elite operate via portable sovereignty stacks, while the structurally dependent remain trapped within brittle national bureaucracies. The rise of new sovereignties could be emancipatory—or it could accelerate digital feudalism.

1. Exit Without Voice – When Sovereignty Becomes Selfish

Historically, political legitimacy has rested on the balance between *exit* and *voice*. You could reform your state (voice), or you could leave it (exit). Micro-sovereignty, especially when engineered through crypto-finance, often fetishises *exit* at the expense of any meaningful *voice*.

This is the fundamental critique: when sovereignty becomes a consumer product, governance risks becoming transactional and exclusionary. Citizenship-by-investment schemes already show us how access to legal protections and mobility can be purchased while millions remain stateless or immobile. If DAOs or network states begin to stratify based on token holdings or invite-only protocols, we risk replacing the monopolistic state with opaque, privately-run technocracies.

In other words, *decentralisation is not the same as democracy*. Without accountability mechanisms, decentralised systems can devolve into "gov-by-whales"—a form of governance where the loudest voices are simply those with the largest holdings. The aspiration of sovereignty must be weighed against its ethical execution.

2. Sovereignty as Stewardship, Not Seclusion

A more mature view of new sovereignty is not as a shield from the world, but as a *structure for responsibility*. Whether one runs a DAO, joins a floating city project, or participates in a digital jurisdiction, the question must shift from "What can I escape?" to "What am I building in its place?"

The Stoics remind us that freedom is not license but discipline. The Taoists remind us that order is not imposed but emergent. These philosophies converge on a common point: *a society worth sustaining must be more than a toolkit for personal risk management*. It must be a crucible for shared meaning, moral seriousness, and adaptive cohesion.

The most promising experiments in decentralised sovereignty are not those promising utopia, but those *rigorously stress-testing the burdens of institutional design*: What are the rights of newcomers? What is the protocol for failure? How are internal conflicts resolved? What happens to dissent?

The power of micro-sovereignty will be judged not by how effectively it enables freedom from others, but by how deeply it cultivates responsibility *toward* others.

3. The Paradox of Stateless Abundance

One final tension bears close examination: *Can there be prosperity without the state?* Conventional economics suggests that states are required to enforce contracts, provide infrastructure, and maintain rule of law. Yet what we now observe is a growing ability for technology to substitute many of these functions—at least in part.

Private security firms, decentralised insurance pools, autonomous dispute resolution, even private cities like Culdesac or charter zones like Neom are re-engineering basic services from the ground up. Critics argue this undermines the public commons. Advocates claim it restores agency, innovation, and adaptability.

But the real question isn't whether these functions can be privatized—it's whether they can be *scaled inclusively*. Without meaningful on-ramps for the vulnerable, or mechanisms to share gains across networks, the post-state future could become extractive rather than emancipatory.

It is therefore not the ambition of post-system prosperity that must be questioned—but *its terms of access*.

4. The Role of the Ethical Architect

This final insight points us towards a role that must now be cultivated: *the ethical sovereignty architect.* Whether designing digital protocols, legal charters, floating jurisdictions, or autonomous communities, builders must now function as cross-disciplinary stewards—part systems thinker, part ethicist, part technologist.

They must ask:

Can governance scale without becoming rigid?

Can freedom be inclusive without being diluted?

Can complexity be humanised rather than weaponised?

In this role, the mission shifts from passive critique of the state to *active authorship of the next institutional paradigm.* It is a role that cannot be fulfilled by engineers alone, nor theorists alone, nor capital alone. It demands moral imagination, institutional humility, and design fluency. These are not utopian demands—they are practical prerequisites for coherence in a volatile world.

Final Thought: Multiplicity, Not Monoculture

If the 20th century was defined by the rise of the nation-state monoculture, the 21st will likely be defined by *sovereignty multiplicity.* The most dangerous error now is to assume that there is one ideal system, one perfect polity, or one exit path. That is the logic that drove centralised empires—and eventually broke them.

What decentralised sovereignty offers is not perfection, but *pluralism.* It allows for jurisdictional diversity, legal experimentation, cultural variance. It creates a laboratory of institutional forms—not to escape society, but to *advance it from more directions at once.*

The rise of micro-nations and decentralised states is not the end of politics. It is the beginning of political authorship—of remaking the conditions of association, governance, and trust from first principles.

For those prepared to think deeply, act responsibly, and build ethically, this is not an escape—it is an invitation.

The Spiritual Dimension of Escape – Considering the Deeper Freedom That Comes from Detachment

To speak of "escape" in a geopolitical or financial context is often to refer to relocation, evasion, or defence—getting beyond borders, regulations, or collapsing infrastructures. But there is another layer, seldom articulated and harder to engineer: the internal act of escape. Not from regimes, but from attachments. Not from systems, but from the self that is beholden to them. This is the *spiritual dimension of exit*—an emancipation not only of body or capital, but of attention, identity, and dependence.

If the preceding chapters have equipped the reader with protocols for resilience and adaptation, this chapter introduces a subtler challenge: *What if true security does not come from controlling the system, but from needing less from it?*

This question is not rhetorical. It is the premise upon which centuries of contemplative traditions have been built. From the Stoic practice of premeditatio malorum to Buddhist detachment from craving, to the Christian Desert Fathers' rejection of empire, the act of stepping away—intellectually, emotionally, spiritually—has long been seen as the foundation of true freedom.

To modern ears, this may sound quaint or even unstrategic. But beneath the noise of geopolitical manoeuvring and technological survivalism lies a more durable truth: *it is not only where you live, or what you own, that shapes your fate—it is how deeply you are entangled in needing things to be a certain way.*

1. The Limits of External Escape

Every act of migration, asset protection, or data minimisation rests on a presumption: that safety lies *elsewhere.* But history shows that even the most elegantly designed exoduses can be disrupted by events beyond one's control—pandemics, regime shifts, market failures, betrayal.

Consider the case of Russian dissidents in the early 20th century who fled to Paris or London, only to face surveillance and exile again. Or the countless Jewish families who diversified their assets in the 1930s, only to have every law rewritten overnight. Or even recent stories of crypto-millionaires with second passports who, despite robust planning, find themselves detained at borders or frozen out of banking networks due to vague allegations or geopolitical retribution.

The external route—however important—is not invincible. *What happens when even your escape plan has a backup plan, and it still fails?*

The uncomfortable answer is this: at some point, strategy becomes insufficient. It must be complemented by a capacity to face loss *without being destroyed by it.* That is where spiritual detachment enters—not as a luxury of monks, but as an essential competence for high-stakes modernity.

2. Detachment Is Not Apathy

To detach is not to withdraw from life. It is to decouple one's identity from outcomes. This distinction is critical. The Stoics did not suggest you stop caring; they suggested you stop being owned by what you cannot control. "You may chain my leg," Epictetus wrote, "but not even Zeus can conquer my mind."

This inner sovereignty—the refusal to allow external events to define internal peace—is the most robust defence against systems in collapse. Unlike assets or plans, it cannot be seized, frozen, or revoked. It cannot be legislated against. And in times of crisis, its effects are disproportionately powerful.

Detachment is not defeatist. It is clarifying. It allows the individual to engage in planning and protection *without illusion*. It reduces the energetic cost of fear. It fosters the calm that allows for effective improvisation. In psychological terms, it cultivates *response flexibility*—the ability to pivot without panicking.

In spiritual traditions, detachment is cultivated through repeated practice: voluntary discomfort, contemplation of impermanence, mindful awareness of clinging. In tactical terms, these may seem esoteric. But ask any survivalist or resistance fighter, and you will find their training includes exactly these traits—calm under pressure, release of ego, non-reactivity to chaos.

Freedom is not simply having options. It is knowing that you are more than your options.

3. The Architecture of Psychological Entanglement

Understanding why this matters requires diagnosing a modern malady: the hidden web of psychological dependencies created by institutions and consumer culture.

From birth, citizens of industrialised nations are trained not just to desire, but to *derive identity* from systems: the school you attended, the career path you follow, the brands you consume, the political affiliations you declare. The social matrix doesn't merely offer options—it defines *what it means to be valid, responsible, successful.*

The escape from this conditioning is not easy. It requires first recognising that systems do not just hold our data—they hold our self-image. Thus, many who escape the jurisdiction of a collapsing state find themselves emotionally unmoored. They have moved their bodies, but not their expectations. They are still haunted by the metrics of a life they no longer live in.

Detachment means auditing not just your bank accounts or digital traces, but your *mental loyalties*: what stories are you still living out? Whose validation do you still require? What would you still feel shame for losing, even if no one was watching?

These are not abstract questions. They are the terrain of true escape.

4. Spiritual Traditions as Operational Technologies

There is a tendency to treat spiritual insight as metaphorical or aesthetic. But when viewed through the lens of resilience, these traditions offer operational technologies.

The Stoics practised *negative visualisation*—imagining loss, exile, illness—as a way to inoculate against fear. The Buddhists taught *non-attachment to identity*, training the mind to witness change without resistance. The Taoists embraced *wu wei*, effortless action, which allows one to align with unfolding reality rather than battle it.

Modern psychology has caught up. Techniques like Acceptance and Commitment Therapy (ACT), Cognitive Defusion, and Mindfulness-Based Stress Reduction (MBSR) are secular echoes of these ancient tools. But the principle remains the same: *the person who can see the wave of crisis, feel it, and not be swept by it—is already free, even if the wave still arrives.*

In this way, spiritual detachment becomes an asymmetric advantage. It reduces mental noise, clarifies decision-making, and restores access to creativity under duress. It also disrupts coercion: systems lose power when their threats no longer define your reality.

5. Building the Inner Citadel

Marcus Aurelius referred to the *inner citadel*—that unassailable space within the self that remains untouched by external force. In a world where algorithms are tuned to provoke, economies are structured to addict, and politics is theatre of distraction, the cultivation of such a citadel is no longer poetic; it is strategic.

To build it requires:

A clear inventory of what you actually need.

A disciplined practice of daily detachment—mental fasting, perspective inversion, moral reflection.

A community of peers who prioritise depth over noise.

A meaningful anchor—spiritual, philosophical, or artistic—that orients you beyond momentary outcomes.

This is not an act of withdrawal. It is an act of *selective allegiance.* You are not refusing to play the game; you are refusing to be defined by it.

6. What Follows Detachment

The final paradox is this: once detachment is cultivated, you may find yourself better equipped to *engage.* You are no longer playing to preserve a fragile self-concept. You act out of clarity, not compulsion. You build systems not to feel safe, but to serve others. You exit not from fear, but to prototype better ways of being.

This is the deeper meaning of the spiritual dimension of escape: it is not a retreat from the world. It is a refusal to be owned by the world as it currently exists.

The Stoic faces collapse not with resignation, but with readiness. The Buddhist faces impermanence not with nihilism, but with compassion. The spiritually detached builder becomes the most reliable architect—not because they fear loss, but because they are not hostage to it.

True escape is not where you go. It's what you're no longer dependent on to feel real.

Rebuilding, Not Just Running – Encouraging the Shaping of the New World Rather than Hiding from It

Escape is often romanticised as a solitary act—withdrawal to the hills, digital invisibility, or quietly expatriating before the system implodes. But the measure of long-term resilience is not merely whether one can leave. It is whether one can build. When systems collapse, the people who shape what comes next are not the ones who hid longest—they are the ones who *emerged prepared to construct.*

If the first impulse of survival is flight, the second must be formation. *Flight preserves the self. Formation extends it outward, into something generative.* That's the difference between a survivor and a founder. Between evasion and evolution. Running might be necessary—but rebuilding is what makes the exit meaningful.

This subchapter turns the lens from retreat to reconstruction. Not to naively advocate utopia, but to confront the deeper responsibility implicit in escape: *You left. Now what will you create?*

1. The Post-Collapse Vacuum

Every collapse creates a power vacuum. Whether political, financial, or social, the disintegration of prior institutions leaves not just broken infrastructures—but broken meanings. Citizens are left not only without governance, but without shared rituals, services, or trust networks.

History offers an abundance of these moments. The fall of the Soviet Union in 1991 left entire generations grappling with identity voids. Yugoslavia's fragmentation gave way to fragile states and violent retribalisation. The end of colonial rule in much of Africa saw hurriedly installed governments collapse under the weight of inherited dysfunction.

These transitions were shaped not by who escaped, but by who returned. Diaspora members who brought capital and skills. Local organisers who filled power gaps before strongmen could. Underground economies that matured into legitimate currencies.

In each case, *the question was not just how to survive the collapse—but who would define the post-collapse norms.*

Running preserves a life. Rebuilding defines the lives of others.

2. The Psychology of Escape Without Rebuilding

For many, collapse triggers a loop: observe warning signs, prepare exit, disengage, relocate, isolate. This is often prudent, but rarely sufficient. Over time, the isolated escapee faces a spiritual dilemma: if you've preserved your capital, health, and optionality—but contributed nothing to your new context—have you truly escaped dependence? Or merely delayed responsibility?

A purely consumerist exit—living abroad on foreign systems, paying for protection, speaking no local language—is not resilience. It is offshored fragility. And more often than not, it breeds paranoia, boredom, or disconnection.

The deeper fulfilment lies in *constructive sovereignty*. That doesn't require founding a new country or building a bunker-based commune. It means designing systems—small or large—that *reduce your reliance on corrupt hierarchies while increasing your value to others.*

Rebuilding may start as a family garden, a decentralised skills co-op, or a privacy-respecting education hub. But the psychology behind it is the same: *the belief that you are not merely a fugitive from the old system—but a custodian of the next one.*

3. Rebuilding as Ethical Imperative

To rebuild is not only practical—it is moral. Those who have the foresight, resources, or flexibility to exit early are among the few capable of creating transitional systems for those left behind.

If the post-collapse world is shaped solely by whoever grabs the most land or yells the loudest, then those who could have done better have failed.

We are accustomed to seeing competence as self-serving. But *exit without contribution is privilege without honour.* The new world will be determined by those who step into its vacuum with vision—not just caution.

In this light, rebuilding becomes a civic act—*not to restore what failed, but to prove something better can function in its place.*

4. What Rebuilding Looks Like in Practice

Rebuilding does not require scale. It requires clarity. The architecture of better systems often begins with *micro-models* that can be tested, adapted, and duplicated:

A regenerative agriculture community that feeds ten families without external supply chains.

An alternative school curriculum that teaches encryption, logic, local law, and nutrition.

A cooperative housing system that de-risks shelter without entangling people in predatory mortgages.

A platform-independent marketplace for local trade and trust-based service exchange.

These are not dreams. These are already underway—dispersed across Catalonia, Chiapas, Chiang Mai. From Zapatista cooperatives to decentralised crypto-villages in Portugal, from remote work zones in the Balkans to agri-tech collectives in Kenya, the seeds are in motion.

The question is not whether rebuilding is possible. It's whether we'll participate—or spectate.

5. From Collapse Consciousness to Design Consciousness

Collapse consciousness is focused on warning signs, failures, retreats. It is reactive by nature—and understandably so. But to remain in that mode is to become paralysed. What's required next is a *design consciousness*: the creative, intentional structuring of new protocols, values, and communities.

Design consciousness asks:

What should a decentralised economy actually reward?

How can reputation be tracked without mass surveillance?

What rituals build trust without bureaucracy?

How do we train young people for leadership in systems that don't yet exist?

These are not philosophical questions. They are design briefs for the post-collapse builder. And every escapee who holds expertise, insight, or capital carries part of the answer.

6. The Role of Narrative and Culture in Rebuilding

Technical solutions are not enough. The success of any new system depends on *shared narrative coherence*—a sense of "why" that binds people beyond transactions.

This means investing in more than survival. It means cultivating stories, symbols, and aesthetics that carry a civilisation's soul. The post-collapse world will need new myths. Not in the sense of fantasy, but in the Joseph Campbell sense of shared organising metaphors.

Rebuilders must therefore think like *cultural architects* as well as system designers. They must ask: *what does it mean to belong here? To be sovereign here? To sacrifice for something again?*

These questions cannot be answered with protocols alone. They require art, philosophy, language, and ritual.

7. The Importance of Local Resilience Networks

Rebuilding isn't only about escaping the global system. It's about establishing *networked alternatives*—clusters of families, micro-communities, or federated collectives that operate semi-independently but cooperate strategically.

Examples include:

Food sovereignty through permaculture networks

Renewable micro-grids that bypass national infrastructure

Skills-based currencies that reward teaching, repair, and mutual aid

Local conflict resolution processes rooted in restorative justice

These do not replace governments. But they *reduce dependence* on their dysfunction—and create parallel institutions that can either support or outlast them.

8. Courage over Comfort

There is one psychological barrier to rebuilding that must be named clearly: *it is far easier to criticise than to construct.* Escape is tidy. Building is messy. Running requires fear. Rebuilding requires courage.

Courage to take responsibility. Courage to try without guarantees. Courage to collaborate with people who are not like you.

This is why so few do it. And precisely why it matters.

9. Rebuilding Is the Completion of Escape

The arc of a meaningful exit does not end at the border or in a digital wallet. It ends when the individual stops living *against* the old world—and begins living *for* the new one.

This shift is the mark of true sovereignty. It is when you stop trying to survive history—and begin to shape it.

And in that act—whether through land, code, trust, or care—you reclaim not just your freedom, but your *authorship.*

Conclusion
Escape as Enlightenment

The notion of escape is too often caricatured—dismissed as mere escapism, burdened by the weight of guilt, or cast as an act of cowardice. Yet true escape, when pursued with lucidity and resolve, bears no resemblance to surrender. It is not a retreat from the world's chaos, but a refusal to allow one's inner life to be tethered to it. Escape, at its most potent, is not reactionary but declarative: a choice to step outside inherited constraints and craft one's agency deliberately, with care and conviction. That is not running away. That is liberation.

This final chapter does not seek to wrap things up neatly, nor does it peddle summary. Instead, it converges—bringing into sharp focus all that has come before: from the threads of sovereignty and jurisdictional agility, through psychological robustness and institutional disentanglement, to the quiet radicalism of civil re-foundation. All of it converging on one central proposition: that escape, when taken seriously, can become a pathway to enlightenment. Not in the esoteric or mystical sense, but in its truest, most demanding form—born of clarity, built upon autonomy, and directed by a deliberate reimagining of one's relationship to the world.

Historically, the Enlightenment was sparked not by comfort, but by rupture. It was a mass intellectual jailbreak—out of feudal hierarchies, out of ecclesiastical hegemony, out of the long sleep of tradition. Its pioneers did not first flee physically; they fled cognitively. And therein lies the resonance. The most vital exits today are not necessarily geographical. They are cognitive, moral, even spiritual. Our firewalls are not just digital anymore. They are conceptual. And the first breach to consider is not in the state, but in ourselves.

We are living through a moment when collapse has ceased to be a thought experiment. It's no longer reserved for speculative fiction or contingency planning. It is measurable, televisual, and for many, already personal. Institutions that once formed the bedrock of modern life—banking, governance, public health, higher education—now seem increasingly unmoored from the actual needs of human beings. To prepare for rupture is no longer paranoia; to ignore it may well be denial. But the real question is not how to escape collapse—it's how to pass through it without surrendering one's soul. How to rise from it with something better than mere survival.

This is not a call to panic. It's a call to precision. Enlightenment begins with seeing—truly seeing. It means shedding received obligations, naming the assumptions that have quietly colonised our inner lives, and breaking the false binary between total compliance and reckless rebellion. In that space between the extremes, there is a kind of clarity. A recognition that security, meaning, and dignity can often be better constructed in parallel to existing systems, not within them. But to do that well requires a discipline that is both architectural and existential: a design of life based on first principles. A conscious positioning in relation to risk, to value, and to freedom.

There is also a moral sleight of hand that must be exposed—the notion that escape is selfish. That to walk away from broken institutions is to forsake responsibility. On the contrary, to remain complicit in systems that degrade the human spirit may be the greater abdication. Enlightened escape is not abandonment—it is discernment. It's a refusal to perpetuate dysfunction. And from that space of moral clarity, one becomes newly capable of building what others, trapped within those same systems, will one day depend on.

Too often, those with the most education, the most status, and the most institutional success find themselves unable to move—stuck in gilded cages. They are over-optimised for structures that no longer serve them, quietly disillusioned but unsure how to break ranks without fracturing their sense of self. This book has not asked anyone to vanish into the woods or disappear behind encryption. Its purpose has been subtler: to remind you that you are not trapped. That alternatives do exist. That exit is not inherently dramatic, nor inherently selfish. It can be strategic. Ethical. Even elegant.

But such a life—consciously untethered—requires inner ballast. Those who endure collapse with grace are not simply those with provisions or passports. They are those who have cultivated, over time, a kind of interior stillness. The ancients were not naive in this. The Stoic discipline of *apatheia*, the Buddhist path of detachment, the Taoist embrace of flow—all of these are not spiritual affectations. They are durable tools. Technologies of thought. If your peace is externally sourced, you are vulnerable to every disruption. If it is internally forged, you can act with calm precision even as the world convulses.

This is why, at its highest expression, escape becomes philosophy. A life defined not by reaction, but by design. Certainly, there are guides aplenty for acquiring second citizenships, diversifying assets, or building remote workflows. But what has been lacking—what this book has attempted to offer—is a template for integrated sovereignty. Where outer manoeuvres are aligned with inner clarity. Where departure is not just logistical, but meaningful. To leave well, one must know not only how, but why. And for whom one becomes on the other side.

We are not the first generation to find ourselves standing at the edge of old maps. But we are among the first to do so with this level of access—digital tools, cultural cross-pollination, and real-time information flowing at global scale. With such capacity comes obligation. Exit must not become mere lifestyle. A digital nomad who extracts without offering, a prepper who hoards and withholds—they are not escaping the dysfunction. They are replicating it. Enlightenment means more than surviving well. It means building something others might join, something not just resilient, but generous by design.

This final chapter, then, is not a door closing, but a lens sharpening. It invites you to see escape not as a binary, but as a gradient—scaling from practical detachment to metaphysical reorientation. It asks you to reconsider what territory really is: not lines on a map, but stories, assumptions, defaults. The most radical escape, it turns out, is from the belief that life must be lived according to inherited scripts.

As we move through the concluding essays, escape will be explored not as a flight from—but as a movement toward. Toward discernment. Toward self-authorship. Toward the quiet power of those who choose to leave, not in anger or fear, but in order to build what they could not find.

Because the highest form of escape is not disappearance.

It is design. And when that design is conscious—grounded, principled, generous—you are not simply rejecting a crumbling order. You are beginning the architecture of what comes next.

Final Reflection: Escape as Conscious Evolution, Not Fear-Driven Retreat

Escape is often mistaken for failure. In popular imagination, to exit is to lose—to flee, to give up, to back down. But this framing belongs to the lexicon of the trapped. Those who benefit from your inertia will always define your motion as retreat. Yet not all departures are acts of desperation. Some are acts of discernment. And when undertaken with clarity, they are acts of evolution.

This book has walked the reader through layers of personal sovereignty—economic, legal, technological, psychological, and even spiritual. But sovereignty is not a toolkit. It is a philosophy. And escape, properly understood, is not the opposite of engagement. It is the *precondition* for meaningful engagement—one not dictated by coercion, legacy systems, or fear of exclusion, but one chosen freely, intentionally, and on one's own terms.

To escape, in this higher sense, is not to vanish from responsibility, but to reject *false obligations*. It is not about hiding from a collapsing world, but about refusing to let a collapsing world define what is possible. We are not advocating for exile. We are advocating for evolution—for a reconfiguration of life where each decision is examined for alignment, each commitment chosen for coherence, and each dependency scrutinised for ethical and strategic merit.

In times of systemic volatility, the urge to flee is natural. But when escape is fear-driven, it tends to recreate the very conditions one tried to leave. People relocate yet remain psychologically ensnared. They change jurisdictions but not paradigms. They build bunkers instead of better lives. And here lies the central thesis of this final reflection: *Escape is not just a direction. It is a transformation.*

Real escape—enlightened escape—is not defined by geographic relocation or the accumulation of emergency provisions. It is defined by *a shift in orientation* from reactive survivalism to proactive sovereignty. This means designing systems—financial, relational, intellectual—that are *aligned with your values rather than inherited from broken institutions*. It means detaching not only from failing governments or toxic economies, but from inherited scripts about success, status, and security that no longer serve.

What begins as tactical preparation must mature into *philosophical coherence*. A second passport is a tool. A decentralised income is a hedge. A family protocol is a strategy. But the real preparation—

what endures—is *a mind trained to see clearly, act independently, and choose deliberately under pressure.*

History provides ample precedent for this deeper escape. Consider the Stoics of ancient Rome—figures like Epictetus, who while born a slave, trained his mind to be freer than that of any senator. Or the early Buddhists, who did not flee cities but developed *internal frameworks* for not being ruled by them. Or the Enlightenment thinkers who, before revolutions were launched, *escaped the control of church and monarchy by withdrawing their intellectual obedience.* What changed the world was not that they ran. It was that they *reframed* what the world could be.

This final act of reframing is what you are now invited to undertake. You have studied escape as a structure—multi-jurisdictional citizenship, resilient income, secure documentation, scenario training. But now the question must turn inward: *Who are you becoming by opting out?* Sovereignty is not just about being unowned. It is about being *self-owned*—ethically, practically, and spiritually.

Self-ownership demands more than evasion. It demands *agency.* It demands asking: Am I building a life I want, or merely hedging against one I fear? Am I choosing systems that honour dignity, or merely gaming those that reward cunning? Have I examined my values deeply enough to lead, or am I still running on scripts I never authored?

Here, the psychological dimensions of escape grow sharp. Those who prepare best are not those who believe collapse is imminent, but those who understand *systems are always collapsing somewhere*—and that *robustness comes from clarity*, not control. To live with sovereign intention is to live *regardless* of whether the grid is stable, the currency is sound, or the courts are just. It is to be structurally ready, but spiritually detached.

Let us also address a deeper danger—the commodification of escape. As geopolitical uncertainty rises, the market for sovereignty grows. But what is being sold is often security theatre: a panic-stirred menu of bolt-holes, crypto vaults, and citizenship packages that distract from the more radical—and more subtle—form of exit: *ethical disentanglement.* Escaping well is not about status insulation. It is about value integration.

It is time, then, to redefine what it means to exit well. A sovereign life is not a sealed life. It is not off-grid for its own sake. It is not contrarian for identity. It is not elite for comfort. *It is intentional at every level.* And its ultimate purpose is not just self-protection, but *self-authorship.* Because in the end, the real escape is not from institutions, governments, or economies—it is from *complicity in scripts that no longer deserve you.*

There will always be external threats—hyperinflation, capital controls, censorship regimes, ecological collapse. But the first escape—and the most enduring—is always internal. It is the moment you stop reacting and start designing. When you stop complying without questioning. When you stop conflating safety with obedience. When you realise the institutions around you may not collapse tomorrow, but *they have already stopped evolving*—and therefore, *you must.*

This book has offered maps, not mandates. Frameworks, not fear. Tools for those who seek to be both safe and principled. The real goal was never to make you invisible. It was to make you *invulnerable to coercion.* And that goal does not end with offshore accounts or encrypted backups. It ends with *clarity of purpose*—a life lived in alignment, regardless of borders, banks, or broadcast warnings.

As we draw this work to a close, we leave you with this proposition: Escape is not the final act. *It is the first sovereign gesture in the construction of something better.* Something decentralised, resilient, and deeply human. A life where freedom is not a loophole but a birthright. Where risk is managed not through fear, but through *frameworks you designed yourself.* And where prosperity is not extracted, but created—from values, relationships, and regenerative systems you chose freely.

So, redefine escape. Not as a fear-driven flight. But as conscious evolution. Not as withdrawal. But as *alignment with a future only the sovereign can build.*

Now—choose what comes next.

About the Author

Elias van is a geopolitical strategist and financial philosopher whose work interrogates the hidden architecture of global finance and power. With roots in economic research, behavioral psychology, and counter-culture movements, Elias has advised private investors, startup founders, and sovereignty-focused families on navigating the silent shifts of collapsing systems. He blends a deep understanding of decentralised finance with ancient philosophies on autonomy and resilience. Known for his razor-sharp insights and anti-fragile worldview, Elias writes not for the mainstream investor—but for the awake and alert. His mission: to help individuals reclaim agency in a world rigged for dependency.

www.ingramcontent.com/pod-product-compliance
Lightning Source LLC
Chambersburg PA
CBHW031339230926
51848CB00002B/304